Why
Iris Murdoch
Matters

WHY PHILOSOPHY MATTERS

Why Philosophy Matters focuses on why a particular philosopher, school of thought, or area of philosophical study really matters. Each book will put forward an original view about why the topic or philosopher they are discussing matters beyond the remits of purely academic debate. Each book shall offer a brief overview of the subject before exploring its reception both within and outside the academy and our authors defend radically different outlooks on where the value of philosophy lies. Why Philosophy Matters is accompanied by an ongoing series of free high-profile events (talks, debates, workshops, etc.) in Bloomsbury. Podcasts of these events will be freely available on the series page.

Also available from Bloomsbury

Iris Murdoch: Philosophical Novelist, Miles Leeson
Iris Murdoch and the Art of Imagining, Marije Altorf
Iris Murdoch's Ethics, Megan Laverty

Why
Iris Murdoch
Matters

Making Sense of Experience
in Modern Times

GARY BROWNING

BLOOMSBURY ACADEMIC
LONDON • NEW YORK • OXFORD • NEW DELHI • SYDNEY

BLOOMSBURY ACADEMIC
Bloomsbury Publishing Plc
50 Bedford Square, London, WC1B 3DP, UK
1385 Broadway, New York, NY 10018, USA

BLOOMSBURY, BLOOMSBURY ACADEMIC and the Diana logo are trademarks
of Bloomsbury Publishing Plc

First published in Great Britain 2018

Cover image © Chinch Gryniewicz / Bridgeman Images. Stormy sea on rocky
misty coastline, near Allihies, West Cork, Beara Peninsula, Republic of Ireland.

A catalogue record for this book is available from the British Library.

A catalog record for this book is available from the Library of Congress.

ISBN: HB: 978-1-4725-7448-0
PB: 978-1-4725-7447-3
ePDF: 978-1-4725-7449-7
eBook: 978-1-4725-7450-3

Series: Why Philosophy Matters

Typeset by Newgen KnowledgeWorks Pvt. Ltd., Chennai, India

To find out more about our authors and books visit www.bloomsbury.com
and sign up for our newsletters.

CONTENTS

Acknowledgements vi

1 Murdoch and lived experience 1
2 Murdoch and metaphysics 27
3 Murdoch and the novel 55
4 Murdoch and morality 85
5 Murdoch and the political 115
6 Murdoch: Her life and times 145
7 Conclusion 173

Notes 195
Bibliography 217
Index 227

ACKNOWLEDGEMENTS

This book has been with me for a long time. Over the years I have read and reread Murdoch's novels, worked through her philosophical writings and have come to know some wonderful people in the Murdoch world of literary and philosophical scholars. For a number of years I have been working on and with the arguments that I have delivered in this book. I am convinced that her work fits together as a whole and that it is a mistake to separate her novels from her philosophy. They combine in addressing related themes even if she was neither a philosophical novelist nor a literary philosopher. Virtually alone in the Anglo-American world of philosophy and literature she has something to say to a lot of people about how we should live. What she has to say is disclosed in her novels, in her theoretical work and in her life. Her life should not be left to those who mock its vitality and its abundance. It is most remarkable for its association with her thought.

I have a mountain of debts, and I am pleased to acknowledge a few of them. I have appreciated the warmth and wisdom of Anne Rowe and Frances White, who know an enormous amount about Murdoch and have been happy to share their knowledge. I have also learnt much about Murdoch from Niklas Forsberg, David Robjant, Pamela Osborn, Sabina Lovibond, Miles Leeson and Nora Hämäläinen. The series editor Constantine Sandis has been a helpful and stimulating companion on this project, and Liza and Frankie at Bloomsbury have always responded to my questions. I would also like to thank Sue Brown, the inter-library loan librarian at Oxford Brookes University, for being so helpful and kind. I am also grateful to Katie Giles, the resident archivist at Kingston University, and to the Library of St. Anne's College for granting me access to the papers of Iris Murdoch.

Once again, I would like to thank my wife Raia, who has been a wonderful support during the project. Without reading a word of what I have written, she knows what I have to say and where I am going. Her patient attention to my explanations have contributed much to my sorting-out of one or two tricky issues. I would also like to dedicate this book to my grandchildren, Isaac, Annie and Theodore, who know how to laugh, smile and occasionally cry – and to mean it when they do all these things. Is there anything more that we can ask of fellow human beings?

CHAPTER ONE

Murdoch and lived experience

Introduction

Why does Iris Murdoch matter? She matters in many ways. Her novels are absorbing and fun. They make us think and feel in all sorts of ways. Her philosophy is serious and engaged. She offers a realistic reading of the psyche, a perceptive understanding of social and political life and appreciates how religion and art speak to us in important ways. Morality matters to her in demanding significant things from us that are ignored by most modern philosophers. Her life also serves as a reminder of what a life guided by philosophy might look like. Most of all, though, she matters because she brings these things together, showing how they arise out of and reflect back upon experience in related ways. Her multiple interests and publications are interconnected in tracking lived experience in modern times. In a letter of 1947 to Raymond Queneau, before she established herself as a philosopher or novelist, she mused, 'Can I really exploit the advantages (instead of as hitherto suffering the disadvantages) of having a mind on the borders of philosophy, literature and politics.'[1] The question is significant, and her subsequent career would answer it in the affirmative. The advantages of a mind that is on the borders of philosophy, literature and politics is that it enables styles and objects of thinking to be linked together. Literature can show the ways in which individuals experience the world, form relationships and recognize or misrecognize moral and political demands. Philosophy can review how literature imagines individuals and their interactions, and can reflect upon the general character of personal development, morality and the political situations in which individuals are entwined. Murdoch strikes a subtle balance between the styles and objects of thinking to which she attends. She does not dismantle the borders, but takes them to be open and mutually accessible.

Murdoch's mind is alert to many sides of experience – the social and political as much as the personal and introspective. She is a dialectical theorist in identifying differences in style and substance and yet connecting these differences so that the value of her work resides in its overall integrity. Her life is of interest because it reflects and contributes to the ways she perceives the world. Her novels are not a disguised form of philosophy, but imagined worlds of intersecting individuals that are aligned with her philosophical analysis of the meaning of individual freedom and moral development. Her multidimensional perspective is exhibited in her reading of the historical context in which her theoretical and fictional writings are situated. Murdoch has been celebrated as a novelist and philosopher but rarely as an historian, and yet all of her work has an historical aspect. Time and its historical appreciation is vital, for Murdoch, because lived experience in all its guises is historical. The character of personal and public life, which is exhibited in the texture of her novels and in the arguments of her philosophical texts, reflects the issues and frameworks of particular historical contexts. Her philosophy is self-consciously historical in its defining but ambivalent response to the assumptions of modern philosophy. As a novelist, she might maintain nostalgia for nineteenth-century realism, but her focus is upon producing fiction for modern times that avoids its contemporary deficiencies. The generic frame for all of Murdoch's work is the modern break with pre-Enlightenment traditions so as to hold subjectivity, freedom and instrumental reason to be foundational for theory and practice. Within this overall frame, she reviews distinctive assumptions in literature, philosophy, politics and religion while also invoking more fine-grained contexts in establishing background conditions for her novels and in reviewing specific forms of recent moral philosophy and metaphysics that bear upon her interests. Throughout her works, she engages with the historicity of the present and reflects upon the past from which it has emerged. She respects the past and attests to the influence of preceding philosophers and novelists but relates past thinkers to the realities of modern and contemporary experience. These realities – war, political repression and cultural innovation – impact upon the present in all its aspects. The past is not outside the present but is internally connected to it. We are what we have become, and this process of becoming is dialectical. The past lives on in the present perspective, which has emerged from reflection on the past.

From the beginning of her intellectual career to its close, Murdoch thought deeply about how the questions arising within the present are shaped by preceding ways of thinking. An enduring feature of her work, in all its guises, is her sense that her present was different from the past, and that reflection in the present requires clarity over the nature of that difference. In her application for the post of tutor in philosophy at St. Anne's College in April 1948, she offers her 'line' in philosophy, which is an account of how she sees the current philosophical situation and of how that context sets an agenda for subsequent inquiry. She observes, 'More recently I have had the time to see the existentialist and phenomenological movements in their historical perspective, and have been attempting to sift the valuable from the useless in their rich but confused philosophical development.'[2] She goes on, 'Kant's revolution has been mainly developed by two philosophical groups (Hegelian idealists and logical positivists) – each attempting in different ways to amend the rigidity of the system.'[3] She explains how her future role will be that of a critical and historical theorist, who is to integrate seemingly disparate forms of thinking in philosophy and who is also to bring this thinking to bear upon moral and political practice.[4] Throughout her life, she aims to integrate Continental and Anglo-Saxon ways of thinking and to bring her synoptic and historical thought to bear upon personal and social experience.

Towards the end of her life, and before the onslaught of Alzheimer disease, in an address to humanities graduates of Kingston University, she reflects on the meaning of the specific cultural context of the late twentieth century. She remarks,

> All these things (politics, reason, and civilisation) have been transformed in the twentieth century, notably in ways that pose dangers to our lives. Hitler and the evil of the Holocaust remains

a potent warning of the threat of political fanaticism to security and ordinary virtue, while the erosion of belief in Christianity due to scepticism over its miraculous doctrines undermines a source of virtue and love. The ongoing development of technology, a tribute to mankind's rationality, also endangers its continued cultivation, in that collateral environmental degradation and the invention of lethal weapons threaten to destroy a rational form of life. Even the creativity of an individual artist is threatened by the development of standardised technology, such as the word processor.[5]

For Murdoch, there is an ambivalence about modern times, in that a development of freedom and reason is to be set against a loss of wider traditional and spiritual ties. The dangers of modernity are accentuated by accelerating technological invention that privileges instrumental progress over reflection on intrinsic value. The eclipse of superstition and supernatural beliefs allows mankind's rationality to come to the fore, but the advance of reason threatens to override mankind's creativity and spiritual reflection.

What animates Murdoch is her sense of loss at the dissolution of preceding unifying myths and the deprecation of religion, metaphysics, morality, political ideology and the literary imagination. The upshot is that individuals possess an immediate freedom from constraining conventions and attitudes at the price of losing touch with orienting beliefs that guide their conduct and sustain their identities. Kant is a pivotal figure of modernity in demanding a critique of the operations of reason to ensure that the empirical limits of what can be known and the rational claims of morality are to be observed.[6] In her Platonic dialogue, *Above the Gods: A Dialogue about Religion* (1997), she projects her reading of contemporary culture onto that of fifth-century Athens. In the dialogue, the sophist, Antagoras, declares:

> Instead of cosmic mythology we have science, instead of picturesque god fables, we have independent moral men making up their minds and choosing their values. We are the lords of meaning, there isn't any higher meaning set up somewhere else. There's nothing high, there's nothing deep, there's nothing hidden – but that is *obvious*, it's what everyone here in this room believes.[7]

Antagoras's reading of his time represents a challenge to Socrates, but also to Murdoch, whose writings respond to the prevailing cultural mood in which God and background beliefs supporting morality, art and religion have been dismissed in the name of freedom.

Throughout her writings, Murdoch identifies processes of 'demythologization' that strip religion, morality and culture more generally of supernatural and unverifiable beliefs.[8] As a 'modern' herself, she sees the logic of these processes, without abandoning a commitment to the claims of philosophy and literature to provide an insight into the human condition. She still sees these subjects as guiding individuals towards a sense of truth and goodness that supersedes a set of instrumental procedures to satisfy desires. To counter the hollowing effects of demythologization, she employs a critical and historical perspective. In so doing, she draws upon Plato to reframe a philosophical conception of moral, religious and artistic life.[9] Murdoch's Plato is a 'modern' Plato, whose thought is reconstructed so as to render it relevant to and in accordance with a culture that demands reason to be kept within the bounds of experience. In reading Plato, she is attracted to his philosophy and takes from it what is pertinent to present circumstances. The use of Plato is integral to her interpretive strategy of reading preceding philosophers that she observes in her journal for 1981–82, 'in philosophy, one goes where the honey is'.[10] Hence Murdoch's Plato reinforces her critique of contemporary philosophy and literature, which she takes to reflect rather than to challenge problematic aspects of modernity. Contemporary philosophy gives up on metaphysics and so abandons its traditional and certainly Platonic commitment to identify patterns of unity within the discordance of experience. Likewise, moral philosophy denies the relevance of moral vision in yielding to an alignment of morality with individual choice and shallow behaviourist accounts of human conduct. She also resorts to Plato in critiquing contemporary fiction for its uncritical submission to modern forms of neurosis and conventionalism, rather than portraying real characters freely interacting with one another.[11]

Murdoch's sense of how time bears upon her work tends to receive marginal if valuable incidental critical commentary. For instance, at the outset of A Philosophy to Live By: Engaging Iris Murdoch, Antonaccio remarks, 'Murdoch was a writer whose fiction and philosophy bear the deep imprint of the twentieth century and the end of the Cold War.'[12] What is neglected, however, is the centrality of the historicity of the present for her thinking in all of its guises. At the outset of *Metaphysics as a Guide to Morals* (1992), she identifies what is distinctive about the present cultural context. She highlights how its demythologization of traditional beliefs threatens to undermine appreciation of the ubiquity of value and of the unity within the diversity of experience. She refers to 'the extreme complexity of the whole idea of demythologization and its challenge to conceptions of transcendence'.[13] Old truths have crumbled and unifying myths are giving way to a deconstructive rational analysis, which disdains the integrity of experience. Murdoch's philosophy deals with the defining aspects of her times, notably the loss of faith in God, the end of 'grand' ideologies, the erosion of artistic realism and the substitution of subjective choice for non-negotiable principles in morality. This process of demythologization is exacerbated by political catastrophes of the twentieth century, which disturb faith in an underlying order to things. After the Holocaust and the Gulag, the very possibility of human goodness is questioned. Murdoch, in her letters and journals as well as in her published fiction and non-fiction, attests to the political catastrophes of the twentieth century that undermine utopian ideals.[14] Murdoch maintains a holistic conception of the unity and goodness amidst the dissonant and disconcerting claims of subjectivity and cultural rationalization. Deconstructive forces are to be acknowledged and negotiated and, at the same time, they are to be resisted.

All of Murdoch's work, her fiction alongside her non-fiction, focuses upon the defining aspects of the present and the contemporary questions that are posed to theory and practice. If, in some sense, philosophy and literature are timeless in relating to truth and reality, they are also historical in that their particular forms emerge from specific historic cultures. Questions arise out of experience, and experience is necessarily present and hence historical. The questions that are posed in the modern world are different from those that have gone before. Modern philosophy has to deal with a world that judges the dogmas of the past to be unacceptable. The intricacies of metaphysical thinking must now recognize experiential limits that condition its work. The modern novel cannot rehearse the self-confident realism of the great nineteenth-century writers, whose fiction reflects the contemporary surge of social forces and the consolidation of Western nation states.[15] If metaphysics is to serve as a guide to morality, it must deal with the current historical situation. In the wake of disintegrating demythologized traditions, Murdoch's philosophy represents a countervailing response, which continues metaphysics in a post-metaphysical age by drawing together forms of thought and action so as to make sense of them as a unity. Her metaphysics does not rely on top-down first-order principles but works with the grain of experience. It does not shirk the dissonance and fragmentation of late modernity but maintains a continuing commitment to orient personal and moral development by attending to unifying notions of truth and goodness that are evidenced within lived experience. Hence religion is to be valued for its orienting capacity to value experience as a whole rather than for its supernatural claims. In the light of the political traumas of the twentieth century, utopian schemes for political renewal are to be abandoned in favour of protecting the rights of individual citizens. Again, representational claims for art are to be modified rather than revived, so that its role in enabling an individual to perceive things accurately is to be cherished, notwithstanding the iconoclastic temper of the contemporary world.

Murdoch's philosophy arises out of her reflection upon modern culture, and her novels, insofar as they aspire to be realistic and truthful, reflect her times just as her critical reflection aims to make sense of her times. Her novel, *The Time of the Angels* (1966), is a case in point.[16] The phrase, 'the time of the angels', conjures up a world that has experienced the death of God, and it crops up again in *The Philosopher's Pupil* (1983), but the sense of a world without God is reflected in all of the novels.[17] The uncertain status of religion in a modern demythologized world is part of the atmosphere within which the action of her novels takes place. What remains in the wake of a waning of belief in the supernatural elements of religion – such as the existence of a personal God, the resurrection of Christ and God's miraculous intervention into the world – is a question that is taken up by the priests, iconoclasts and moralists who populate her novels. The rational temper of the modern age and its corrosive effect upon traditional beliefs constitutes a contextual component of the world that individual characters negotiate in her novels. Forsberg, in *Language Lost and Found – On Iris Murdoch and the Limits of Philosophical Discourse*, conceives of Murdoch's novels as pursuing a kind of philosophy in registering a loss of traditional concepts in the ways that their characters struggle to make sense of their world. He remarks, 'What drives my work here is the thought that a loss of concepts is something that permeates our culture and is not something that can reduced to a loss of a certain set of words that we can do without.'[18] Of course, Murdoch's novels are indirect rather than direct expressions of how she understands the world. They reflect rather than expound the issues of modern identity that are discussed directly in her philosophical writings. But her novels aim to be truthful in composing pictures of how individuals negotiate the world, of how they cope with its contingencies and of how they explore the freedom and respond to the challenges of modern times. The novels' characters question the orienting myths of preceding times and work within contemporary conventions and social practices that allow for choice and freedom in contrast to the previous rigidity and constraints. The historicity of the present is a feature of her novels just as it underlies her philosophical thinking.

In succeeding sections of this Introduction, I develop aspects of my overall argument, which will be pursued in later chapters. Murdoch's conception of the relations between philosophy and fiction will be outlined. Identifying the relations between the two is crucial in that recognizing their connections contributes to an understanding of the integrity of her overall perspective. Yet it is also important to be clear that this does not entail one being reduced to the other. Murdoch does not merely translate her philosophy into fiction, though her novels and her philosophy are interrelated ways of seeing things. I will also expand upon her understanding of the cultural context of late modernity, which underlies both her fiction and non-fiction. Thereafter I will review how her first philosophical publication, *Sartre – Romantic Revolutionary*, and her first novel, *Under the Net* (1954), share common ground while remaining distinct. I conclude this Introduction by setting out the agenda for the rest of the book.

A philosophical novelist?

Commentators on Murdoch take a view on how her philosophy is related to her fiction. After all, she is a notable practitioner in both fields, and the question of the relationship between the two bears upon how we interpret her as a philosopher and as a novelist. Opinions are divided. Some commentators see her as putting her philosophy into her novels, while others deny a connection. On the face of things, Murdoch seems pretty clear on the relationship. In interviews she characteristically denies that her novels are philosophical. For instance, in an interview with Stephen Glover that was published originally in *New Review*, she responds to the suggestion that she imports her philosophical theories into her novels by declaring, 'I hope not. I think it's a very dangerous thing to do, and I certainly don't want to mix philosophy and fiction – they're totally different disciplines, different methods of thought, different ways of writing, different aims.'[19] Again, in an interview with Bryan Magee for the TV programme *Men of Ideas*, she confesses to an absolute horror of putting ' "philosophical ideas" as such into my novels'.[20] Certainly, it would be misleading to reduce the role of Murdoch's fiction to that of a vehicle for transmitting an underlying philosophy. Literary scholars, such as A. N. Wilson and Conradi, tend to take her fiction as representing her pre-eminent achievement and play down her philosophical powers and interests.[21] They are right to attest to the quality of her fiction. Murdoch's imaginative creativity as a novelist supersedes a merely instrumental conception of her turn to literature. Murdoch's novels invoke imaginative worlds, decked with evocative descriptions and absorbing conversations between interlocutors, who demand our attention because of their credible individuality. Conversely, scholars such as Leeson, Nussbaum and Antonaccio take the novels to convey her philosophical ideas. There are variations on this theme. Heusel, for instance, identifies Murdoch's fiction as applying the doctrines of the later Wittgenstein. Certainly, Wittgenstein fascinated Murdoch, whose work she knew from her studies in Cambridge where she mixed with his former students. Arguably, Hugo Belfounder in *Under the Net* and Rozanov in *The Philosopher's Pupil* incarnate aspects of Wittgenstein's charismatic persona. Perhaps, Wittgenstein's later philosophy, which allows for a diversity of uncoordinated language games that preclude an overriding pattern to things, is also intimated by the multiple, unschematic frames that structure her novels.[22]

Murdoch's novels feature conversations of a philosophical nature. The meaning of God, the nature of morality and the future of the planet are subjects of debate, and individual characters in the novels are writing books on philosophy. These imaginary texts within the novels resemble themes in Murdoch's philosophy. They are on Plato, the transcendence of the good and how to maintain a sense of the good and moral perfection without relying on the existence of God. Individual characters and the diverse themes of the narratives also recall Wittgenstein. Yet, is this enough to justify terming Murdoch a philosophical novelist? As Forsberg suggests in *Language Lost and Found – On Iris Murdoch and the Limits of Philosophical Discourse*, it is questionable to assume that Murdoch possesses a self-contained set of doctrines that can be transferred easily to another form.[23] Her moral perfectionism, for instance, is more of a reminder for us to consider closely how we think about goodness and evil in our individual experience rather than a generic formula for living. Murdoch, in her philosophical writings, recognizes differences between art and philosophy and critiques novels that follow a tight theoretical or ideological agenda. Art, for Murdoch, is a means of perceiving and imagining reality. Visual and literary artists present the world realistically, and our engagement with a work of art enhances our appreciation of reality. Murdoch's novels do not rehearse a set of doctrines without regard for the intricacies of their imagined worlds and the interplay between their characters. Murdoch may put philosophical ideas into the conversations of her fictional characters and even allow for their writing philosophical Murdochian tracts and uttering phrases that are associated with her ideas. Yet her philosophy is contained in neither fictional speeches nor in fictional texts. We need to specify how the novel for Murdoch is separate from and yet connected to her philosophical writings.

Murdoch's distrust of novels that convey philosophical messages is set out clearly in her essay, 'Against Dryness'. In this essay she inveighs against crystalline novels, which dictate the interplay of characters and plot so as to express a position or point of view of the author.[24] She is also opposed to journalistic novels, which rely on detailed descriptions of the conventions in which narrative plot lines are developed. Both journalistic and crystalline novels tend to reduce imaginative literature to something else – theory, ideology or sociology – whereas Murdoch imagines the novel to be autonomous. Indeed Murdoch establishes the autonomy of the novel as well as the internal relationship between philosophy and the art of the novel, by philosophical means. She philosophizes about the differences between philosophy and literature. Standardly, she takes philosophy to be concerned with attending to conceptual affinities and differences between forms of experience so that, for instance, it discriminates between public and personal morality and recognizes how art, religion and philosophy are distinct but related ways of understanding experience. Art is not reduced to philosophy, and its independence is established by philosophy.[25]

While philosophy makes sense of the general contours of lived experience, the novel, for Murdoch, focuses uniquely upon its particularities. The messy, endlessly particular and contingent experiential world is captured in novels that articulate complex and interwoven plots where characters develop lives, and intermittent patterns are constituted by their overlapping relations to one another. In 'The Fire and the Sun – Why Plato Banished the Artists' (1977), Murdoch explains how the artist is attuned to 'the hardness of the real properties of the world ... where the mystery of the random has to be accepted'.[26] She takes art to contribute to the realization of truth and goodness by its capacity to show the particular reality of our experience, and the novel is well fitted to frame narratives that show the contingency, plurality and freedom of individual characters. She proposes a theoretical frame for understanding novels, which invokes a reworked Kantian idea of the sublime, whereby the straining of the form of a novel against the variety of particulars that are developed in a narrative shows the reality of our experience. In 'The Sublime and the Beautiful Revisited', Murdoch concludes: 'A novel must be a house fit for free characters to live in; and to combine form with a respect for reality with all its odd contingent ways is the highest art of prose.'[27] If Murdoch distinguishes the novel from philosophy, she does so by means of philosophy. She provides a philosophical account of its experiential role in attending closely to experience. More than this, the relationship between the novel and philosophy is dialectical. Philosophy allows us to see the value of the novel and art in general, while the novel, in opening us to reality and a world outside of ourselves, can prepare us for philosophy. Literature is distinct from philosophy, and philosophy registers its separateness, just as literature, in making sense of experience, serves as a vehicle to enable a philosophical perspective that is open to experience.

Philosophy, for Murdoch, respects the contingency and randomness of reality along with its intimations of unity and goodness. It is sensitive to the magnetism of goodness within experience, even if the pursuit of moral perfection is not to be encapsulated in any particular experiential enactment. In the light of this recognition, philosophy is to eschew general formulas for moral conduct that sideline the responsibilities of individuals to attend closely to other individuals and the particular circumstances in which they are situated. In her philosophical writings, Murdoch suggests that what is required for moral development is a virtuous and loving attention to others and the reality of their circumstances.[28] And the quality of attention or inattention to others in particular circumstances can be shown imaginatively in novels. Murdoch's novels show many characters interacting with one another, and in so doing they either attend to or neglect others' needs and concerns.

In 'The Fire and the Sun – Why Plato Banished the Artists', Murdoch suggests that an artist can be adept in depicting the prevalent tendency of individuals to act selfishly. She observes, 'good literature is uniquely able publicly to clarify evil'.[29] And she goes on to say, 'He [the artist] lends to the elusive particular a local habitation and a name.'[30] Murdoch's own art that is expressed in her novels is philosophical neither in deriving from a philosophical blueprint nor in conveying her own expressed doctrines or messages. Rather, Murdoch's novels disclose particular events and characters realistically. They reflect contemporary reality in the freedom that is explored by her characters who break with traditional religious and moral attitudes in pursuing an uncertain moral path that tends to be impeded by their distortive self-absorption. The novels are true to the nature of experience, and thereby they invite readers to consider the possibilities of moral progress or self-delusion in the modern world. In so doing they show something of the meaning of Murdoch's, philosophical perspective at a local level without being reduced to it. For instance, the personal development of Ducane in *The Nice and the Good* (1968) shows how moral progress is possible amidst a disturbed political context and within a moral atmosphere that defers to the pleasure of nice, bourgeois attitudes.[31] On the other hand, demonic figures, such as Julius King in *A Fairly Honourable Defeat* (1970) and Carel Fisher in *The Time of the Angels*, show how morality is not simply about enabling choices. Morality is altogether more serious. There is the possibility of evil. Some individuals pursue goals that are fundamentally at odds with the welfare and care of others.[32] We all know of occasions when we sense the presence of something evil.

In *Sartre – Romantic Rationalist*, Murdoch relates how the novel can convey concrete aspects of life that tend to be overlooked by abstract formulations. Indeed, in part, her interest in Sartre derives from his use of literary expression. Sartre, she maintains, can turn to the novel as he is interested in reviewing the texture of consciousness and lived experience. Hence his fiction in portraying lived experience and the permutations of consciousness can complement philosophy. She observes,

> The novelist proper is, in his way, a sort of phenomenologist. He has always implicitly understood what the philosopher has grasped less clearly, that human reason is not a single unitary gadget, the nature of which could be discovered once for all. The novelist has had his eye fixed on what we do and not on what we ought to do.[33]

The novelist, for Murdoch, gets to grips with what Beauvoir referred to as the 'metaphysics of lived experience'.[34] A novelist imagines individuals in realistic contexts, which are concrete and specific rather than abstract and general. She maintains, 'He [the novelist] has that natural gift that blessed freedom from rationalism which the academic thinker achieves, if at all, by a precarious discipline.'[35] Murdoch's novels provide a phenomenological review of imagined experience, shedding light on the contours of personal and social life. In her philosophy, she draws upon this imaginative capacity.

Murdoch's recognition of the interplay between philosophy and the novel is confirmed by her attraction to Plato. Notwithstanding Plato's critique of art, she sees Plato as an artist himself, approving of his use of the dialogue form. It is a form that imagines philosophical questions as arising out of the conversational interplay between individuals.[36] Murdoch herself wrote Platonic dialogues and is alert to how philosophical questions arise out of and re-engage with experience. The questions to which Murdoch's philosophy are addressed arise out of the post-war culture of the Western world. Central to this culture is the demythologization of religion, morality, philosophy and politics, whereby traditional values are losing sway and the previous security of principles is being disrupted by assertive subjectivism. Moral subjectivism takes over as beliefs in an objective goodness and a transcendent God disappear and the great ideologies of socialism, communism and fascism retreat before an instrumental liberalism. This eviscerated form of liberalism licenses subjective choice over a way of life that respects the liberty to develop individuality.[37] Murdoch's novels reveal a context in which traditional ways of life and principles are being eroded. They exhibit themes that are central to her philosophy because they show a world of particular individuals, situated at a point in time in which the culture of modernity renders moral, political and religious practice directionless. Just as her philosophy deals with demythologization and the ideal of a pilgrimage to goodness from the subjectivism of the contemporary world, so her novels depict characters who contend in unique situations with the confusions of modern culture.

Murdoch, as Forsberg intimates, in her novels and in her philosophy, is intent on capturing what is lost or being lost in contemporary culture.[38] In this respect, her novels and her philosophy are complementary projects. The nature of this complementarity is exhibited nicely in the novels *The Time of the Angels* and *A Fairly Honourable Defeat*. In *The Time of the Angels*, the demonic Carel Fisher is possessed with the idea of the death of God and the absence of moral limits, while his brother Marcus is working on a book to justify morality in the absence of a personal, transcendent God. Rupert Foster, in *A Fairly Honourable Defeat*, is composing a text on Plato and the good, while his former colleague, Julius King plays havoc with people's lives in his unrestrained manipulation of people's self-regard. On the face of things, the projects of Rupert Foster and Marcus Fisher resemble Murdoch's philosophy in their focus upon her own engagement with developing a sense of religion and goodness to fit with a demythologized world. Yet, neither Rupert nor Marcus is portrayed sympathetically. While the impetus of their writing may be honourable, we realize by the close of these novels that they are pusillanimous and vain, and their abstracted philosophies do not bear significantly upon the worlds around them. Chaos and immorality are unmoved by their words. The texts within the texts of Murdoch's novels do not encompass her philosophy, just as it is not disclosed in doctrines that are aired in her characters' conversations. Her novels, however, do imagine individual lives concretely so as to show the phenomenological possibilities of her philosophical analysis of moral perfectionism, and in particular they show the fallibility and susceptibility to self-absorption and hence the moral difficulties of individuals operating in a messy world.

Sartre and *Under the Net*: Philosophy and the novel at the outset of Murdoch's career

Murdoch's perspective on philosophy and the novel is evident at the outset of her career. She sees philosophy as more than an exercise in logic or semantics. It offers something to live one's life by, and this guidance appears all the more urgent in the immediate post-war world, when everything had been turned upside down. Similarly, her first novel reflects a critical turning point in post-war British society. Traditions and institutions are failing, socialism is an indeterminate word rather than a motivating doctrine, and individuals strike out alone without institutional support and a guiding philosophy. Her first works of philosophy and literature signpost her concerns. Subsequent philosophical texts focus on the post-metaphysical and deracinated ethics of the late twentieth century and are motivated by the priority of re-establishing a metaphysical underpinning for morality. After *Under the Net*, Murdoch's novels continue to explore the post-war world, where underlying myths of religion, philosophy and politics are decomposing and egoistic characters struggle to explore new possibilities of freedom.

From the beginning, Murdoch's philosophy differs from that of her counterparts in Oxford and Cambridge. They were wedded to a post-metaphysical analytical framework, which renounced traditional metaphysics and reduced ethics to a set of formulas enabling the freedom of self-interested individuals. In contrast, Murdoch's approach recognized how philosophy is to attend to the quality of experience and serves as a guide to how one might live a life. In a letter to Raymond Queneau in 1946, in which she recounts her excitement on reading Sartre, which is at odds with the cold rationalism of Oxford philosophy, she observes, 'But oh the way he throws his terms about ... would make Oxford hair stand on end. My cold critical judgment has not yet caught up with my emotional assent. (Now and then I think let it go to hell anyway why not read philosophy just for the emotional kick).'[39] Murdoch's own philosophy can be read for its emotional kick. She saw philosophy and literature as possessing a kick. They have something important to say about experience. She read Sartre and Beauvoir alongside Anglo-American philosophy, and while she absorbed the analytical precision of the latter, she also retained the existential kick of the former. If in the 1940s Murdoch was drawn to Sartre, she was also critical of him. Byatt, among others, is right to emphasize her critique of existentialism in that it was never sufficient for her to conceive of freedom in terms of 'indifference'.[40] *Under the Net*, her first novel, can be read as showing the limits of an existentialist attitude in that Jake Donoghue is so self-absorbed in his own pursuit of an individualist form of freedom that he ignores or misconstrues what is happening around him.[41] Yet, Murdoch values Sartre as well as rejects much of what he has to say. Sartre's *Being and Nothingness* is a phenomenological review of personal existence and the possibilities of freedom, which captured the mood of the times by looking for existential meaning while eschewing traditional forms of spiritual comfort.[42] In commenting upon *Being and Nothingness* to Queneau, Murdoch is ambivalent in testifying to its merits while criticizing his sense of freedom. She observes,

> He is seductive and captivating ... I don't want to concede that all awareness is self-awareness, and I find his concept of freedom vague and transcendental ... I'm also very drawn to the Sartrean concept of anguish and to the portrait of man alone in the universe faced by choice, architect of his own values.[43]

Sartre's phenomenological analysis of existence spoke to the generation that had experienced the Second World War. It was a generation that sought freedom and authenticity without reliance upon outmoded and discredited authorities. Murdoch's critical reading of Sartre reflects her sense that philosophy and literature more generally must engage with the present as an historical phenomenon in recognizing what is distinctive and urgent about its character.

Murdoch's first book, *Sartre – Romantic Rationalist*, introduced Sartre to an English-speaking audience, and it remains a considered introduction to Sartre and existentialism. As with her consideration of other philosophers more generally, her criticism also serves as a way of setting out her own ideas. She follows Sartre's engagement with Husserl, Heidegger and Hegel and admires the intensity of his phenomenological multilayered review of existence. Yet she poses critical questions to his philosophy, which reflect her training in analytical philosophy and her down-to-earth appraisal of experience. She highlights a tension between Sartre's intensive pursuit of individual freedom and what she terms the ordinary virtues of everyday life, whereby obligations to family and friends are conditions of self-development rather than barriers to an individual's exercise of self-control. She observes, 'Sartre by-passes the complexity of the world of ordinary human relations which is also the world of ordinary moral virtues.'[44] For Murdoch, 'Sartre's man is depicted in the moment-to-moment flux of his thoughts and moods … at this level freedom seems indeed like randomness, the freedom of indifference.'[45] In a later essay 'On "God" and "Good"' (1969), Sartre's notion of freedom is likened to that of contemporary Anglo-American theorists of morality in his focus on will and choice as sovereign instruments in determining value, even though their philosophical styles contrast.[46] Moran, in his article 'Iris Murdoch and Existentialism', takes issue with Murdoch on Sartre and existentialism, holding that the existentialist emphasis upon choice is warranted by the continuous responsibility an individual must assume for their lives. He remarks: 'For it is because of what I referred to earlier as the "unbounded" aspect of human freedom, the fact that the person always orients himself one way or another toward both his capacities and obstacles, that the Existentialist sees an element of choice in all the continuities and discontinuities of a person's gestures, postures and attitudes.'[47] Moran might well be right in highlighting the conceptual link between freedom and agency, which perhaps Murdoch underplays in her moral writings. Her reading of Sartre and existentialism is questionable, but it is also plausible in pointing to the social context of freedom and her own alignment of freedom to a vision that goes beyond merely individual choice.

Murdoch's early work on Sartre represents her enduring approach to philosophy. Philosophy, for Murdoch, is not an abstract exercise without reference to lived experience. What she values in Sartre is his focus upon making sense of an individual's experience. Likewise, she accepts Sartre's break from preceding forms of metaphysics and from an uncritical acceptance of conventions. She is at one with aspects of his reading of the present. The free development of individuals is central to the modern world. Yet, she breaks with Sartre in insisting that an individual is not to be abstracted from social and political practices that contribute to their identity and freedom. Moreover, Murdoch subscribes to a renewed form of metaphysics, which is to be distinguished from pre-Kantian forms of reasoning, but which continues the work of Plato and Hegel in connecting significant aspects of experience in guiding an individual to align with truth and goodness.[48] Where the Sartrean individual sees others as impediments to freedom, Murdoch imagines an individual's cultivation of friendship, family ties and political obligations as being constitutive of their identity. Moreover, she perceives art and religion as attuning an individual to the possibility of grasping the truth of things and of other people.

Under the Net announces Murdoch's arrival as a novelist, and her arrival was interpreted variously. Ryan, in his introduction to the Vintage edition of the novel (2002), recalls and rebuts its original critical reception as a work of an angry young man.[49] If Murdoch was neither angry nor a man, she engaged with the spirit of her time like other emerging post-war novelists. But she saw the time differently. Spear in *Iris Murdoch* remarks:

> The further we travel from the 1950s, the clearer it is that while the novels of the 'Angry Young Men' of that time were the forerunners of the disillusioned 'University novels' of the later decades of the twentieth century, she herself was in the process of creating a novelistic world unique to her own art; her created world attempts to grapple, not with the so-called realism of the 1950s and 1960s, but rather with the malaise that lies at the heart of life, the 'real' realism in which we, all of us, have faced the changes brought upon us by the Second World War, by the holocaust, by the fear of the atom bomb, by the gradual erosion (however much it may be denied) of the old class system.[50]

Spear's focus upon the realist and historical dimension of *Under the Net* and of Murdoch's fiction as a whole is enlightening. *Under the Net* is not a philosophical tract in which Murdoch dispenses her philosophical views. Rather it is a narrative of how a young man, Jake Donoghue, reflecting contemporary existential attitudes, negotiates the atmosphere of the post-war world, where long-standing traditions and beliefs have receded. *Under the Net* is, however, notable for containing express discussion of philosophy and for including two characters who are memorable philosophers. When Jake needs a bed at the start of the novel, he goes to Dave Gellman. Dave is a philosopher who does extra mural work for a university in London. He is a sympathetic character, who never seems to lose contact with a student and who knows many artists, intellectuals and left-wing political people. Students like and admire him even if he devotes himself to critiquing the grounds of their metaphysical beliefs by his own brand of linguistic analysis. His hard-headed philosophical questioning aims to destroy unifying theories, and he also aims to put students off pursuing a philosophical career.[51] The other philosopher is Hugo Belfounder, who is not a professional philosopher, but Jake sees him as a rigorous theoretician who offers a distinctive, philosophical perspective. Belfounder had a 'theory of everything but in a peculiar way. Everything had a theory but there was no master theory.'[52] Hugo is profoundly anti-metaphysical – a radical undoctrinaire philosopher who nonetheless has a distinct point of view. His critical hostility towards generalization renders him suspicious of language itself. How can it capture the reality of particular things? It is a net that covers things.

The representation of philosophers and philosophical positions in *Under the Net* does not entail that Murdoch is espousing an express philosophical doctrine. She does not share the views of Gellman or Belfounder. Their views are not the heart of the novel. In fact, Murdoch is a metaphysician to whom their doctrines are opposed. What the novel does display is the rootless individualism of its central protagonist, Jake Donoghue, who wanders across London without a fixed purpose and enduring social ties. He believes in socialism but indeterminately. He is elusive, and his elusivity represents the general elusivity of the present. The novel is also the first of a number of first-person narratives, where the narrator is revealed to be unreliable. The unreliability of Jake Donoghue's perception of things stands for the general unreliability of all of us in attending to what is happening. By the end of the novel, Jake himself, and the reader, are aware, albeit dimly, that his assertive subjectivity masks his misreading of virtually all the key characters and relationships in the novel. The novel does not spell out a philosophy, but it serves as a reminder that, in a radically individualist culture, securing a grip on one's relations with others is problematic. In his sensitivity to resist conventions and relationships that compromise his individuality, Jake is insensitive to friends and lovers. He lacks awareness of whom he loves and who is in love with him.

Jake's Bohemianism might seem romantic and heroic, like existentialism, but he is revealed to be egoistic and floundering amid the deracinated relationships and practices of the post-war world. His individualism is uneasy, as he resists conventions and avoids stereotypical acquisitive behaviour to insist upon authentic existential choices, which obscure his real relations with others. Murdoch's first novel, like her first philosophical work, anticipates what follows in her career. As in *Under the Net*, all of her novels relate to her philosophy, vividly showing what it might amount to in an individual case while not rehearsing philosophical doctrines directly. The author relates to her readers indirectly. Characters are shown to be involved in fluid situations that allow for individual choices that tend to lack realistic assessment of self and others. Myths that have previously supported institutions and practices are now questionable, and their recessiveness tends to leave individuals without the resources to handle their freedom. And yet the novels do not simply yield to what has been lost in the transition to modernity. There are suggestions of the possibilities of moral progress and a humour that lightens the incompatibility between individual ambition and the realities of the world.

The dialectic of Murdoch's life and work

In the following chapters, I develop the themes that have been set out in the preceding pages. This book will attend to the critical and dialectical way in which Murdoch integrates forms of thought and action and their historical development. In doing so, the value of her work in specific ways will be highlighted along with the overall value of her integrated conception of experience and how we are to understand it and live within it. In Chapter 2, 'Murdoch and Metaphysics', her metaphysics is reviewed. For Murdoch, metaphysics provides an overall way of understanding experience, linking religion, art, personal development, morality and politics to one another and to an overall unity of experience that allows for difference and contingency. The historicity of metaphysics is significant for Murdoch in that she makes clear that she approaches metaphysics via a reading of its history. Murdoch's approach to metaphysics is post-Kantian, and she assumes that any viable form of metaphysics in the modern era must respond to the post-metaphysical context of modern times. She takes metaphysical understanding to depend upon experiential forms of support.

Merely logical reasoning cannot generate experiential truths; rather, experiential evidence allows for ways of reading experience as exhibiting truth, goodness and unity. Her historical perspective is evident in her practice of metaphysical thinking in that she develops her thinking by engaging in sustained criticism of preceding and contemporary philosophers. Metaphysics is a holistic reading of experience in which differing elements of experience are linked together in terms of their common revelation of their underlying value and goodness. The inclusivity of this holistic perspective entails that the dissonant, the wayward and the contingent are to be recognized as part of the whole, and their impact is evident in the imperfection of every experiential enactment of the good.

Notwithstanding the centrality of morality to Murdoch's conception of metaphysics, Chapter 2 will not focus upon her ethics, which is set out most memorably in the essays contained in *The Sovereignty of Good* (1970), for her moral philosophy will be considered in Chapter 4. Rather, it examines *Metaphysics as a Guide to Morals* and her unpublished 'Manuscript on Heidegger'.[53] These two texts, which were composed towards the end of her life, furnish a retrospective account of what she takes to be central in metaphysics. They are at one in respecting modern limits on the way in which metaphysics operates, in that Murdoch takes metaphysics to draw upon experience to support its arguments. She is also clear that metaphysics is not a mere academic exercise. It matters. It matters in that it provides an overall picture by which one can live one's life.

Chapter 3, 'Murdoch and the Novel', reviews how she understands the novel. It asks and answers the questions of how her own novels fit with her philosophical ideas and how she perceives art in general. The novel, like art more generally, plays an integral role in Murdoch's conception of experience and the possibility of achieving moral progress. Murdoch's sense of the interrelations between the novel, visual arts and philosophy will be explored. While many texts of Murdoch will be examined, the focus will be upon her series of essays on literature that are collected together in *Existentialists and Mystics* and her book 'The Fire and the Sun – Why Plato Banished the Artists'. The essays show how intensively Murdoch was engaged in reflecting upon the possibilities of literature and, in particular, the novel. She offers a reading of the novel, which is historical in character. She focuses upon the crisis of the novel in the contemporary world, offering a critique of the contemporary novel, eschewing the didactic tone of one of its most prominent idioms. As an alternative, she looks to work with the sublime whereby the interplay of particular human characters resists the author's inclination to impose a formal conception upon the intricacies of human interaction. She relishes the way in which the novel can intimate the richness and freedom of lived experience. Her own novels are guided self-consciously towards capturing the nature of lived experience, notably its randomness and contingency. The novels also frame pictures of individuals whose conduct and reflections bear upon themes of her philosophy. They reflect the processes of demythologization that act upon twentieth-century culture. Again, insofar as the novels are realist, they reflect aspects of her philosophy that are designed to comprehend experience. Characters are shown as seeking the good and straying from it in ways that show how the pilgrimage to goodness is a particular and arduous road. The novels disclose the singularities of roads to goodness and particular personifications of evil. Murdoch understands the visual arts as representing truth and goodness, and her novels engage with the visual arts in developing imaginary but realistic images of experience. Art as a whole in representing the world truthfully allows for an appreciation of reality, which enables individuals to be clear on things. In her novels, individuals who visit art galleries and think about paintings are shown to be contributing to artistic endeavour and to artistic appreciation of reality.

Central to Murdoch's view of the world is morality and goodness, and she takes the visual arts, literature and philosophy to contribute to the moral life. Hence in Chapter 4, 'Murdoch and morality', Murdoch's distinctive moral theory is analysed. Contrary to standard contemporary views, which rehearsed forms of subjectivism, Murdoch was committed to a perfectionist view of moral life, where individuals aim to achieve the good, which goes beyond a merely subjective perspective. It involves the critical determination to see things from other than one's own point of view. Her most famous philosophical essays that are collected in *The Sovereignty of Good* set out a challenging view of morality, which draws upon Plato's notion of the Good as the magnetic force that metaphorically expresses the standard for moral goodness. These essays are discussed alongside a review of the ways in which the pursuit of the good and its pitfalls enter into her novels, such as *The Good Apprentice* (1985) and *The Bell* (1958). Murdoch's moral philosophy remains as relevant today as when it was written. It combines a radical critique of standard assumptions with a plausible experiential argument for a perfectionism that answers to our sense that we need to look hard at ourselves and others in our moral conduct.

An underexamined aspect of Murdoch's work is her appraisal of the political world. In Chapter 5, 'Murdoch and the political', her views on politics are examined. Her early communism and later espousal of liberalism are acknowledged by commentators, but what tends to be ignored are the ways in which she explores politics in her theoretical writings and how politics enters her novels. Politics occupies a definite place in her scheme of things. In her early political thinking of the 1950s she looks to a renewal of socialist ideology, while recognizing that in the post-war Western world radical ideology has lost its previous appeal. Subsequently she develops a liberal political theory in which a limited form of politics is espoused that concentrates upon providing security and rights in the public realm so that individuals can pursue personal moral development. Her politics is influenced by historical developments. In her letters she reveals concerns over the tyrannies of the twentieth century, which have prevented individuals from exercising freedom. Her early commitment to socialism faded. In her first novel *Under the Net* socialism is an unexplained and unjustified commitment by characters who cannot provide an account of its credibility. Subsequently she lost faith entirely in the socialist project and, indeed, in the capacity of politics to provide a utopian solution to the human condition. Her novels contain many references to Holocaust survivors, who testify to the calamities that can befall radical ideological projects. Questions of public morality are rehearsed in her novels, ranging from the status of refugees, the nature of rights, the balance to be struck between private and public morality, life and death issues, sexual freedoms, and what a citizen owes to the state. *The Flight from the Enchanter* (1956), *The Nice and the Good* and *An Accidental Man* (1971) contain subtle discussions of a number of these issues. *The Book and the Brotherhood* (1987) concerns the writing of a book that purports to provide a general theory of politics. It is financed by a group, the brotherhood, whose own beliefs in socialism and grand theory have receded, but the author David Crimmond produces a radical and challenging critique of the political system. Is the project of grand critical political theory still viable? This is a question that is asked in the novel. The political questions and issues that inform the novels are not resolved conclusively, as they appear within complex events and are taken up by characters who are neither exemplary nor simple representatives of a viewpoint. Murdoch deals with these political questions because they are important in the modern world and impact upon people's lives and other aspects of experience. Her treatment of politics is subtle and valuable.

If Murdoch's philosophy and novels are ways of making sense of lived experience then it makes sense that Murdoch's own life reflects the issues with which she deals in her philosophy and in her imaginative writing. This is the case. In Chapter 6, 'Murdoch: Her life and times', her life is reviewed. For better or for worse Murdoch's life is in the public domain and has been the source of several conflicting standpoints. One narrative sees her as a brilliant young woman, succeeding as a philosopher in a very male world of Oxford philosophy, making an ideal marriage with an Oxford eccentric and then succumbing at the last to Alzheimer disease. At the last this formerly brilliant mind becomes hopeless and abject, and is cared for by her loving partner. By and large, this is the story of the film of her life that relates to the moving memoirs of her husband, John Bayley.[54] This narrative was quickly debunked by A. N. Wilson who referred to her sexual promiscuity and frenzied sociality. The publication of some of her letters has added to the complications of the way her life is to be understood. In their Introduction to a selection of her letters, *Living on Paper – Letters from Iris Murdoch 1934–1995*, the editors Horner and Rowe observe: 'They give us a portrait of a woman who lived unconventionally and according to her own moral code; of a complex individual whose reactions to others and events were often intense and frequently irreverent; of a woman whose ideas and values changed profoundly over the years.'[55] Perhaps unsurprisingly this balanced assessment of her life was not accepted by some reviewers who have concentrated on the sexual revelations in the letters. While Murdoch's life and letters can be understood in multiple ways, what they do show, and in ways that are relevant to the themes of this book, is Murdoch's personal involvement with events and attitudes to experience that feature in her writing. While in her philosophy the general character of morality is discussed and in her novels imaginary characters confront moral issues, in her letters we have evidence of how morality and reflection on morality vitalise an actual life, namely, Murdoch's own. She owns to moral failings, empathizes with others and has to deal with loss, of her parents, and a loved one. Again, the letters provide first-hand experience of refugees surviving as victims of Nazi atrocity in the uncertain world of displacement centres. Her novels involve numerous migrants of many kinds, whose precarity and dislocation pose moral and political questions for themselves and others. The letters do reveal her intense personal and sexual relations with others, and this readiness to embrace loving relations may be questionable at times but also testifies to her capacity to enact the love of which she writes in her theoretical and fictional writing. The fluidity of her sexuality reflects her clear-headed analysis of homosexuality and her support for its legalization in her article, 'The Moral Decision about Homosexuality' (1964).[56] Murdoch's life attests to her reflection on experience, which includes consideration of political events of the day, and her concern to develop as a moral person. The life matters because it shows how making sense of experience matters. Indeed, her metaphysics, her literary art, her moral and political thought and her life inter-relate because she integrates them all into her overriding concern to enhance engagement with experience.

In the course of this book, many different kinds of writing by Murdoch will be consulted. Given our sense of the complementarity of her fiction and non-fiction, her novels and philosophical writings will be drawn upon. Given the interrelated nature of her interpretation of differing areas of experience, reference will be made to particular texts and arguments in differing chapters. Unpublished writings will be cited, along with published texts. These unpublished items include her 'Manuscript on Heidegger' and her letters and journals as well as papers relating to Murdoch that are kept at St. Anne's College. Given that Murdoch did not want her letters, journals and 'Manuscript on Heidegger' to be published, we use these sources after some reflection. Their use is justified in that they relate to themes that are explored in this book and generally harmonize with what is maintained in her published texts. Some of the unpublished writings are of significant value. Her 'Manuscript on Heidegger' is a considered and thoughtful exploration of the possibilities of metaphysics in a post-metaphysical context as well as an informed and considered study of Heidegger. Indeed, it merits publication in that it sheds light on Heidegger and on Murdoch's conception of metaphysics, without wandering away from how she discusses metaphysics in her Gifford lectures which were later published as *Metaphysics as a Guide to Knowledge*. Her journals vary in character. Some of the early journals of the 1940s contain intensive notes on philosophy, including a record of her thoughts on Cambridge philosophy, the existentialism of Sartre and Marcel and analysis of Hegel and Husserl. Later journals tend to be more epigrammatic and less scholarly but provide a record of her thinking on a variety of subjects. Her letters vary. Some are short on intellectual or personal reflection, but the letters to Queneau stand out for their discussion of her intellectual interests at the outset of her philosophical career. Where possible I have drawn upon the selection of letters in *Living on Paper – Letters from Iris Murdoch 1934–1995* as they are published and accessible, though all of the letter runs in the Iris Murdoch Archive are worth consulting. The use of her unpublished writings allows for an intensive analysis of the themes that underlie this study. Iris Murdoch matters because she provides an integrated, historically attuned exploration of experience in the modern Western world in fictional and non-fictional texts. She tried to live by the principles that she theorized. Her ideas and life remain worthy objects of study.

CHAPTER TWO

Murdoch and metaphysics

Introduction

Murdoch's metaphysics is dialectical and historical. Its dialectical quality is exhibited in the series of internal relations it establishes between forms of experience. The personal and the public, the disordered and the ordered, unity and plurality, and past and present are some of the constituents of her relational perspective. The object of metaphysical understanding is present experience, which at the same time presumes a past from which it has emerged. The historicity of the present entails the time-bound operations of metaphysics, in that its questions arise out of reflection upon contemporary experience and its form develops historically by a critical engagement with past metaphysicians. Murdoch takes metaphysics to be holistic in its review of how partial forms of experience are only fully intelligible in terms of the location within the whole. Metaphysics identifies the contributions of religion, art and morality to its own integrative understanding of experience. Religion frames a conception of reality as a whole and inspires and sustains moral practice. In modern times, however, supernatural elements of religion cannot be sustained in the light of the prevailing rationalist temper and a critical philosophical perspective sets limits to a religious perspective as well as identifying its significance. Likewise art is understood critically by philosophy so that its sentimental and consolatory forms are dismissed, but its awareness of underlying unities is respected. Morality incorporates interrelated public and personal forms, which are anchored by a presumption of underlying goodness and unity. Murdoch's metaphysics is not a world-denying neo-Platonism, in which the ideal is divorced from the apparently real. Her reading of Plato allows for a modern sensibility that links speculation on the absolutely good to experience and takes the ideal to be a projection from and reflection back upon the actual. Theory and practice, imperfection and perfection and past and present are mutually implicated in an integrative metaphysics.

Murdoch was aware of the delicacy of her metaphysical thinking. She takes on board a thoroughly modern perspective, in which the limits of knowledge are recognized and empirical information is valued. Simultaneously she draws upon Platonic metaphysics to resume an ambitious conception of philosophy's role in framing a broad metaphysical picture of a multidimensional but unitary reality. To establish and explain Murdoch's metaphysical perspective we will focus upon Murdoch's last published philosophical text, *Metaphysics as a Guide to Morals* (1992) and her late unpublished 'Manuscript on Heidegger'. In these texts Murdoch frames a considered view of how metaphysics can operate in modern times. In related ways, these texts establish a historical context in which her metaphysics is to be offered. In *Metaphysics as a Guide to Morals* she highlights the processes of demythologization that have reduced the ways in which we understand ourselves. Science, technology and a stripped down notion of philosophy set the tone for a rational instrumentalism in which orienting schemes of metaphysics are excluded. In responding to this context she enlists a form of Platonism, which is framed so as to meet the philosophical temper of the moment. In the 'Manuscript on Heidegger', which she prepared for possible publication in 1993, she provides a careful commentary on how Heidegger's post-metaphysical scheme of metaphysics signposts a way of dealing with the contemporary philosophical impasse.

Along the way in these texts Murdoch invokes numerous preceding philosophies and reviews past thinking from the perspective of the present and offers discontinuous commentary on her own position in the light of her predecessors. The upshot is that commentators find it difficult to thread a path through what Tracy has referred to as the 'occasional appearance of meandering formlessness' in *Metaphysics as a Guide to Morals*.[1] Her thinking darts between past and present and between commentary on past philosophers and exposition of her own thought. In respect of this tendency to move noiselessly between second order commentary and first order theorising Rosen advised against publication of the 'Manuscript on Heidegger'.[2] However, there is a rationale for Murdoch's way of proceeding. Past and present, for her, are not located in isolated worlds. A present aspiration to undertake metaphysics is to be made in the light of current readings of past endeavours and the past can be scrutinized and resumed so as to challenge orthodoxies of the present. The interpreter of past texts is not preparing them to be exhibited in a museum where they are not to be touched. The historical turn against metaphysics can be remedied by recasting past forms of thought to counter the contemporary demythologizing currents that threaten the integrity of experience. Murdoch practises a form of Gadamerian hermeneutics in approaching the past in the light of the present and using the past to comment upon the present.[3] There is to be a fusion of horizons. For Gadamer, there cannot be, as Collingwood maintained, a rethinking of past thoughts because thought is always connected to its contexts in ways that render present perceptions of past thought distinct from their original form.[4]

Murdoch's working through of her own philosophy by reworking the ideas of past practitioners is a method that fits with the historical nature of metaphysics and the historical perspective that she brings to its study. Occasionally it can distract readers, for instance, when she delivers an uncompromising and highly partial reading of Derrida to highlight her sense of an historical trend within modernity to deprecate moral agency and the conditions that make agency possible.[5] Her use of the past to highlight deficiencies of the present in *Metaphysics as a Guide to Morals* and the 'Manuscript on Heidegger' is matched by what Antonaccio terms 'the movement between metaphysics and empiricism'.[6] Unifying theory is tethered to particular observations about the world and consciousness so that Murdoch's metaphysics relates to the lived experience of individuals. Hence, our analysis of Murdoch's systematic presentation of her metaphysics will be supplemented by reference to observations in her journals and letters and to passages in her novels. The novels do not so much represent a condensed philosophy as serve as mirrors of what it means to live in a modern world in which individuals look for meaning in a world without a personal God, respond to political events and look to make moral progress in a world of contingency, particularity and comedy.[7] The uneven juxtapositions of experience that are the stuff of her literary imagination are also part of her metaphysical perspective.

Metaphysics as a Guide to Morals

At the outset of *Metaphysics as a Guide to Morals*, Murdoch sets out the context within which it is written and the situation to which it is addressed. She observes, 'This subject or problem interests us now because the pluralization or demythologisation of history, art, religion, science, which is characteristic of our age, largely takes the form of an analysis of old and prized unities and deep instinctive beliefs thought to be essential to human nature.'[8] Metaphysics like religion, ideology and art suffers from a prevailing cultural mood that disturbs allegiance to intellectual and moral order and established authorities. In the wake of the growth of science and technology, religion strains to sustain its most sacred tenets, art renounces its ambitions of realism and ideological commitment to utopian renewal retreats before the material delivery of goods and the protection of individuals from public domination. In her journal of 1947 she refers to the precarious status of metaphysics and the tendency to degrade mysteries into problems.[9] Metaphysics has to operate in the wake of the processes of demythologization that have marked the modern world. Murdoch's concern to recast metaphysics so as to preserve its status, and to respect the mysteries that were being dissolved by an increasingly scientific and materialist spirit, persisted throughout her career.

Murdoch recognizes the peculiarity of the modern context in which she operates. Indeed, she accepts the post-Enlightenment situation. The critical scrutiny of all claims to knowledge is to be embraced. The supernatural elements of religion cannot be maintained in the light of reason and the authority that is enjoyed by science in establishing the empirical facts pertaining to the natural world. After Kant and his critical scrutiny of the claims of reason metaphysical claims cannot be upheld by dint of a priori reasoning. She accepts Kant's deflationary critique of the claims of reason, maintaining, 'Kant's metaphysic is a model of demythologisation, wherein God, if present, is secluded.'[10] In a journal entry for 1947, she remarks, 'We cannot return to Aquinas as if Kant, Hegel and Marx had never happened.'[11] While recognizing that these demythologizing tendencies are neither to be ignored nor simply denied, she is aware of their menace in that they threaten to undermine the claims of art, religion and metaphysics to orient individuals in the direction of truth and goodness.

In the light of the menacing aspect of modernity she rehearses a forceful critique of Derrida in a chapter of *Metaphysics as a Guide to Morals* that is entitled 'Derrida and Structuralism'. The title itself shows hostility in that Derrida himself was a severe critic of forms of structuralism and his post-structuralism was pitched against all forms of thinking that presume essentialized forms of meaning underlying the flexibility of language.[12] Yet Murdoch is suspicious of Derrida's deconstruction of authorial meanings of texts. Derrida's method is to disturb authorial authority by tracing the ways in which the language of the text goes beyond any particular restricted viewpoint, including that of the author. What worries Murdoch are the implications for agency and an agent's affirmation of values in the light of this latest demythologizing tendency. She observes, 'The notion that every sentence we use bears, indeed consists of, the invisible traces of other meanings created by a vast non-human system carries serious implications ... Value, morality, is removed by the structuralist picture if taken seriously. This removal of value is in a quiet way, characteristic of this age.'[13] Murdoch sees Derrida's deconstruction of traditional metaphysics and authorial authority as symptomatic of the age and its tendency in a multiplicity of fields to undermine traditional myths. While the myths might have rested upon uncertain foundations, their demolition leaves values exposed, and in consequence they are taken increasingly to represent nothing more than changeable and disordered forms of desire.

Murdoch's metaphysical remedy for the problems of modernity is paradoxical. She embraces a form of Platonic metaphysics. How is this possible? Plato, after all, is pre-modern. Murdoch herself understands its seemingly paradoxical nature, given her recognition that we cannot return to a pre-Kantian form of metaphysics. Towards the end of *Metaphysics as a Guide to Morals*, she provides an answer. It is historical and dialectical. She sets out the rationale for her interpretation of past metaphysics. She notes, 'In thinking about the work of great metaphysicians one has to seek a balance between "faithfulness to the text" and a tendency to invent one's own metaphysician.'[14] This balance involves avoiding the rehearsal of old, unassimilated dead ideas and being overly 'inventive' and substituting one's own thoughts for those of the thinker whose work is being interpreted.[15] She admits, 'In my own case I am aware of the danger of inventing my own Plato and extracting a particular pattern from his many-patterned text to reassure myself that, as I see it, good is really good and real is really real.'[16] She goes on to say that she wants 'to put his [Plato's] argument into a modern context as a background to moral philosophy, as a bridge between morals and religion, and as relevant to our new disturbed understanding of religious truth'.[17]

The upshot is that Murdoch uses Plato to respond to the processes of demythologization that undermine faith in God and in objective goodness in the modern world. Plato is invoked because he provides the metaphors, which allow individuals to make sense of experience. A Platonic perspective encourages individuals to develop their understanding of its truth and unity while having faith in nurturing their virtue in the light of the Good. Plato's images and comprehensive vision of experience lend themselves to the task which Murdoch sets herself in the light of the current destruction of religious mythology and affiliated large-scale readings of experience. In so doing she adopts a particular reading of Plato, which, as her reading of Plato on art in 'The Fire and the Sun – Why Plato Banished the Artists' (1977) suggests, is informed and considered, but also accentuates the openness of Plato's philosophy so that it allows for modern scepticism over dogmatic metaphysics.[18] Invoking Plato is both courageous and risky. Her reliance upon Plato is susceptible to misapprehensions. Tracy observes how Platonism has been taken to represent exactly the kind of vague overly ambitious philosophy that analytical philosophy in its earliest most strictly observed modes was supposed to undo.[19] Conradi in his study, *Murdoch – A Life*, notes how 'Iris's and Plato's voices become a single indistinguishable composite intellect.'[20] Bernard Williams in his review of 'The Fire and the Sun – Why Plato Banished the Artists' bemoans Murdoch's lack of engagement with the scholarly literature on Plato and questions the Platonism of her own defence of art. He observes, 'Miss Murdoch, retaining a schematically Platonic language at least, but with something of a modern blank where the Cosmic Thing used to be, defends art against Plato.'[21]

Murdoch's Plato in *Metaphysics as a Guide to Morals* plays a positive role in developing a metaphysical counterpoint to modern scepticism rather than serving as an uncontroversial scholarly study of his dialogues. It is an interpretive procedure that informs her reading of many philosophers in this text. Her metaphysics emerges from her criticism of other thinkers, whom she stylizes so as to make a contribution to contemporary issues. She sees Hegel as resembling Plato in that he is a metaphysician, whose metaphysical style bears upon the project of reviving metaphysics in a modern context. Her reading of Hegel is critical in that she is suspicious of his assimilation of forms of experience and historical development into a final absolute comprehension of truth. This finalization of truth is something to which Murdoch is opposed. Her own metaphysics is constructed so as to maintain the freedom of individuals and to be open to the contingency of events. Hence her critical reading of Hegel is a means of highlighting her own position just as her sympathetic interpretation of Plato is a vehicle for its expression. Murdoch herself draws attention to the significance of a comparison between Plato and Hegel for the formulation of her own standpoint. First, she observes what they have in common as metaphysicians in remarking, 'For both Plato and Hegel the need and desire to understand (to understand *everything*) presents a conception of what is real as a series of progressively higher levels.' Hegel's *Geist* (better translated as 'spirit' rather than as 'mind') is like Plato's Forms (Ideas) which generate both logical-epistemological understanding (as universals) and (as desired by Eros) spiritual understanding and moral motive.[22] However, Hegel is taken to diverge from Plato in maintaining a closed system. Murdoch declares, 'Hegel must count himself a Platonic thinker, and his image of progress must remind us of Plato's Cave. However Hegel's omnivorous dialectic is unlike Plato's dialectic. Hegel's Reason proceeds by a continuous discarding of possibilities; doubts, ambiguities, rambling of any kind are officially not permitted and cannot be left "lying about." '[23] Where Plato is open and ambiguous, leaving many possibilities for further enquiry, Hegel is closed and confining. For Murdoch, Hegel's systematic treatment of experience closes down possibilities and while he is insightful in considering the history of social and political life, his linear reading of historical development informs a utopian reading of history by Marxists, which permits a repressive treatment of those who espouse alternative historical scenarios. Of course, this reading of Hegel is controversial. Hegel has been read as an open theorist, who accommodates freedom and contingency.[24] Murdoch herself reviews his thought more sympathetically in early journal entries.[25] But the primary point in Murdoch's reading of Hegel in *Metaphysics as a Guide to Morals* is that it sets up a contrast with Plato and allows for Murdoch's expression of her own commitment to a world of freedom and contingency to emerge clearly in opposition to this constructed image of Hegel.

Murdoch is a dialectical thinker, like Plato and Hegel, in that she connects areas of experience with one another and allows for a deeper understanding of aspects of experience to emerge from the construction of a progressively broader and more differentiated picture of things. She follows Plato rather than Hegel in allowing for freedom, contingency and interpretive openness in tracing interconnections within experience. Of course her interpretation of Plato reflects her own preference for open-mindedness, and a persuasive rather than fixed and dogmatic style of thinking, just as her reading of Hegel deflects from the ambiguities of Hegel's own position.[26] In interpreting Plato as allowing for freedom, Murdoch takes the forms of Plato's philosophy as 'separate and distant' from the particular constituents of lived experience.[27] This separation of an ideal rational and moral order from the experiential world allows for individual freedom. The moral and intellectual development of individuals is never completely realized, because the forms represent a standard of perfection that is not to be achieved. Hence the possibilities of human agency always remain open. In contrast, Hegel's system represents a scheme of philosophical knowledge that absorbs individuals within its absolute achievement. The philosophical explanation of historical progress detracts from the contingency of an individual's situation and their capacity to exercise freedom.

Murdoch's reading of Plato and Hegel discloses her own metaphysics. She shares with her dialectical predecessors a commitment to an inclusive style of metaphysics in which the whole of experience is to be understood. Forms of thought and action such as art, religion and moral and political practice constitute the loving pursuit of truth and goodness. Philosophy comprehends the interrelations between them and their underlying unity. The ascent towards truth is an arduous dialectical journey, which can be intimated by images such as Plato's cave, which conveys our propensity to misperceive things and the immensity of the struggle to orient oneself towards the good. Experience is awkward, discontinuous and difficult to negotiate. The ego is a relentless purveyor of fantasy and orchestrator of false unities that mask the reality which individuals should embrace in loving relations with others. Murdoch invokes Freud to reinforce her message about the propensity of individuals to be self-deceptive and their susceptibility to egoism, fantasy and neurosis.[28]

The contrast that Murdoch draws between the aspiration to truth and unity, and the actual world of everyday contingency and muddle, is a vital aspect of her metaphysics. At the outset of *Metaphysics as a Guide to Morals*, she observes, 'We fear plurality, diffusion, senseless accident, chaos, we want to transform what we cannot dominate or understand into something reassuring and familiar, into ordinary being, into history, art, religion, science.'[29] The dialectic between experiential diffusion and plurality and a countervailing aspiration to unity is central to Murdoch's metaphysics. The plausibility of her metaphysics turns upon a phenomenological reading of experience that acknowledges both of these experiences. The recognition and pursuit of unity and order is complicated and muffled by the prevailing cultural mood that demythologizes images of unity that run counter to scientific research and empirical knowledge. Antonaccio in *A Philosophy to Live By – Engaging Iris Murdoch* sees Murdoch as combining brute and sometimes recalcitrant empirical reality with a theoretical reading of experience that points to underlying unities. She observes, 'There is in short, a two-way movement between "theory" (or metaphysics) and its opposite (that is "untheory").'[30]

There can be no magical, supernatural formulas to counter the disruption and diffusion to which metaphysics responds. What is demanded is a philosophy that connects forms of experience by conjectural images of a unifying truth that are suggestive rather than principles deduced systematically by a watertight logical procedure. Murdoch offers a set of suggestive connections between modes of experience, which draws upon a reading of Plato as a similar philosopher with an artistic bent, who was alive to the conjectural status of his own ideas. The truth of her metaphysis depends upon its consonance with the lived experience of individuals rather than upon a set of rational deductions that are imported into experience from the outside. To convey her sense of experience and the possibility of advancing so as to see more clearly its order and unity she invokes Plato's *Phaedrus*, which elaborates figuratively the possibility of an individual ascending from an appreciation of sensuous beauty in the visible world to a complete intuition of the essential form of beauty.[31] Murdoch herself traces unity and value in a series of states of mind: in conscious awareness, personal and public morality, art and religion as well as within the philosophical dialectical appreciation of their interrelations that is achieved by a perception of ultimate goodness. Her reading of Schopenhauer in *Metaphysics as a Guide to Morals* is notable because she recognizes his status as a pivotal modern theorist, who works within a post-Kantian framework. He is taken to conceive of the thing in itself behind phenomenal appearances as being the Will to Live, which is articulated in Ideas and is present in all forms of life. But life in this picture of the human condition is an egoistic struggle for existence, which is deeply miserable, and against which some relief is offered by art. The only complete escape from the misery of existence, however, is to achieve an ascetic denial of the Will, which is a mystical state beyond virtue. Murdoch appreciates Schopenhauer's recognition of the imperfections of existence and the different registers with which he operates. He allows for compassion in morality, which is a down to earth acknowledgement of the need to relieve suffering and his writing allows for lightness and humour. Above all she respects his modern sense of metaphysics, when 'he speaks of our finite nature together with our passionate desire to understand "the world" which we attempt to intuit "as a whole"'.[32]

Murdoch's metaphysics unites forms of experience within a whole so as to make sense of experience and to guide moral life. In *Metaphysics as a Guide to Morals* she introduces a distinction between differing forms of moral life, distinguishing between public and personal morality. Personal morality had been the subject of her celebrated essays on morality that are contained in *The Sovereignty of Good* (1970), which sets out a perfectionist ideal of morality against a backdrop of contemporary moral theory that reduces morality as so many ways of facilitating the satisfaction of the chosen ends of individuals. Personal moral progress towards perfection can be assisted by art, which, for Murdoch, but not Plato, can inspire insight into the world. Artistic appreciation, like morality in the contemporary world, tends to be reduced to the status of the mere preferences of individuals. But for Murdoch, art and its appreciation connect with how things are. She cites selected letters of Rilke, which attests to the power of Cezanne's work. Rilke observes how a Cezanne self-portrait has a humble objectiveness resembling a dog looking into a mirror and simply recognizing another dog. For Rilke, Cezanne did not sentimentalize. The sentimentalist school painted as if they were professing their love for their subject rather than simply allowing it to be.[33] For Murdoch painting contributes to truth by showing reality, simply and truthfully allowing it to be, without elaboration or preaching. The recognition of reality opens a person to the possibility of loving relations with others and a sense of how experience exhibits an order within its disorderly motion.

The question of how personal morality relates to the public world of politics and the law is not explored in the essays of *The Sovereignty of Good*. Her introduction of the notion of public morality in *Metaphysics as a Guide to Morals* is to be explained by her concern to provide a complete account of morality within experience. Its appearance is also prompted by her reflection upon twentieth-century history and the harm that has been inflicted upon individuals by a series of repressive tyrannies, which continue into the latter part of the century. She traces the internal relations between personal and public morality. The security that is provided by a decent public order, whereby historically changing axiomatic rights are protected, affords the possibility of personal moral development towards the good. Her letters provide evidence of her concern to reduce the suffering that has been inflicted upon individuals by tyrannical Fascist and Communist regimes.[34] In the light of the awful treatment of individuals at the hands of states in the modern world, Murdoch opts to concentrate political resources on protecting basic human rights rather than on utopian schemes.

Throughout her work, in her novels and in her philosophy, Murdoch combines a realistic assessment of individuals, their frailties and limits, with a countervailing recognition of their aspiration to align with truth and goodness. A bleak vision of human frailty and egoism, which blocks the path to enlightenment, is narrated in *The Sacred and Profane Love Machine* (1976). It shows how individual conduct is caught up in the mechanics of egos satisfying their desires and concocting fantasies. Blaise Gavender is a psychiatrist, who has lost belief in the doctrines underlying his practice. He lives a double life in maintaining two relationships and households – one with his dutiful wife Harriet and their child David, and the other with his mistress Emily and their child Luca. To dissemble his double life he resorts to inventing clients and their stories, and these invented stories are suggested by his neighbour Monty, a second rate novelist.

Harriet is taken in by Blaise's deceit, and when the truth of the situation is revealed, she suffers and struggles to deal effectively with the revelation. She is killed in a terrorist attack at a German airport, while protecting Luca, the child of the profane mistress. Monty, who has abetted Blaise's lies, writes worthless stories that do not stretch or enable his personal development. The atmosphere of the novel is bleak and the bleakness is transmitted through all of the characters. The close ties between the characters and what they stand for is suggested by the title and by its reference to the Titian picture, 'Sacred and Profane Love'. Titian employed the same model for his images of both sacred and profane love, which suggests a connectedness between the sacred and the profane, just as the bourgeois family life of Blaise and Harriet is connected to the illicit affair of Blaise and Emily. All the relationships in the novel are unbalanced, possessive, mechanical and untruthful, especially those orchestrated by Blaise. Harriet does develop some intermittent insight, and Monty realizes something of the truth of his miserable relationship with his wife, Sophie and his own role in her death. These moments of insight, openings to truth and to goodness, suggest an ascent from egoism and lies, yet the characters remain engrossed in egoism and caught up in lies and fantasy so as to preclude anything but a fragile hesitant change of attitude. Such an opening is intimated in the following conversation between Harriet and Monty after the truth about Blaise's double life has been revealed. 'You can't – I think – imagine', said Harriet slowly,

What it's – like – to be me – now. I realize a lot of things about myself. Obvious things, perhaps. I married very young. Blaise has been my only man. I suppose that in a way that meant I never grew up. It seemed perfect. If Blaise had been what he appeared to be perhaps it would have been perfect, a kind of perfection anyway. I would never have needed to grow up and change and see the world as terrible, for it is terrible, it is terrible in its nature, in its essence, only sometimes one can't see. Some people never see. You have always known this, and I knew you knew, long ago, something I could not name in you attracted me and it was this, that you knew. As Blaise never did. Blaise pretended to. He played at it, with his patients, but he was too self-centred and too fond of pleasure really to see it. Blaise has always lived in a dream world.

'We all live in dream-worlds', said Monty.[35] This passage highlights the awfulness and burdens of what is demanded in moral life and in facing up to reality. Harriet is burdened by her immersion in conventions and lack of individual reflection upon her own situation. Monty is a fantasist whose love for his wife has been twisted out of shape and so he has been left the awfulness of his own egoism and artistic failure. Like Plato's, Murdoch's philosophy is not easy. It recognizes the misery and occlusions of existence. Her novels are often at their most poignant and insightful when they imagine individuals caught up in situations that hurt most of all because of their own characters' propensity to fantasy and to avoiding truthful recognition of difficult things.

The wretchedness of Harriet in *The Sacred and Profane Love Machine* resonates with the description of the void in *Metaphysics as a Guide to Morals*, which deals with possibilities of extreme wretchedness within experience. Murdoch declares, 'What I refer to here is something extreme: the pain, and the evil, which occasion conditions of desolation such as many or most human beings has met with.'[36] In the chapter, 'Void', Murdoch observes how individuals can feel dissipation in the wake of the pain and dislocation of bereavement, remorse, and guilt. Murdoch invokes Kierkegaard, Weil and Conrad as authors who have testified to such acute affliction. Weil's notion of the void is an evident influence upon Murdoch, though her notion as set out in *Gravity and Grace* assumes an expressly religious guise that is not shared by Murdoch. Weil sees the void as an extreme otherness that evokes God's renunciation of himself in creating the world.[37] Murdoch's novels testify to the intensity of suffering that can be experienced in the wake of human catastrophe. They exhibit many examples of extreme suffering through bereavement, guilt, remorse and self-loathing. *The Sacred and Profane Love Machine* shows the misery of being caught up in lies. In *A Word Child* (1975) the principal protagonist, Hilary Burde, has to suffer the awful repetition of responsibility for the death of a loved one on two occasions.[38] *The Good Apprentice* (1985) begins with Edward Bertram's culpability for and guilt at the death of a friend, who has leaped to his death following Edward's placing a drug surreptitiously into his friend's sandwich. By its close Edward has made some progress in releasing his soul from the grip of desolation and in so doing he has registered some moral progress.[39] Murdoch is alert to the responses of individuals to such suffering and the possibilities that are afforded for freeing themselves from the power of the self. In her philosophical discussion of the void she maintains that, if possible, egoistic responses must be relinquished. Following Weil, she observes that such experiences can lead to an unselfing on the part of an individual if they renounce fantasy and egoism and attend to reality in reorienting to goodness and clarity of vision. She warns, however, of the dangers of a sadomasochistic engagement with suffering. This latter warning reflects reservations about Weil's perspective that qualifies her great admiration for Weil that had been expressed in her radio talk of 1951.[40]

In the light of the dissonance within experience and the obstacles to making moral progress, Murdoch recognizes that religion can contribute to enabling the development of individuals. She is, however, mindful of the strain exerted upon Christianity by the impact of science and Enlightenment reason, which undermines the credibility of its supernatural elements. She maintains that religion can play a powerful role in serving as a motive of good conduct, for the practice of religion can imprint images of goodness on the minds of the young, which are retained in later life. The significance of religion is that it reaches deeply into things and can underpin a sense of the integrity of experience. Religion supplies spiritual energy. Murdoch observes, 'The mystery of religion (respected, intuited) is a source of spiritual energy. An orientation toward the good involves a reorientation of desire.'[41] With the onset of secularism and the decline in Christianity Murdoch fears that the loss of Christian moral and spiritual practice might deprive individuals of an opportunity to be inducted into a pathway towards the good. She identifies the reinforcement that religion provides to morality, 'High morality without religion is too abstract, high morality craves for religion.'[42]

Murdoch fears that with the onset of secularism and the decline in Christianity the loss of Christian moral and spiritual practice might deprive individuals of an opportunity to be oriented towards the good. She accepts the demythologization of religion and the unacceptability of a supernatural God in an age of science where the limits of empirical knowledge are to be accepted. But she hopes that insofar as its doctrines clash with science and reason then their literal truth can be dropped and they might be understood metaphorically so as to retain their power to support the spirituality of life. She observes, 'Perhaps I believe Christianity can continue without a personal God or a risen Christ, without beliefs in supernatural places and happenings, such as heaven or life after death, but retaining the mystical figure of Christ occupying a place analogous to that of Buddha.'[43] She is more sanguine about the amenability of other world religions to the requirements of the age. Buddhism, for instance, is taken to be suited to the demands of a demythologized religion, and she observes how Judaism and Islam have avoided the path of image-making. In revering the name but not the image of God they avoid some of the problems that affect Christianity. The philosophical mysticism of the Hindu religion is oriented towards the world of experience and hence does not require a strained supernaturalism.

Murdoch's novels are replete with characters that react to the demythologization of religion. In *Nuns and Soldiers* (1980) the complex action of the novel is set in train when Guy Openshaw, a strong and magnetic presence to his wife and friends, dies. The loss of his stern commanding presence resembles the death of God in that these dependent people are set loose and free to choose and act in self-chosen ways. At times they feel lost. His wife consorts and eventually settles with a footloose artist and she is supported by her friend Anne Cavidge, who has withdrawn from a Convent and struggles with her religious beliefs. We are thereby seen to inhabit a universe in which we are free but suffer grave difficulties in a world that is not supported by a strong and disciplined religion.[44] In *Henry and Cato* (1977), Cato Forbes, a fledgling priest, has doubts over a personal God and Christ's risen presence while he struggles with his passion for Joe, a beautiful delinquent.[45] In *The Book and the Brotherhood* (1987), Father McAlister can offer the consoling spirit of Christianity to Tamar Hernshaw, who is disturbed by the abortion which she has experienced, while he himself has broken with the literal untruth of the Christian dogma.[46] Murdoch's fiction also draws upon Buddhism to show the force of mystical practice. James, the saintly cousin of Charles Arrowby in *The Sea, The Sea* (1978) is everything that his egoistic cousin is not. He is a disciplined and spiritual ex-army figure who has turned to religion in the East and has developed an intense spirituality. He is equipped with a mystical power, which he aims to relinquish but uses to soothe troubled waters. Notably he employs it to rescue Charles, who has been jealous of him since childhood.[47] Again in her last novel *Jackson's Dilemma* (1995), a strange and unduly neglected work,

Murdoch testifies to the power of religion, through the mysterious figure of Jackson, another character steeped in the force of Eastern religion. Quietly and mysteriously he helps various characters negotiate disquieting situations and helps the central character to find peace.[48]

Perhaps the most telling illustration of Murdoch's approach to metaphysics is the section of *Metaphysics as a Guide to Morals* in which she revisits and reflects upon St. Anselm's ontological proof for God. She sees the force of Kant's critique of the argument, which denies the attribution of existence to a thought. The thought of God's perfection does not justify ascribing existence as a predicate of the subject. Mere thought does not constitute existence. In passing, Murdoch recalls Hegel's resurrection of the ontological argument to represent the determining power of thought, where the onward reach for perfection is propelled by internal self-moving powers. She is more positive about Collingwood's justification of the ontological argument in his *An Essay on Philosophical Method*.[49] In his discussion of the argument Collingwood highlights two things that Murdoch takes on-board. First, Collingwood specifies that in commenting on St. Anselm, he was 'divesting his argument of all specifically religious or theological colouring'.[50] Second, he emphasizes that St. Anselm was applying the argument 'not to thought in general but only to the thought of one unique object'.[51] The object to which it is directed is metaphysical thinking. Murdoch concurs with Collingwood in assuming that the ontological proof cannot justify the presumption of a personal, existing and other-worldly God. Rather, she imagines philosophy, in reflecting upon the idea of goodness and our experience of ethical life, can make a sort of transcendental argument for the reality of goodness and its unifying presence. Hence when a person is considering how to act and aims to follow the good, imagining that there is a right course of action that is to be followed, then it makes sense to presume a paradigm of goodness that legitimates the quest for that right course. Metaphysics works with these presumptions and intimations within experience rather than by prescribing how experience is to be taken. In a commentary on Murdoch's use of the ontological argument Mulhall expresses this interplay between actual experience and the assumption of a unifying goodness or 'God', in Wittgensteinian terms. He observes, 'One might say: what connects the logical grammar, the meaning of the concept of "God" to our lives is a certain kind of experience.'[52]

Murdoch's use of the ontological argument is revealing of her approach to metaphysics in two ways. On the one hand, she is uninterested in speculation about a thoroughly transcendent personal being. God, in this sense, is not part of her philosophy. At the same time she aims to make sense holistically and dialectically of forms of experience that testify to the urge for perfection in human activities and to conceive of a related idea of goodness that supersedes a mere subjective satisfaction. These themes inform her celebrated three essays – 'The Idea of Perfection', 'On "God" and "Good"' and 'The Sovereignty of Good over Other Concepts' – which were published originally in 1964, 1969 and 1967 respectively and were published retrospectively in *The Sovereignty of Good* (1970) and subsequently included in the edited collection, *Existentialists and Mystics* (1997).[53] In these essays she critiques existentialism and Anglo-American language philosophy for seeing ethics as a means to service individual choices. Metaphysics for Murdoch draws pictures that make connections within experience and intimate an underlying unity and goodness, while acknowledging the world's refractoriness and plurality. This metaphysical capacity is not a clearly specifiable intuition that can be reached by logical thought, but there are intimations of it within experience. Moral life, for Murdoch, turns upon what is revealed by loving attention to others, and it implies a unity between individuals that supersedes mere individual calculation. Moral life is more than a mere succession of ways of calculating individual or even general happiness. It leads us away from absorption with the self and orients us towards a notion of goodness that supersedes egoism and thwarts a tendency to fantasy. Morality is central to metaphysics because it exhibits the magnetic force of a Goodness that supersedes the partial, the imperfect and the subjective and presumes an idea of perfection. The dynamic Eros or love, which is manifested in sexual attraction, can lead to respect and love for others. There is a pathway that leads from the lower self and its focus upon its own desires towards a higher self and a loving appreciation of others and of goodness. For Murdoch what enables metaphysics to draw a dialectical pattern in experience and to connect seemingly disconnected features are the intimations of goodness that are felt and considered by individuals in their ordinary lives.

Murdoch and the 'Manuscript on Heidegger'

Towards the end of her life, Murdoch completed a 'Manuscript on Heidegger' but decided against publication, and since her death it has yet to be published as a whole.[54] However, her 'Manuscript on Heidegger', should neither be abandoned nor discarded as the work of an old and failing thinker. No doubt Murdoch had reasons not to publish the manuscript and Stanley Rosen advised Peter Conradi against its publication for a number of plausible reasons, principally its tendency to combine commentary on Heidegger with open questions and comments that serve less as direct engagements with Heidegger's texts than as reminders to Murdoch herself of significant issues and themes arising out of them.[55] The value of the Manuscript, however, resides in the very features that were taken to justify its non-publication. It yields access to Murdoch's philosophical ideas as well as providing incisive commentary on Heidegger and in so doing confirms and develops her own thoughts on metaphysics. She presents a considered review of Heidegger's writings, notably of *Being and Time*, and takes Heidegger's texts as provocations to reflect upon her own conceptions of metaphysics and moral life. In aligning and distinguishing herself from Heidegger she discusses her own views on metaphysical ideas while allowing for their continuities with preceding philosophical speculation. She shares with Heidegger a common context for philosophical speculation, namely the crisis of metaphysics and a more general fracturing of traditional beliefs. Just as she interprets Plato in the light of her own concerns and reading of modernity, so she interprets Heidegger in the light of her own commitment to continue metaphysics in a disenchanted and anti-metaphysical age. In her own words, 'In philosophy, we go where the honey is.'[56] If Heidegger is a philosopher of late modernity, exploring metaphysics in a post-metaphysical context and identifying values without reference to traditional means of support, then Murdoch too identifies with his project and its cultural and historical context. She also shares aspects of his substantive thought. Insofar as Heidegger is decidedly a philosopher of late modernity then Murdoch identifies herself as one too. She too is committed to a form of metaphysics, which can be sustained in a post-metaphysical age, as she set out in *Metaphysics as a Guide to Morals*. She remarks, 'Metaphysics must live, it is good for us and Heidegger's work is a very important step along that dark forest path.'[57] Like Heidegger, she sees herself as a post-Enlightenment philosopher. She is critical of Heidegger, however, for his isolation of the individual from traditional religious sentiments and from wider social obligations.

Appraising Heidegger

Murdoch reads Heidegger by means of her own philosophical training and interests, which are broad and span traditional metaphysics, contemporary Continental and analytical Anglo-American philosophies. Her synoptic philosophical aspirations reflect her early ideas on her own determination to integrate a range of philosophical styles.[58] Murdoch's expertise in the history of philosophy allows her to recognize how Heidegger, if he may be said to continue metaphysics, aims to avoid preceding historical errors such as the reifying or systematizing of concepts so that they become detached from the world, as he imagines being the case with Plato, Descartes, Kant and Hegel.[59] In his later writings, Heidegger's critique of this philosophical impulse encompasses Nietzsche's own critique of metaphysics, whereas Murdoch appreciates the explanatory force of Nietzsche's diagnosis of the nihilism within modernity.[60] Murdoch is sympathetic to what she sees as Heidegger's project of continuing metaphysics by working with and critiquing its traditional forms, just as she appreciates his maintenance of a this-worldly experiential frame. She shares this approach to metaphysics. Murdoch, however, asks down-to-earth questions of Heidegger's methods. For instance, she wonders, 'Why bother about Being?'[61] She notes that empirically minded philosophers would be inclined to dismiss Being as a non-question. Murdoch is impressed by Heidegger's engagement with actual experience, which avoids dualisms. His starting point, *Dasein*, a Being for whom Being is an issue, at one stroke avoids the problems of reintroducing the object to the subject and the world to the individual. She observes, 'The concept of Dasein in Sein und Zeit solved or dissolved old philosophical problems or pseudo problems.'[62] Heidegger's *Dasein* is expressly in the world, where things are at hand and other subjects are near, and hence abstractly constructed philosophical problems such as that of knowing other minds and of certifying knowledge claims are side-stepped. These problems are the kind of pseudo-problems that Wittgenstein also critiqued and they are the product of a misleading philosophical impulse to examine experience, as it were, from the outside. She appreciates what may be seen as a dialectical engagement with terms and standpoints. Her appreciation of Heidegger, however, does not inhibit her questioning of his phenomenological method. Her training in analytical philosophy reinforces her critical disposition so that she asks how the route taken by Heidegger's phenomenological approach is to be justified.[63] She finds no ready answer.

Murdoch is receptive to Heidegger's critique of traditional forms of metaphysics for their tendency to fix upon concepts that are taken to be external to the flow of experience. Likewise she is appreciative of Heidegger's existential engagement with experiential conditions. She observes that metaphysics and metaphysicians such as Heidegger, Hegel and Plato provide a unifying way of mapping experience, one that aims for coherence between the various projects and forms of experience that compose a life rather than a correspondence between knowledge and its object. She recognizes how her own metaphysics is a commitment to continue this currently undervalued tradition.[64] She is sympathetic to Heidegger's situated philosophical standpoint, which avoids the otherworldliness of metaphysical and religious standpoints that are no longer sustainable in the current cultural context, where literal belief in God and transcendent moral principles are anachronisms. She is, however, critical of the credentials of his phenomenological approach, and of the transcendent status attached to Being in the later writings. What exercises her about *Being and Time* itself and to which she devotes most critical attention is its failure to be inclusive in considering social and ethical relations. She impugns Heidegger for failing to deal with ordinary people and patterns of moral life. She observes, 'Heidegger lacks, even rejects an essential connection with ordinary people and ordinary life.'[65] In doing so Murdoch reinforces her own commitment to ordinary life and the capaciousness of metaphysics. In her criticisms of Heidegger she also continues her critique of existentialism. Her critique of Heidegger is of a piece with her preceding critique of Sartre. Heidegger's frame in *Being and Time* establishes a normative dualism between authentic individual *Dasein* and the social world of everyday life. Heidegger counterposes an authentic courageous commitment on the part of an individual to face up to the existential conditions of Being in the world, notably in an engagement with the prospect of their own death to a countervailing everyday world into which people fall and in which 'they' submerge authentic feelings behind the small change and idle talk of social interaction. Heidegger sets up what Murdoch takes to be an uncharitable contrast between a socialized world of idle chatter where existential questions are ignored and the care exerted by authentic *Dasein* in experiencing the call of conscience and anxiety and in facing mortality.[66]

Murdoch's critique focuses upon a problematic feature of Heidegger's analysis. Heidegger observes the inauthentic public way of imagining death where 'dying which is essentially mine in such a way that no-one can be my representative, is perverted into an event of public occurrence which the "they" encounters'.[67] The inauthenticity of the 'they' is related in this observation in *Being in Time*. 'The "they" gives its approval and aggravates the *temptation* to cover up from oneself one's ownmost Being-towards-death.'[68] Murdoch expands upon her critique of Heidegger's dichotomy between authentic *Dasein* and the public 'they' by observing the absence in *Being and Time* of a consideration of ordinary morality. She questions why is there no mention of notions such as justice, mercy, love and welfare.[69] She wonders how a standpoint that can avoid perennial philosophical dualisms such as mind and body, and subjectivity and objectivity reduces the complex social world and its moral dilemmas to a contrast between the 'they' everyday world and a singular heroism in facing up to anxiety and the prospect of one's own death. Murdoch's critique of Heidegger's impoverished treatment of the relations between the individual and public self revisits her earlier critique of Sartre.[70] Her early critique of Sartre and this later critique of Heidegger share a concern at a neglect of the plurality of ways in which social life and political life is conducted. Her critical reading of *Being and Time* is intensified in her consideration of Heidegger's later work. The later Heidegger is taken to relinquish his perception of *Dasein* as the shepherd of Being so as to release a transcendence that establishes a gap between human beings and an external realm of value. Murdoch argues forcefully against forms of transcendence. She takes the cultural world of the late twentieth century to testify to the truth of Nietzsche's conception of the death of a God that is separate from the world. She observes its contemporary cultural resonance by observing how clergymen standardly interpret God and Christ's resurrection in metaphorical terms. Murdoch concludes that a metaphysics that harmonizes with contemporary convictions, must take its bearings from worldly human endeavour and moral aspirations, that is, from the projects and dilemmas of everyday life.

Murdoch is critical of Heidegger because he 'lacks even rejects an essential connection with ordinary people and ordinary life'.[71] Moreover, he either omits or misrecognizes the plurality of experience. This shortcoming is evident in his failure to reckon with or anticipate the fall of Soviet communism. For Murdoch the political provision and maintenance of basic liberties are significant aspects of our experience and they are ignored by Heidegger. Murdoch highlights the social and moral progress that has been made in the West, which is to be respected in any comprehensive metaphysical review of the human condition. She notes how significant progress has been made in establishing equality between the sexes and ethnicities and how differing forms of sexuality are no longer repressed but tolerated. She observes, 'We are aware of the holocaust. We are also aware that in the West, attitudes to women, children, blacks, homosexuals have markedly improved. We have many paths to goodness.'[72] For Murdoch, a synoptic metaphysics, which takes its bearings from the experience of ordinary human beings, must take account of the public world and the imperative of securing liberty, justice and social welfare.

In appraising Heidegger Murdoch rehearses her own thinking on metaphysics, which confirms her ideas as they are set out in *Metaphysics as a Guide to Morals* and elsewhere. She reaffirms the value of metaphysics in a contemporary context where the empirical sceptical bent of Anglo-American philosophers undermines its status. For Murdoch metaphysics furnishes a synoptic perspective weaving together diverse strands of thinking and forms of practice. She takes Plato and Hegel to be paradigmatic metaphysicians offering large-scale visions of reality that frame coherent unifying frameworks for understanding changing experiential circumstances at a number of levels. She acknowledges here as elsewhere that metaphysical systems, such as Hegel's, run the risk of becoming overly schematic but she concludes that at its best metaphysics is open and inclusive rather than closed and narrow.[73] She is clear that metaphysical schemes of thought have to take their bearings from the human world and the ordinary individuals who compose it. Metaphysics offers coherence but the unity it imagines should not be constraining. She invokes the notion of the Platonic Good as a unitary concept, which is not removed from experience and human endeavour, but functions as an intensive concept, imparting meaning and purpose to a plurality of valuable activities. She recognizes its provenance in Plato's metaphysics but her Platonism represents a particular reading of Plato, which follows the advice that Parmenides imparts to Socrates in the *Parmenides*. Forms cannot be external to sensible things if they are to have meaning and exert motivational force, and the energy of love flowing through a variety of activities is what Murdoch takes to be the Platonic model of metaphysical unity.[74] In critiquing Heidegger Murdoch rehearses her own sense that metaphysics in order to deliver an inclusive conception of the moral life must embrace ordinary individuals, who are envisaged as energized by loving relations and who engage in personal and public forms of morality. In so doing her discussion is of a piece with her analysis of public and personal forms of morality in *Metaphysics as a Guide to Morals*. Likewise in the 'Manuscript on Heidegger' her references to the Holocaust and Soviet tyranny and the need to attend to the public sphere to protect individuals, recall remarks in *Metaphysics as a Guide to Morals* that express admiration for the premium that is to be placed on public security by Hobbes and Hume.[75]

In the novel *The Time of the Angels* (1966), the effect of abandoning notions of God and dogmatic truths upon ordinary lives is played out in a drama that reveals disturbing experiential possibilities. Its central character Carel Fisher, the widowed rector of an eerie East London Church, draws on the thought of Heidegger in abandoning belief in God for an existentialism that lauds raw existential power over dogmatic truths and traditional morality. In the course of the novel his detachment from ordinary moral scruples is revealed progressively. He declares his iconoclasm in conversation with his brother Marcus, who is himself writing a philosophical book arguing for objective goodness while accepting the loss of former religious truths. Carel talks of the death of God releasing a multiplicity of angels, and a frenzied chaotic disorder upon the world. The extent of Carel's disdain for standard forms of morality emerges when his daughter Muriel discovers that he is having an incestuous sexual relationship with his ward Elizabeth, who in fact is his daughter. Carel has also had a sexual relationship with the orphaned maid, Pattie, over whom he exerts a continuing power. She cannot move on from his coercive presence. At the outset of the novel, while cleaning Carel's room, she stumbles, literally, over a copy of Heidegger's *Being and Time*. Later, she glances at a page of the text, which makes no sense to her at all. It appears 'senseless and awful'.[76] Murdoch nether endorses nor condemns the doctrines that are maintained by Carel or those that are held by Marcus. Marcus's metaphysical understanding of morality appears to approximate to Murdoch's own positon, while her late and unpublished study of Heidegger shows her interest in Carel's philosophy.[77] However, the truth or falsity of doctrines is not what is at issue in the novel. *The Time of the Angels* explores an imaginary world which is set in post-war London and shows interrelations between individuals who take up ideas that are part of a modern cultural context and arise out of events of the twentieth century. Heidegger's thought can excite a demonic heroism that is blind to ordinary morality. This abstract possibility is recognized in Murdoch's late philosophical study of Heidegger but it assumes a dramatic form in the novel and impacts upon members of a family and individuals, who are connected to the central protagonist. The unhappiness of Pattie's troubled childhood is compounded by her personal and sexual domination at the hands of Carel. His conduct is licensed by his contempt for ordinary morality, just as his flouting of the incest taboo disturbs an already vulnerable young woman and unsettles his other troubled daughter. Carel's unbridled existentialism, which is sanctioned by the contemporary revolt against traditional moral and religious traditions, legitimates his operation of lordly power over others. Yet Marcus's metaphysical justification of a continuing sustaining goodness appears powerless in the light of his ineffectual conversations with Carel and his failure to protect or even visit his ward, the vulnerable Elizabeth.

The novel is not a vehicle for Murdoch's philosophical ideas. There is a difference between a novel and a philosophical text. Murdoch in her philosophical examination of Heidegger's thought shows a sympathy to Heidegger's post-metaphysical project of uncovering how Being appears to *Dasein* and yet this is not taken up in this novel, though it does surface in *Jackson's Dilemma*.[78] In *The Time of the Angels* Murdoch's own philosophical ideas are beside the point in shaping the plot. Philosophical ideas, even if they are valid, neither necessarily triumph in the actual world nor in a novelist's imaginary one, and the point of a novel is to explore imaginary but realistic worlds that bear upon our own. The narrative of *The Time of the Angels* is set in a cultural context that is recognizable from Murdoch's philosophical analyses of the modern world. What is presumed in the novel is the evanescence of religious belief, itself a sign for a wider cultural transformation, encompassing morality and social relationships. All of the characters in *The Time of the Angels* are working with religious and moral issues that are involved in the cultural transformations, which Murdoch diagnoses as constituting her times. Eugene Peshkov is a displaced Russian, whose family has suffered from the major disturbances of recent European history. The theft of his icon by his amoral son, Leo, is a metaphor for the iconoclastic temper of the times and the disruption and loss caused by revolution and the Holocaust in the twentieth century.[79] Carel, Marcus, Pattie, Leo, Muriel, Elizabeth and Eugene Peshkov are particular characters, whose fate is shaped by the contingent events in the novel. They do not function as representatives of a didactic scheme but as individuals whose actions are animated by particular thoughts and feelings. Yet the drama of their interactions reveals the moral and religious landscape of a late modern world in which the nature of the world after god, and the pursuit of the good in the wake of a loss of faith, are imagined in ways that resonate with how Murdoch perceived the times in which she lived. It reveals a connection between Murdoch's philosophy and her novels.

Conclusion

Murdoch detected honey in Heidegger, and in her 'Manuscript on Heidegger' the honey that she detects concerns the possibilities for metaphysics in a post-metaphysical world. Her reading of Heidegger and her own philosophy turns upon her sense of their historical contexts. As is noted by Broackes, she tends to locate philosophers including herself in wider cultural contexts.[80] Murdoch sets out a metaphysics in and for a modern world that she diagnoses to have lost touch with large scale, ordering beliefs in religion, morality, politics, art and philosophy. Her metaphysics charts this loss and looks to redeem the situation by connecting forms of experience with the world as a whole so that a way might be signposted to perceive its unity and goodness. Her study of Heidegger shows how she looks to resolve issues that are thrown up by the general tenor of cultural development and historical events. She recognizes the decline of metaphysics and looks to resume its potential by turning to the history of philosophy. She looks to historic metaphysicians, most notably Hegel and Plato, while also drawing upon Heidegger's undertaking of metaphysics in a post-metaphysical age. What she takes from Heidegger's *Being and Time* is a reinforcement of her commitment to work within the limits of experience. The Kantian critique of dogmatic metaphysics is to be respected. She is impressed by Heidegger's starting point, *Dasein*, which assumes a being in the world for whom being is an issue. While Murdoch does not subscribe to existentialism, she recognizes how Heidegger's notion of *Dasein* avoids the dualisms associated with sharply delineated distinctions between subject and object, and the individual and society. The point of Heidegger's perspective on Being can be illustrated by contrasting it with Hegel's negation of pure Being as an empty category that lacks determinacy.[81] Hegel's dialectical manoeuvres over Being presumes it functions as a categorial description of the world rather than as constituting an existential issue. Murdoch sees the point of taking it as raising an existential issue. But if she takes the honey from Heidegger she is also alert to the drawbacks of his philosophy and her criticism of his standpoint emphasizes features of her own metaphysics. Heidegger's distinction between the everyday social world and authentic *Dasein* speaks to those who experience high anxiety about existence and who attend to the conditions of their own finitude and question everyday attitudes that ignore or sidetrack existential questions. Murdoch reckons this distinction amounts to a failure to deal with ordinary morality and everyday people. It points to what Murdoch holds as important in her own metaphysics, namely a commitment to be inclusive. Murdoch's own metaphysics in *Metaphysics as a Guide to Morals* recognizes the role of social and political practices that allow for social interaction and the safeguarding of basic human rights.

Metaphysics as a Guide to Morals replicates features of the 'Manuscript on Heidegger' in that it recognizes the prevailing loss of faith in large scale beliefs in many fields and sees a reconstituted metaphysics as a way of dealing with the loss of concepts that underpin morality and personal development. Her metaphysics is distinct from what Kant termed dogmatic metaphysics and aims to draw support from aspects of lived experience that point towards its underlying unity and goodness. Her argument is a kind of transcendental argument in that she works from what is acknowledged in experience towards unificatory principles that do not deny the muddle and dissonance that compose much of our lives. At the same time, as in her 'Manuscript on Heidegger' she works with and through preceding philosophers, including Wittgenstein, Schopenhauer, Kant and most centrally Plato.[82] Just as in the 'Manuscript on Heidegger' she acknowledges the authority of Plato and offers a sympathetic and modern interpretation of his ideas, in which forms are not separated from particulars. Hence in *Metaphysics as a Guide to Morals*, in the light of a cultural loss of unifying doctrines, Murdoch aims to revive a modified Platonism that is shorn of hard and fast dogmatic doctrines. If Murdoch takes her bearings from Plato and other historic metaphysicians at the same time she is working within a particular cultural and philosophical context. Her metaphysics works with the grain of the current demythologization of the world, while offering a metaphysical picture that allows for a presumption of goodness and unity. She offers a philosophy to live by to counter the pervasive turn towards empiricism and subjective assertion at the expense of philosophical speculation and religious faith.

In pointed contrast to Heidegger Murdoch's metaphysics incorporates moral and political experience. Murdoch's philosophical perspective encompasses psychological, social and political factors that either disturb or enable the psyche's possibilities of achieving insight and loving relationships. She sees art, religion and philosophy as underpinning moral development, for they register unity and truth, which supports a morality that is oriented towards an objective notion of the good rather than submitting to subjectivism. Her later subscription to a form of political liberalism is motivated by reflection on political events and a recognition of the imperative of achieving a political settlement in which repression and insecurity can be avoided while securing an egalitarian entitlement to rights. In *Metaphysics as a Guide to Morals* and in her 'Manuscript on Heidegger', and in her letters and journals she testifies to the courage of East European dissidents who resist the repressive force of Soviet communism. While Murdoch's reading of social and political history is selective and controversial, it nonetheless forms an important component of her thought, which distinguishes it from that of Heidegger's. Her reflection upon the character of her own cultural context and her recognition that philosophy is to recognize developing historic assumptions about politics as axioms to be instituted casts doubt on Lovibond's view that Murdoch is out of sympathy with a vision of society as self-instituting.[83] Murdoch might well not share radical political sentiments, but she takes politics seriously and recognizes that political life is made and remade by historical political actors. Murdoch's very engagement with Heidegger is inspired by and reflects back upon a reading of the contemporary social situation. Throughout her career Murdoch as a philosopher and novelist is acutely aware of the decline of traditional beliefs and practices. The modern Western world is one in which religious beliefs can no longer be routinely invoked and relied of. Morality is disturbed by the uncertainty pertaining to the source of support for its pronouncements. Society is becoming increasingly materialistic in the wake of technological progress. Individual freedom is asserted more loudly if there is vagueness over its value and direction; egalitarianism appeals against the injustice involved in the past and present treatment of minorities. Subjected groups demand more attention. Murdoch's writings are designed to accommodate these developments, while identifying a means to preserve a reasonable form of metaphysics. In so doing she sees metaphysics as providing a means to understand experience as a whole, and thereby serving as a means to guide personal moral development.

CHAPTER THREE

Murdoch and the novel

Introduction

Ray Monk, in his introduction to *A Word Child* (1975) offers this
perceptive observation on the relationship between Murdoch's novels
and her philosophy, '*Of Course* her novels are not philosophical
treatises. But equally obviously, there is a great deal of philosophy in
them.'[1] The remark rings true but the devil is in the detail. How do
the novels contain philosophy? And why are they not philosophical
treatises? The second question is easier than the first. Murdoch set
herself against writing novels, which were philosophical treatises
and she achieved her ambition. The novels are open-ended and
have a large cast of characters that are not coerced into performing
to one overarching didactic theme. The philosophy within them
derives from their representation of lived experience. They show
modern life from the inside, as characters trying to come to terms
with disquieting desires and disorienting situations. Men with
homosexual leanings struggle to repress or express their sexuality.
Marriages feel the strain against a modern tide of freedom. Political
ideals are stretched in a world where loyalties to public ideals are
no longer clear-cut. Women suffer at the hands of tyrannical men
and occasionally are emboldened to question inequalities of social
structures. Religious truths are subjected to rational criticism, while
moral commitments are questioned. This literary exploration of the
modern world matters to philosophy because the lived experience
of the modern world is the object of philosophical analysis.
Murdoch's metaphysics analyses the meaning of lived experience

and her philosophical reading of modern forms of experience goes hand in hand with the imagined modern worlds of her novels. The one understands and theorizes what the other discloses.

Murdoch's philosophy may be one to live by, but it is far from a substitute for life, and her novels show what modern life is like.[2] Murdoch herself offers a number of essays on the nature of art and literature, in which she explains how they are related to but different from philosophy. Of course, her very philosophical explanation of the relationship between literature and philosophy shows one of the ways in which they are connected. The nature of literature matters to Murdoch as a philosopher. Her philosophical approach to literature and art is historical in orientation. Just as in all of her philosophizing, she establishes where we are and where we have come from. Philosophical understanding itself can be engendered by the close attention to things and individuals that is undertaken in good art and literature. And, in a dialectical turn, philosophy recognizes that art constitutes a route to intellectual and moral insight. This conceptualization of art and literature has a historical pedigree. Preceding philosophers and artists have reviewed the nature of art and Murdoch's own thinking is worked out by attending to a series of thinkers. Even Plato, as a critic of art serves as a notable stimulus to her own thinking, and she uses her reflection upon Plato's suspicions to confirm her own estimate of its positive qualities.

The content of art is historical insofar as it imagines experience in time, and the form of art is historical in that it is modified over time. Murdoch is sensitive to these historical dimensions of art. In her own reflections upon art and literature, she reviews artists and thinkers such as Plato, Tolstoy, Kant, Hegel and more recent figures such as Derrida and Sartre. Her own novels feature exemplary modern attitudes and situations, highlighting aspects of modernity such as its demythologizing spirit, its uncertain morality and the meandering freedom of its individuals. In her theoretical essays on the novel she provides an incisive commentary on the changing styles and possibilities of the novel as an expressive medium. And being a philosopher with a facility for making conceptual connections, she links the contemporary malaise of the novel to the disruptive culture of the late twentieth century.

The agenda for the rest of this chapter follows from what has been said above. Murdoch's views on the novel will be focused upon, and her understanding of art more generally will also be explored. First we will review a series of essays and talks, 'The Novelist as Metaphysician' (1950), 'The Existentialist Hero' (1950), 'The Sublime and the Good' (1959), 'The Sublime and the Beautiful Revisited' (1959) and 'Against Dryness' (1961), in which Murdoch discusses post-war literature.[3] In these essays the transformation of the novel from its nineteenth century heights to its disturbed post-war condition and a proposed remedy for the malaise of the late twentieth-century novels are set out. Subsequently her own art as a novelist will be considered in the light of her assessment of what the contemporary novel requires. Her own writing strategy was inspired by the view that the novel can act as an entertainment and a way of making sense of things. She aims to engage the reader so as to focus his or her critical attention upon realistic characters and story lines and hence to consider how things are. The novel, for Murdoch, is not a means for an author to transmit their philosophy Rather it is to open up to experience, and show freely interacting characters that are not squeezed into a pre-formulated authorial structure. For Murdoch, moral life suffers if individuals are obsessed with examining their own identities. They need to look outside of themselves, to see other people and to take account of them. The novel can show the nature of people, and so readers of a good novel can look outside of themselves and consider what other people and their lives are like. In so doing they can become attuned to the reality of others rather than immersed in their own desires and fantasies. Murdoch thinks that the visual arts as well as the literary arts can expand our appreciation of a world outside of ourselves. Her commitment to artistic realism is at odds with Plato's strictures against art, and so her criticism of Plato's tirade against art in 'The Fire and the Sun – Why Plato Banished the Artists' (1977) will be reviewed at the end of this chapter. It combines a critique of Plato on art with her own powerful defence of its worth.

Murdoch on the novel and history

Murdoch's philosophical prowess renders her unusual among novelists in that she offers a philosophical perspective on the nature and development of the novel. In a series of theoretical pieces Murdoch addresses the question of literature and its identity in the post-war world. In doing so, she critiques prevailing styles of fiction and intimates a way in which the novelist can operate so as to represent a changing society without sacrificing the novelist's calling on the altar of philosophical abstractions. In the essays she is alive to how novels respond to a wider cultural mood. In 'The Novelist as Metaphysician', Murdoch identifies the contemporary existentialist novel as reflecting the disconnected individualism of contemporary post-war society. In Sartre's novels the notion of meaning looms in a peculiar way that is characteristic of the disturbed character of post-war society. Meaning is detached from and disrupts attachment to wider beliefs and relationships. She sees Sartre as focusing upon 'this point at which our beliefs, our world pictures, our politics, religions, loves and hates are seen to be discontinuous with the selves that may or may not go on affirming them'.[4]

Sartre's portrayal of an individual, who is not only divided from the world, but also from her own transactions with others, represents a disquieting but more general development. It reflects the divided disjointed atmosphere of the post-war world and fits with a wider cultural malaise. In removing the individual from traditional values and wider commitments, Sartre's novels are seen to capture a feature of the current mood. Sartre's stripping away of informing social ties yields an atomized individual, who neither notices nor engages with others. It is an unencumbered individual, who in fiction, as in post-war reality, is discontinuous and divided from wider world pictures. She takes the point of Sartre's novel sequence, *les Chemins de la liberté* to reside chiefly in the question: 'Is there a meaning in history, and what is the individual who cannot answer this question to do about it?'[5]

The radio talk, 'The Existentialist Hero', goes along similar lines. She notes how pre-eminent French contemporary novels are populated by deracinated characters. She observes, 'These are people from after the deluge. The values of the nineteenth century are gone. The destruction for which Nietzsche called has taken place.'[6] There is a flaw in these novels. They are not remiss in reflecting aspects of contemporary society, for that is what novels are to do. Rather it is the way in which they do so. They are programmatic in valuing the lone individuals, severed from emotional ties to friends and wider society, and who do not engage with a reality outside themselves. The form is as dubious as the content. Its didactic, philosophical point of view undermines the integrity of the novel and leaves no room for the reality of characters. Murdoch maintains that the characters and narratives of these novels are drawn too tightly so as to reflect the standpoints of their authors. She observes, 'These characters and the universes which they inhabit are made excessively transparent. We can see a little too precisely what is being done.'[7]

The existentialist novel suffers from being all too existentialist. It is motivated by a philosophy that determines what is said and done within its pages. Murdoch is not that kind of philosophical novelist and we know she isn't, because she explores its rationale and finds it wanting. Its form is overly schematic, shaped by philosophical interests rather than artistic imagination. Its content suffers because its substance derives from a philosophy that is itself skewed by its replication of a problematic culture. In the modern post-war world values are devalued by being taken to be mere assertions of individuals, rather than relating to a wider recognition of other people and systems of belief. Conversely, Murdoch's own philosophy implies a world that is open and unregulated by philosophical imperatives. For Murdoch, experience is contingent and open and allows for the reality of distinct characters that are not formulaic projections of an author's standpoint. The novel, for Murdoch, is to respond to the nature of experience and frame plausible characters and action within a realistic setting. Even Murdoch's early novels which have been seen to incorporate existential themes show a range of characters, whose nature is not dictated by a single formula. Her portrayal of characters is different from existentialist novelists such as Sartre and Camus. Murdoch's first novel, *Under the Net* (1954), appears similar to existentialist novels in that its protagonist Jake Donoghue eschews traditional values and defining social ties, and yet by the end of the novel no clear philosophical message is delivered. All that can be said is that Jake's involvement in complex and disappointing interactions with others appears to reveal the partiality of his standpoint.[8] In *The Sandcastle* (1957) the central protagonist, Mor, a teacher at St. Bride's school, undertakes critical self-examination on falling in love with Rain, a young painter visiting the school. Yet its narrative is not absorbed by a single perspective. The plot opens up to include Mor's family as a whole, and by its close the family is reunited and the interplay between family members and their perspectives shapes the action rather than a particular philosophical point of view.[9]

In two essays at the end of the 1950s Murdoch invokes Kant's aesthetics to review the novel. Throughout her career, and in a variety of contexts, Kant, for Murdoch, represents the movement of philosophy and culture to a decidedly modern frame. He sets the modern limits to which knowledge is subject. In 'The Sublime and the Good' she admires Kant's aesthetics, which recognizes modern freedom in the free play of thought that is taken to be integral to aesthetic judgment. Kant distinguishes aesthetic judgment from empirical, scientific judgments by observing how judgments of the beautiful in art are not determined by the standard operations of the empirical judgments that are analysed in the *Critique of Pure Reason* where determinate categories are brought to bear upon a product of sensibility.[10] Aesthetic judgments of beauty do not appraise phenomena in terms of their consonance with standard qualities. Rather they represent the common sense occasioned by the free movement between the productive imagination and rational conceptualization, whereby an object is judged to be beautiful because of a feeling of aptness or fit between the terms of the judgment. Sensibility and conceptualization harmonize. Aesthetic judgments are indeterminate and the beautiful is decided by the free play of individual judgment.

Kant also sets out an alternative aesthetic judgment, that of the sublime, whereby a judgment is made on the sublimity of a situation or scene. The sublime is occasioned by a tension between the rational urge to bring order and determinacy to an understanding of some exceptional phenomenon such as the sight of an immense mountain or of experiencing overpowering waves on the sea and the sheer impossibility of bringing such phenomena under rational consideration by measurement of any kind. One is overcome by a feeling of the mismatch, which bestows a feeling of discordant awe over the impulse to bring even the wildest phenomena under the rule of reason. Kant is on to something in both these forms of aesthetic judgment. The beautiful is of a different order from standard categorial judgments that determine our empirical understanding of the world. We are aware of indeterminacy in response to certain phenomena. And the exercise of judgment in aesthetics seems to go beyond the mechanical operations of empirical judgment. It appears to testify to human freedom. Nonetheless Murdoch is critical of Kant on the grounds that his aesthetics is non-historical and it fails to make artistic representation of humanity and human freedom central to its operation. Hegel's sense of tragic conflict between individuals points in the right direction. It puts individual human beings at the centre of things. Yet Hegel in his *Phenomenology of Spirit* sees historical development as resolving tragic encounters.[11] Murdoch resists the absorption of individuals into history. She argues that art is the apprehension of reality, and the highest art concerns the apprehension of the freedom of human individuality. Great art is the tragic recognition of another individual. She observes the art of Tolstoy or Pasternak to be 'the non-violent apprehension of difference'.[12] She rehearses a pocket history of the notion of freedom from the Greeks to the Romantics. She observes how the great nineteenth-century novels tracked human freedom as it related to social and political movements and modern Romantic art concentrates on the individual. Murdoch respects the freedom that is granted to the individual in modernity but modern forms of Romanticism engender the vices of conventionalism and neurosis. The individual simply identifies with contingent conventions or else is absorbed by neurotic obsession with the self. What she holds up as the true sublime is the tragic compassionate recognition of difference in the form of free individuals. Recognizing individual lives in all their richness serves as an appropriate ambition for artistic creativity.[13]

In 'The Beautiful and the Sublime Revisited', Murdoch re-engages with Kant in a broad review of the historical origins of the contemporary literary imagination. Drawing on her preceding analysis of the sublime, she reaffirms its possibilities but critiques its Kantian formulation. Kant and several philosophers and cultural critics are dealt with in a characteristically Murdochian way. She sets out their theories to provide an intellectual context for the contemporary novel but she criticizes and reworks them in articulating her own ideas. She imagines the novel as contributing to the recognition and expression of human identity in the modern world. She explains the overall cultural context in which novelists currently operate by sketching a contrast between paradigmatic but distinct ways of conceiving of individuality. She contrasts the empirically minded ordinarily language conception of the individual with the Romantic image. Both fail to do justice to individuality. The empirically minded liberal notion, deriving philosophically from Hobbes, Hume and Mill, imagines freedom to consist in the protection of individual interests. The modern Romantic counterpart, however, which internalizes Hegel's totalizing vision of history, undertakes an intensive exploration of individuality that leaves no room for a genuine appreciation of others.

The literary legacy of these impoverished notions of the self, as they are filtered through existentialism and symbolism, results in an inadequate reading of the self. Murdoch bemoans the passing of classic nineteenth-century novels but their utility in the present is limited due to their derivation from a Hegelian notion of historical progress. In any event the clock cannot be turned back. Contemporary novelists either concentrate upon furnishing contextual information or frame crystalline ideals or myths. Of course some contemporary novels are impressive. Camus's *The Outsider* is a case in point. It is absorbing but it is very focused and rigidly controlled to convey Camus's sense of an absurd and meaningless universe, in which its protagonist, Meursault, is caught up. In the novel, readers find out next to nothing about Meursault's girlfriend, his victim, his mother or even about Meursault himself. What we find out about is Camus's attitude to the universe. For Murdoch this is interesting but it reflects a self-absorbed Romanticism and how the novel has lost touch with real people. In turn it reflects a society in which individuals are losing touch with a wider society.

What emerges from Murdoch's analysis is the imperative of finding a way for the novel to imagine real characters that can enhance our sense of the world outside ourselves. In looking to resolve the tension between the novelist's creative use of form to frame an encompassing narrative, and the quest to create characters that are real and not merely puppets of an authorial puppeteer, she turns to Kant and a reformulated notion of the sublime. Kant's sublime focuses upon the awe experienced in contemplating some overwhelming natural scene such as the Alps. For Murdoch, however, the novelist is to create something more appropriately sublime, namely developing stories that do justice to the richness of human individuality. She declares, 'It is indeed the realisation of a vast and varied reality outside ourselves which brings about a sense initially of terror, and when properly understood of exhilaration and spiritual power ... the sight not of physical nature, but of our surroundings as consisting of individual men.'[14]

The novelist, for Murdoch, can contribute to our understanding of the world and hence to our moral development by creating imaginary worlds that are realistic, in which there are characters that are different from ourselves. Authors and readers need to direct their vision outside of themselves. The sublime is an appropriate expression for what is being sought, in that it is a feeling that resists overt rational articulation and which testifies to the mystery of experience. Jordan, in her essay, 'Mess, Contingency and Iris Murdoch', highlights how Murdoch aims to limit artistic form by incorporating contingency and muddle. She observes, 'Form, then, at least in its "crystallised" aspect, is the enemy of contingency. The fact that life is contingent, messy, unpredictable, is familiarly difficult to comprehend. And Murdoch limns it as antithetical to the artistic impulse – the temptation to create form, myth, narrative, story.'[15] It is to ask much of novelists to aim to achieve something so intangible and arduous but it is a task that Murdoch sets herself in following in the footsteps of a great novelist such as Tolstoy.

Murdoch's most celebrated essay on the modern novel is 'Against Dryness' in which she highlights the close ties between the contemporary novel and the accompanying social world. She observes, 'We live in a scientific and anti-metaphysical age in which the dogmas, images and precepts of religion have lost much of their power.'[16] She recounts factors in recent history that militate against individuals identifying themselves in terms of wider allegiances. She notes, 'We have not recovered from two wars and the experience of Hitler. We are also heirs of the Enlightenment, Romanticism and the Liberal tradition. These are the elements of our dilemma: whose chief feature in my view, is that we have been left with far too shallow and flimsy an idea of human personality.'[17] Modern individuals, for Murdoch, are shallow. They lack a moral vocabulary to make sense of their thoughts and feelings. She maintains:

> What have we lost here? And what have we perhaps never had? We have suffered a general loss of concepts, the loss of a moral and political vocabulary. We no longer see man against a background of values, of realities, which transcend him. We picture man as a brave naked will surrounded by an easily comprehended empirical world. For the hard idea of truth we have substituted a facile idea of sincerity.[18]

Existentialists and their English liberal counterparts reflect the prevailing cultural norms in their philosophies, and they do not consider the narrowing focus of individuals upon themselves and their subjective choices as loss. Rather, they celebrate the contemporary recognition of choice and subjectivity. But, for Murdoch, sheer choice in itself is inadequate to orient an individual's relations with the world and with others.[19]

In 'Against Dryness' Murdoch again reviews the literary present and its relation to the past. The Enlightenment is a cultural turning point, signposting a novel cultural identity. It celebrates reason and the advent of a 'rational' person, who is stripped of consolatory religion and deracinated from traditions, and conceives of reason in instrumental terms, unencumbered by cultural constraints. A person's identity is self-made, relying only upon their own instrumental actions. Murdoch takes the present situation to mimic that of the eighteenth century in that 'we retain an unfounded faith in our rational power, in technology but we are left with individuals, "stripped and solitary"'.[20] While the present reproduces the eighteenth-century Enlightenment, it is set apart from the social and literary world of the nineteenth century. The nineteenth century represents a century of change in which social and national movements swept individuals along with them, so that individuals were interwoven with a dense social background. She observes, 'The nineteenth century (roughly) was the great era of the novel: and the novel throve upon a dynamic merging of the idea of the person with the idea of class.'[21] Novelists such as Tolstoy, Dickens and Eliot represent the fates of individuals as wedded to wider developments in that they participate in events that bring about dramatic social and political change.[22] In the nineteenth century, close ties between individual and society allowed for a novelist's representation of characters as upholding political commitments whereas in the contemporary modern world society, individuality, society and the novelist have gone separate ways. Modern moral life and its fiction are alienated from wider beliefs and social structures.[23]

The contemporary novel, for Murdoch, reflects a loss of moral and political concepts, endowing meaning to an individual's life. The informing context of an intersubjective moral world that imparts meaning to a person's identity has been lost. The upshot is that the contemporary novel fails to identify anything but lone individuals struggling to assert themselves. Freedom is little more than self-assertion, and is detached from an informing context of interpersonal relations. As Byatt emphasizes, Murdoch sees freedom as a matter of degree in that individuals, in engaging with concepts and social practices establish ascending degrees of freedom.[24] In a devastating critique of contemporary assumptions, Murdoch maintains, 'We are not isolated free choosers, monarchs of all we survey, but benighted creatures sunk in a reality whose nature we are constantly and overwhelmingly tempted to deform by fantasy.'[25]

The contemporary novel reflects the deracinated state of contemporary society, and lacks the assurance of what has gone before. The great realist novels of the nineteenth century convey the confidence in society of the characters whose lives they track. Eliot, Dickens and Tolstoy imagine an ebb and flow in their characters' lives that reflect the tides of social movements. The contemporary novel is different. Its characters are isolated, not looking outwards towards others, but immersing themselves either in conventions or more likely in interminable self-analysis.

Murdoch identifies two paradigms of the contemporary novel, neither of which matches up to what was produced in the nineteenth century. Contemporary novels are either journalistic or crystalline. The journalistic novels are crammed with detail and its characters are lost in conventions at the expense of an insightful evocation of interpersonal situations within which personal qualities can be shown. Crystalline novels, on the other hand, absorb individuals within tightly controlled plots, showcasing the theories of their authors. In these standard forms of the novel individual characters are portrayed standardly. The crystalline novel is didactic in propounding a thesis or point of view, and the journalistic one is informative. In neither case does the contemporary novel allow individual characters to develop or to engage freely and developmentally with others. Some crystalline novels, such as *Darkness at Noon* are memorable and register significant points. Soviet tyranny was thoroughly repressive and Koestler's fiction helped to counter current myths of its beneficence. But the imagined characters of Koestler and Camus are lightly drawn so as to make points, which are the pre-formulated doctrines of their authors. Murdoch protests, 'Against the consolations of form, the clean crystalline work, the simplified fantasy – myth, we must pit the destructive power of the now so unfashionable naturalistic idea of character.'[26]

Murdoch had no intention of putting philosophical doctrines into her fiction. Yet the novel, for Murdoch, can open up to the world. Good literature reflects the world as it is and allows the reader to consider situations and characters that reflect experience. In exhibiting reality the novel performs a task that is connected to philosophy in that it is attuned to experience. Philosophy theorizes about the nature of morality, relating modern conceptions to what has gone before, and highlighting the significance of combating egoism and of attending to others. While the novel does not present a philosophical perspective it can imagine realistic situations and the distinct realities of human character as its protagonists assume or renege on responsibilities in a distinctively modern setting.

Form, content and the reader in Murdoch's novels

For Murdoch, in imagining things concretely the novel is closer to lived experience than philosophy. Its proximity is registered in its humour. Its province is lived experience as a whole so it embraces laughter and joy along with despair and misery. Murdoch herself proclaims that metaphysics demands a sense of humour that is sadly lacking in the general run of philosophical texts.[27] Certainly humour lightens the mood of novels that also show the most serious disturbing forms of experience. It is a tribute to Murdoch's artistry that she can juxtapose the search for salvation with farcical scenes catching the changing moods of a conversation and the inexorability of altering circumstances. Hence in *The Good Apprentice* (1985), Harry Cuno's desperate desire to advance his romantic affair with Midge McCaskerville is stymied by a tryst turning sour for the participants but not for the reader, as Harry and Midge bump into Harry's sons and confusion and embarrassment ensue.[28] Again, Austin Gibson Grey, the central character in *An Accidental Man* (1971) suffers a number of accidents, which are unforeseen, risible but also symptomatic of his lack of responsibility for others. The reader is amused by the accidental nature of Austin's life and self-images, but by the end of the novel these accidents and contingencies affecting the novel's characters, give the reader cause to reflect upon the role of accidents in the economy of our moral lives. How much responsibility can be taken for what happens when we do not control events? This is a complex question but it is also the case that we can laugh at the occurrence of accidents even if reflection upon them makes us think of our responsibility for what might seem merely accidental.[29] *Bruno's Dream* (1969) deals with death in multiple and moving ways, notably in its focus upon the old man, Bruno, who is struggling to come to terms with his past and his impending death. Yet it is also a novel of intersecting romances and strange comic happenings. Gerstenberger in her book, *Iris Murdoch*, is surely right to note how this juxtaposition of elements is deliberate and powerful on Murdoch's part. She observes, 'Murdoch has, in *Bruno's Dream*, come close to a successful joining of domestic comedy and macabre elements.'[30]

If Murdoch is realistic as a novelist in enlisting humour as an element of our experience, she is also prepared to imagine situations that are serious. Her realistic portrayal of characters who are evil in their manipulation of others is arresting. Given the refractoriness of experience to the realization of ambitions, and the propensity of things to go to the bad, the novel is well suited to portray human failings and warped characters. Her novels are highly memorable for their realistic but chilling portraits of demonic characters, such as Mischa Fox in *The Flight from the Enchanter* (1956), Charles Arrowby in *The Sea, The Sea* (1978), Carel Fisher in *The Time of the Angels* (1966) and Julius King in *A Fairly Honourable Defeat* (1970). These demonic figures exploit the uncertainties of complex situations and the susceptibility of individuals to defer to strong-willed characters.[31] The modern world, for Murdoch, is perhaps more inclined to respect the sheer strength of the will, stripped of a countervailing consideration for others, given the destruction of traditional supports for morality, such as belief in God and conventional paradigms of goodness. Mischa Fox preys upon the marginal and vulnerable in society, including those who have been displaced as refugees by totalitarian states; Carel Fisher tyrannizes his maid, Pattie; Charles Arrowby exerts a dominance over colleagues and especially women, while Julius King, perhaps unhinged by his experience in a concentration camp, plays mischievous and hurtful tricks on apparently virtuous friends.

Murdoch, in her fiction, gives thought to the question of form and to the question of how the modern novel might best be constructed to depict the world of experience. She is appreciative of the realism of the nineteenth-century novel but she was enough of a realist to know that realism could not simply be revived. As Rowe and

Horner point out in their essay, 'Iris Murdoch and Morality', 'It is important not to misunderstand Murdoch's calls for a continuation of the realist tradition in early essays, like "Against Dryness". Her aim was never to produce a kind of pastiche of the nineteenth-century novel, nor did she ever do so.'[32] In her own work, Murdoch allows for a variety of authorial devices to evoke characters and situations and to disrupt seemingly authoritative narratives. While her use of these devices in the late twentieth century, seemed to fit with the postmodern turn in literature, her use of a variety of voices and devices are not motivated by a postmodern scepticism. In her essay, 'Houses of Fiction: Iris Murdoch and Henry James', Priscilla Martin is right to suggest, 'Murdoch's self-reflexive fiction always strives to retain a referential function rather than to cast doubt on the capacity of fiction to refer to the real world.'[33] Murdoch's techniques as a novelist are designed to do at least two things – she aims to evoke plausible realistic readings of individuals and modern settings as well as to provoke the reader to think about the action of the novels. Murdoch employs a variety of narrative strategies so as to invite the reader to think hard about the characters and so to recognize individuals outside themselves.

Occasionally Murdoch employs a first person narrative technique to point up the fallibility of the narrator and to show how individuals can and often do misperceive the world. The first person narrator tends to be confident and assertive but lacks sensitivity to his situation and to that of others so that by the end of the novel, the reader questions the perspective of the narrative voice and is led to question the attitude of the narrator. For instance, in *Under the Net*, Jake Donoghue's perspective on things unravels as he is forced to realize that he has misunderstood his situation, misconceiving the relations between himself and his friends. In so doing his assertive and egoistic perspective is also questioned and the reader is left to contemplate the importance of attending to others. This narrative technique is not used to undermine representative claims but to show the complexity of a world in which individuals do not always see clearly how their world is constituted. Hence the device is used to show how things are. Likewise in the novel *The Black Prince* (1973) the narrative is apparently written by one of the characters, Bradley Pearson, who, while in jail, is writing a narrative of events that have led to his incarceration after being found guilty of murdering a fellow novelist, Arnold Baffin. At the close of the novel, Pearson's account is questioned by a number of other characters, who offer alternative perspective. Rowe and Horner conclude, 'Thus the experimentalism of *The Black Prince* implicitly deconstructs Murdoch's favourite mode, realism.'[34] It is by no means clear, however, that realism is undermined. In her journal Murdoch herself raised doubts about how we are to understand realism.[35] By the end of *The Black Prince* it is not clear who has murdered Arnold Baffin. Pearson appears as an unreliable narrator well before the close of the novel. His high-flown prose and avowedly lofty motives jar with how he ignores the feelings of Julian, the young woman with whom he has had a relationship. Murdoch conveys the unreliability of a number of the narrative voices in the novel. It is this unreliability of human beings who are prone to fantasy and self-justification rather than attending lovingly to others, which Murdoch's novel is aiming to convey. And she does this realistically.

One of Murdoch's most admired novels is *The Sea, The Sea*. It is a complex novel in which the device of an unreliable narrator is deployed so as to provoke readers to question the narrative as it unfolds. The form and content of the novel work together in that the unreliable narrative matches the narrator's behaviour, which is partial and selfish. The narrator, Charles Arrowby, is a theatre director, who has retired to a remote house overlooking the sea. Ostensibly he is leaving behind the busy world in order to become good. His drive to become good is not connected to any traditional beliefs or icons of goodness. His impetus to become good appears to rely upon no more than his own self-image. His self-imposed insulation from others and his lack of any substantial vision of life qualify him as being quintessentially modern. His narrative purports to be a memoir, though the text also serves as a diary in that he jots down his thoughts and notes randomly on what is happening. What is not random is the strength of the narrator's egoism, which informs his memories and distorts his writing. Heusel argues persuasively that his narrative is to be read as an index of our susceptibility to fantasy and the sheer difficulty of seeing things outside ourselves accurately. She observes,

> *The Sea, The Sea* is arguably a novel about the way writing novels is a form of wish fulfilment ... The novel demonstrates the way a mind works when it insists on rationalizing rather than on

simply processing materials – the space between perception and cognition. Insofar as all human beings are victims of illusions, Charles is typical.[36]

Charles's capacity for fantasy is represented by his delusory imagining of a sea monster, which serves as a metaphor for his distorted vision. Titian's painting of a heroic Perseus rescuing Andromeda from a sea monster, which hangs in the Wallace Collection which Charles visits towards the end of the novel, conjures up his delusive self-image and is a graphic representation of the force of the novel's engagement with delusion and misguided egoism. Charles projects his own misguided rescuing of his childhood sweetheart from what he takes to be an oppressive marriage as a heroic enterprise resuming mythical deeds. But he misunderstands Hartley, his childhood sweetheart, her marriage and his own self.[37] Insight into the self and just perception of others are constitutive features of morality and yet Charles's narrative reveals him to lack both of them.

Murdoch's novels use multiple techniques to show the nature of reality and notably to highlight our fallibility and susceptibility to misread things. Often she uses a third person narrative technique. In doing so she is concerned to open the narrative to a variety of perspectives and to the interactions of a number of characters. In 'The Sublime and the Beautiful Revisited', Murdoch points to how the form of the novel should allow for the freedom of its characters. The form should not impose a pattern that drains the life out of them. Reality is not to be subsumed by form in that the real distinct otherness of individuals should stand out. Murdoch's novels tend to make room for multiple characters, whose stories interweave so as to allow them to be appreciated. Yet, characteristically, characters in the novels misperceive themselves and others so that even where they are bent on becoming good they are undermined by their inability to really see others. It is this quality of vision that Murdoch takes to be of importance in morality and for the novelist in relating a truthful vision of things. The interweaving of characters and their propensity to misperceive things can be seen, for example, in *The Bell* (1958) and *Henry and Cato* (1976).

In *The Bell*, a celebrated early novel, a number of characters participate in a spiritual community at Imber Court next to Imber Abbey in Gloucestershire. Their spiritualism, as Nicol maintains, shows a restlessness with modern life and the quest for spiritual meaning in an increasingly atheistic world.[38] Their search for spiritual meaning, however, reveals their flaws and shows experiential obstacles that lie in the way of becoming good. The community's leader, a former teacher, Michael Meade, is troubled by a preceding unconsummated love affair with an adolescent pupil, Nick Fawley. His homosexuality is chaste and repressed, in response to the prevailing social and legal climate of sexual repression. Michael becomes attracted to a young visitor to the community, Toby Gashe. Dora Greenfield, who is unhappily married to a hectoring art historian, Paul, is another visitor to the community. According to old myths the original bell of the abbey fell into a lake in which a nun had drowned herself following the exposure of her illicit love affair. Its recovery is prophesized to bring similar calamity in its wake. Dora and Toby raise the original bell from the lake. Disaster ensues in the wake of a number of interrelated developments. Michael's quest for religious supersession of the self fails as he neglects to talk to Nick when he arrives at the community, and the latter's suicide leads to the closure of the community. The unsophisticated Dora, however, finds the strength to break from Paul and the repressiveness of her marriage. Her assertion of freedom is inspired by her increasing awareness of herself and her situation. The closure of the spiritual community registers the frailty of spirituality in the modern world, when sustaining traditions have been eroded. In his reading of *The Bell*, Nicol remarks on its qualified realism. He observes, 'The novel's realism is offset by features of the gothic romance.'[39] Certainly Murdoch's interweaving of myth into the narrative opens the possibility of alternative interpretations of events. But ambiguity does not undermine a realistic portrayal of Michael Meade's human failing in not attending to Nick and Dora's struggle to free herself from illusion. The narrative accommodates a variety of characters and perspectives on events.

In *Henry and Cato* Murdoch develops a narrative of intertwined modern themes in relating the stories of two childhood friends and their families. One part of the story concerns Cato Forbes and his family. Cato has converted to Catholicism to the disgust of his stern father, who regards religion as a backward step for humanity. Caro's turn to the priesthood is compromised by his own doubts about the foundations of his faith and by his sexual attraction for 'Beautiful Joe' an adolescent delinquent whom he meets in his pastoral work. On the other hand, Henry Marshalson, is a different kettle of fish. He is a shallow self-centred individual who returns from the USA to inherit the family fortune after the death of his elder brother. His long-standing resentment at his mother leads him to sell the family home, to renounce his fortune and to repudiate his mother's values. He sees his actions as liberating but they are unsupported by a reflective insight into himself and others. The two characters and their families intersect when Beautiful Joe kidnaps Cato apparently as part of a gang and demands a ransom, which Henry is persuaded to provide. Cato manages to free himself only when Joe is threatening his sister Colette who has come to his assistance. In struggling with Joe, he kills him. At the end of the novel Colette marries Henry and the two families are united even if intergenerational quarrels remain. The intersecting characters show different sides to modernity and its limiting perspectives. Cato's troubled relationship to the church dramatizes the contemporary demythologization of religious belief and his equally troubled sexuality reflects the uncertain status of homosexuals in an increasingly liberal but still heterosexual culture. Cato's self-absorption prevents him from seeing Joe as a separate individual, and Henry's self-centredness shows the hollowness of modern freedom. The intersections between the two families allows for comedy as well as the tragedy of Joe's death, and show Murdoch's capacity to combine many aspects of experience within a narrative. As Sage notes in her essay, 'The Pursuit of Imperfection: Henry and Cato', 'While the plot appears sensational, the counterpointing of the two protagonists' situations generates a comedy that underlies their characters reality.'[40] There is no philosophical message in *Henry and Cato* and *The Bell* other than that of showing human actuality and the propensity of individuals to fall short of their aspirations because of their failure to recognize themselves and others. Murdoch's later novels tend to be longer and contain even more characters than her earlier ones. Novels such as *The Good Apprentice*, *The Philosopher's Pupil* (1983), *The Book and the Brotherhood* (1987) and *The Green Knight* (1993) can be forbidding because of their density but they show Murdoch's determination to portray characters that work with and beyond the form of a novel that is imposed by the author.

Murdoch sees the visual arts as linked to literature in their capacity to depict the world realistically so as to enhance our awareness of what is other than ourselves. This capacity to depict reality does not preclude showing its ambiguities. The compatibility of the visual arts and the novel, their mutual interest in concentrating attention on reality is shown by Murdoch's presentation of the visual arts in her novels. Her novels are distinguished in part by their incorporation of paintings in her narratives. Rowe in her study, *The Visual Arts and the Novels of Iris Murdoch*, remarks, 'The use of paintings as interpretative tools highlights a distinctive narrative method; in each novel Murdoch brings into close perspective one aspect of human experience in turn, and the paintings provide a key to a particular critical reading of the text.'[41] Murdoch habitually invokes paintings in her novels to highlight aspects of the plot, to show the sensibility and development of characters or to characterize an entire work even if it is overly schematic to say that the paintings and novels highlight singular features of human experience. In *The Nice and the Good* (1968), Bronzino's allegory of *Venus, Cupid, Folly and Time* plays a pivotal role at different moments of the narrative. *The Nice and the Good* is about many things, including the countervailing claims of public and private morality, but in the aftermath of the Profumo sex scandal, which rocked politics and high society, one of its themes is sexual indulgence and its implications. At the outset of the novel the central protagonist, Ducane, is involved in an unsatisfactory love affair and is investigating sexual excesses at Whitehall. Many of the other characters have to contend with sexual encounters past and present, and two of them, Paula and Richard Biranne, review their troubled relationship while attending to Bronzino's painting, The painting itself represents not so much one thing but many. It shows the excitement of sexual experience while also intimating its moral implications. At the end of the novel after experiencing much anguish, and having been excited previously by the painting's sensuality, the Birannes view the painting in a different light. The painting is as ambiguous as experience as a whole and reflects ambiguities in the narrative.[42] In a rare comment on one of her novels, Murdoch in her journal suggests that the novel along with the painting points to the many-sidedness of experience, where the nice and the good are mixed together.[43] There is no definitive interpretation of this painting, just as there is no single interpretation of any work of art, including a Murdoch novel. What her novel indicates realistically is that carnal sex exists alongside other forms of love and that the world of bourgeois niceties exists alongside the goodness of attending to one another's needs.

Murdoch's use of visual art is also shown in *The Bell*. Dora's development as a person is reflected in her engagement with a painting in the National Gallery. Dora is an art student and Gainsborough's *Chasing Butterflies* is a favourite painting. Within the narrative and at a testing time for her, when she is uncertain of her marriage and of an affair that she had started, she revisits the National Gallery and looks again at the painting. She sees the painter's loving portrayal of his daughters running through woods. Dora is reassured as she reacts to the loving clarity of the representation and experiences what Rowe terms, 'appreciation of the beauty and individuality of others and of the world outside ourselves, to which Murdoch insists we turn our eyes on the Platonic path to goodness'.[44] For Murdoch a painting demands the engagement of those who look at it and interpret it, just as a novel calls upon its readers to reflect upon its meaning. Dora's view of the Gainsborough changes over time in that while revisiting it she notices anew the confidence of the girls and in turn she is emboldened to face up to things.[45]

The title of Murdoch's novel *The Sacred and Profane Love Machine* (1974) invokes the Titian painting, *Sacred and Profane Love*, in which a naked woman sits opposite a clothed one, with Cupid stirring the waters by which they sit. Interpretation of the painting is as delicate as interpreting the novel. It suggests an interplay between the sacred and the profane, because the model is the same for each of the figures that are depicted and perhaps intimates the erotic dynamism of life, in which identity is turbulent and yet may be amenable to a perception that recognizes the ambiguities of existence. Murdoch's novel is disturbing in its evocation of the dual life that is led by Blaise Cavender, a disenchanted psychiatrist who is married to a dutiful wife, Harriet and a son, David, while also maintaining a mistress, the unconventional Emily and their child, Luca. In the course of the novel the relationships are turned upside down as Blaise is forced to admit the deception and decides to live with his lover and to abandon his wife. The novel, like the painting may be said to suggest the ambiguities of identity, the power of sexual drives and our capacity to be attracted to apparently opposing forms. It is by no means clear that either the novel or painting is susceptible of definitive interpretation, and yet they are insightful in conveying the real ambiguities of existence.

Great paintings, like insightful novels invite onlookers and readers to think and to consider the truth of what they are experiencing. Murdoch remarks in her conversation with Bryan Magee, 'I think good art is good for people precisely because it is not fantasy but imagination. It breaks the grip of our own dull fantasy life and stirs us to the effort of true vision.'[46] She sees the visual arts as contributing to the possibility of individuals moving towards an appreciation of truth and reality rather than being absorbed by their own interests and fantasies. Murdoch sees great paintings and literature to be related in their capacity to incite in individuals a concentration upon what is other than themselves and to reflect on what this means. Murdoch's novel, *The Sandcastle*, deals with a love affair between a middle-aged schoolmaster Mor and Rain, a young portrait painter, who is at the school to paint a portrait of the retiring headmaster. Rain discloses how she sees and projects herself in paintings. But Bledyard, the art history teacher, gives a lecture in which he reflects upon one of Rembrandt's later self-portraits. He observes, 'Now here', said Bledyard, 'if we ask what relates the painter to the sitter, if we ask what the painter is after, it is difficult to avoid answering – the truth.'[47] Byatt comments perceptively on Murdoch's view of art, 'This respect for truth, and the sense that the idea of truth-telling is meaningful, are very much Murdoch's own.'[48] Byatt is insightful in drawing attention to the affinities between painting and the novel. Certainly for Murdoch, they both matter because they enhance perceptiveness for by attending closely to them we can be delivered from distracting self-absorption. They propound philosophical ideas, but, indirectly, they stir thought and promote a recognition of reality, which opens a pathway to goodness and knowledge.

Murdoch on Plato on art

Murdoch sees the value of the visual and literary arts in enhancing our capacity to perceive reality with a clarity that releases us from the grip of fantasy and delusion. They attend to truth and reality. Yet she also recognizes that there is a case against art. In *Metaphysics as a Guide to Knowledge* she contends with what she sees as contemporary poststructuralism's deconstruction of the very notion of creative agency and acknowledges how the advance of technology threatens individuality and produces rival forms of trivial entertainment.[49] Plato, however, poses perhaps the greatest challenge to the claims of art to contribute to truth and the good society. The challenge comes in two forms. On the one hand, Plato delivers a powerful critical broadside against art, and on the other hand, Murdoch herself is drawn to Plato and his ideas. Murdoch's philosophy contains countless references to Plato. She draws from Plato to construct her metaphysics and Plato's concept of the Good underpins her moral perfectionism. Murdoch does not duck the challenge. She responds to Plato's arguments against art in her study of Plato on art, 'The Fire and the Sun – Why Plato Banished the Artists'. In this book, she reflects upon Plato's metaphysics and his views on art and provides her own robust defence of the status of art.[50] In addressing these topics, her strategy is to show their interconnections. She explains how Plato's metaphysics denies the truth-claims of art and she counters with its determined defence. Ironically, however, her own defence of art depends upon a Platonic notion of the interconnections between truth and goodness and her reading of Plato allows for his artistic prowess to supplement his reflections and to suggest a figurative way of intimating the deepest truths.

Murdoch's trademark way of reading predecessors, and notably Plato, in the light of present day interests is not to everyone's taste. Conradi has declared, 'In *The Fire and the Sun* it is difficult to know where Plato ends and Murdoch begins.'[51] In his review of 'The Fire and the Sun – Why Plato Banished the Artists', Bernard Williams praises Murdoch for raising an important question about serious art and its capacity to contribute to human goodness but then criticizes her for mixing it with an account of Plato. He complains, 'In the place of pursuing this question (about art and goodness) on its own and our terms, Miss Murdoch's chosen plan gives much room to a curious account of Plato's philosophy.'[52] He continues by critiquing Murdoch's Plato. He takes it to neglect much Platonic scholarship and to be overly allusive and insufficiently supported by scholarly references to provide a reliable guide to Plato. Doubtless Murdoch might have provided more references to the scholarly literature on Plato, but Williams might have been more open to the spirit in which Murdoch was writing. Murdoch reads Plato as having something important to say about truth, goodness and art that resonates with her contemporary situation and she spells out what makes Plato important in the present context. In so doing she fuses her own thinking with that of Plato in a way that is both troubling and yet highly stimulating both for a reading of Plato and for considering art in modern times.

Murdoch rehearses Plato's metaphysics economically, allowing for Plato's indirectness and the changing formulations of his key doctrines. She is right to emphasize these aspects of Plato's work, even if she does not document the scholarly evidence for the ordering of the dialogues. She takes Plato's theory of the forms to be central to his philosophical project, denoting a way of seeing reality as essentially rational, but also recognizes that the theory did not receive a definitive statement. The particulars of sense experience are not seen as truly real but their status is not dealt with definitively. In the *Phaedo* and in the *Republic*, they are taken to provoke reflection by posing problems over their changeable appearances. Murdoch notes how in the *Republic* Plato's own recognition of his lack of a clear-cut understanding of the forms goes along with the arresting imagery of the Cave, the Line and the Sun, which convey the drift of his thinking in metaphorical form. The Cave stands for the world of sense experience in which truth is not the object of attention. Rather, the shadows cast by firelight at the back of a cave, in which individuals are shackled, pass for reality. These prisoners in the cave, if they are to grasp reality, must liberate themselves and enter the outside world, in which there are real objects. The ultimate source of knowledge and truth, though itself beyond reality and truth, is the Good, which is likened to the Sun. In the later dialogues such as the *Sophist* and the *Parmenides*, Murdoch notes that Plato envisages the forms to be interrelated so that change and difference can be incorporated into the world of reality and the key Platonic image of sight and the crucial virtue of attentiveness are less prominent.

Murdoch also discusses Plato's notion of Eros, the emotional psychical energy that propels individuals to develop and move from the particulars of sense experience and phenomenal beautiful things to an appreciation of the form of beauty. If Plato shows an appreciation of love and beauty, he is at the same time a consistent critic of art as a form of activity. The *Ion*, an early dialogue undermines the claims of a reciter of Homerian poetry to possess knowledge as, under questioning, he is unclear about the meaning of the poetry that he recites. The *Republic* offers a sharp critique of art. In the *Republic* Plato determines knowledge to be certain and objective by correlating it to the essentialized forms rather than to phenomenal appearances. Knowledge is to be acquired by philosophical insight, hence for Plato philosophers, who are to be trained to develop knowledge of the forms and the Good, are entitled to rule. Just as psychical justice is to be achieved by having reason rule over spirit and desire, in the community philosophers are to rule over spirited auxiliaries and the rest of the population. Philosophical rule for Plato guards against the dangers of ignorance and license. It has to deal with art, because art poses a challenge to philosophical wisdom, making claims of its own to represent and express reality and yet it only works with appearances rather than the essences of knowledge. Plato observes how artists characteristically cannot explain the rationale of their thinking. They are not aligned to the truth that is captured by philosophers. In the *Republic* Plato is committed to establishing a just community that is aligned with truth, and which is discernible to philosophical understanding. Art is unreliable in its presentation of truth and the gods. Homer relates stories that show the gods to be deceitful and unregulated irresponsible representations of the gods will not be allowed to circulate.[53] Art is to be censored. Murdoch observes how this critique of art justifies the tight control over art that is to be exercised in the community that is advocated by the Athenian Stranger in the late dialogue, *The Laws*.[54]

Murdoch expresses some sympathy for Plato's critique of art. Like Plato she takes art seriously and measures it against its claims to contribute to truth and goodness. Good art for Murdoch is justified in Platonic terms. It is to be measured in terms of its contribution to truth and morality. Like Plato she is also mindful of how art can be unreliable and wilful in expressing and promoting fantasies and egoism over self-control. Artists can also pander to the lowest common denominators revelling in pornography or what is merely easy on the eye. Novelists can offer facile plots and exciting characterization without conveying a countervailing sense of truth. Murdoch's sensitivity to the ways in which art can be subverted by the failings of artists is evidenced in her own novels. Her novels include portraits of a number of novelists, who abuse their art by producing fantasies or cheap undemanding stories. In *The*

Sacred and Profane Love Machine, Monty Small is an unreliable and undistinguished novelist, who invents facile undemanding stories. She recognizes how it can be easier and more entertaining to display self-aggrandisement and concoct fantasies rather than to testify to self-restraint and truthfulness. After all she follows Plato and Freud in acknowledging human liability to fantasy and egoistic projections.[55] In *The Black Prince*, Arnold Baffin pours out potboilers while Bradley Pearson holds back from writing due to his commitment to an abstract perfectionism that cannot be realized.

Novelists, for Murdoch, as she indicates in 'Against Dryness', can also fail by rehearsing an overly schematic structure, which bypasses reality. An overly neat formal structure that coerces the content is disrespectful of what is genuinely other. Moreover, artists are notoriously unreliable. Murdoch, however, holds out for art. In 'The Fire and the Sun – Why Plato Banished the Artists', she maintains that great art can contribute to the good, because it focuses attention and enhances perception. 'Art, great art,[56] is and should be realist just as metaphysics attends to what is real. Murdoch works with a contemporary version of Platonism, without, as Williams disparagingly remarks, the Cosmic Thing.'[57] If art possesses the same object as philosophy, namely, reality, it has its own style. In its distinguishing concern to represent the detailed nature of experience in all its imperfection, it is uniquely suited to capturing the way in which the drama of human life is susceptible of multiple pressures that disturb the pursuit of perfection. Life is full of multiple causes and incidents and it isn't susceptible to neat treatment. Art can capture the messiness of life while still recognizing its unity.

Murdoch sees the force behind Plato's treatment of art. She recognizes how art can resort to trivializing the spiritual and television is a caricature of art's focus upon detail in its endless proliferation of senseless images.[58] Yet she recognizes art to be a unique means of freeing people from the grip of desire. In an unreligious age without prayer or sacraments, it represents their clearest *experience* of something grasped as separate, precious, beneficial and held quietly and possessively in attention.[59] Art, for Murdoch, purifies the intelligent imagination and is an antidote to egoism. In defending art against Plato, she complicates the picture of Plato. She points out how Plato himself is an artist, who confesses to an ignorance of the requisite dialectical philosophical knowledge to which he is committed. She highlights how Plato expresses his most significant thoughts figuratively in the images of the Sun and the Cave.[60] Moreover, Plato wrote dialogues and the dialogue is a form that is akin to art in its presentation of character and scene so as to bring discourse to life. For Plato, discourse rather than text is the way in which to convey truth. Murdoch also observes how the *Timaeus*, which she takes, contra Williams, to be a late dialogue, imagines a demiurge as creating the world artistically from various elements, using the forms as a guide as to what should be done. The demiurge contends with the wandering cause that disrupts the task and renders the world is fractious and contingent. Murdoch herself is sympathetic to the use of metaphor in philosophy to express what fuses reason and emotion at the edge of our understanding. She also welcomes the analogy of the world's creation with the creative process of art. The true artist constructs with an eye to truth and realistic vision, which entails seeing the world in its true and moral light but also deals with materials that are to hand and which do not admit of a single crystalline story.

Art for Murdoch represents the particulars of the world, which are not to be reduced to a single line of vision. It is suited to recounting a narrative of development towards the good, which encounters distractions and obstacles along the way. Artists are to furnish a picture of the human condition that is truthful to mankind's capacity for goodness but are also to be attentive to contingencies and the possibilities of failure. The artist is a mirror to the world and should be attentive to reality and truth but mindful of the possibilities of egoism and fantasy that beset mankind. Just as all experience is historical and subject to change, art, for Murdoch is also subject to historical development. Historic Christian visual art has given determinate shape to images of Good and the Trinity, though in doing so it has threatened to deaden what is worshipped.[61] Modernity has altered things because the decline of belief in the major myths of Christianity removes artistry from Christian worship and what we are left with is something of a void. The void in visual art is increasingly filled by artists questioning the nature of art and ignoring the possibilities of conveying truth.[62] Modern literature, in tracking the hollowness of contemporary individualism, tends to produce impoverished narratives that deflect from an authentic representation of character. The true artist is mindful of their role in aligning with truth and goodness and also of the diffuse plurality of the world. Murdoch set herself the task of being true to the mission of art.

Murdoch expresses her ideas on art by engaging with Plato because she sees Plato as a kindred spirit in his sensitivity to the interplay between artistic imagination and philosophical truth. He is an artist himself, appreciates the pitfalls of art and knows the value of truth and the pursuit of a perfectionist morality. Her admiration for Plato and his capacity to deal with the many-sided nature of things is evident in her own Platonic dialogue, 'Art and Eros: A Dialogue about Art'. In this dialogue she rehearses much of what is conveyed more prosaically in 'The Fire and Sun – Why Plato Banished the Artists'. The dialogue consists in a conversation between a number of characters including a mature Socrates, a young puritanical Plato, Manitas a man of politics, Callistos a beautiful youth, Deximenes, a hardened cynic and Acastos a serious-minded youth. The participants in the dialogue represent different ways of taking art and just as in Platonic dialogues all of the participants contribute to its overall understanding. Mantias urges that art should be political, in inculcating citizenship and providing appropriate role models for youths. He states the case for censorship, 'Of course the state must control art. If it doesn't it is wasting a precious source of power. All that emotion in the theatre today, wasted just rising up uselessly into the sky!'[63] And he makes an ad hominem point to his interlocutor Acastos that the rights of minorities should be defended in plays.[64] Socrates insists however that they need to be clear on the nature of art before they can prescribe its uses. Acastos presses the case for art as the pursuit of truth. Plato, who has been sitting away from the others is incited by this comment to highlight the abuses of art. He observes how bad art 'is nothing, it's fantasy … And of course bad art can be harmful like pornographic muck'.[65] For Plato, art as a whole, even good art, is dangerous because it is ambiguous. He warns, 'Art is the highest escape route, it's the last exit and that is why it is the most dangerous.'[66] He observes, 'Art is dangerous to philosophy, it's dangerous to religion.'[67] Characteristically, Socrates has the last word and Murdoch through Socrates, responds to Plato by saying, 'It may be that the only art you would praise is practised in heaven when Apollo and the Muses.'[68] He goes on to say how art is fitted to an earthly existence, 'And perhaps the language of art is the most universal and enduring kind of human thought. We are mixed beings as you said yourself, mixed of darkness and light, sense and intellect, flesh and spirit – the language of art is the highest native natural language of the condition.'[69]

In *Metaphysics as a Guide to Morals* Murdoch is insistent upon this continuing role of art. She observes,

> Art is informative and entertaining, it condenses and clarifies the world, directing attention upon particular things. This intense showing, this bearing witness, of which it is capable is detested by tyrants who always persecute or demoralise artists. Art illuminates accident and contingency, and the general muddle of life, the limitations of time and the discursive intellect, so as to enable us to survey complex or horrible things which would otherwise appal us. It creates an authoritative public human world, a treasury of past experience, it preserves the past ... It calms and invigorates, it gives us energy by unifying, possibly by purifying our feelings. In enjoying great art we experience a clarification and concentration and perfection of our own consciousness. Emotion and intellect are unified into a limited whole.[70]

Conclusion

Murdoch is a novelist and a philosopher, though she does not use her novels to transmit a set of philosophical doctrines. Art, like philosophy, for Murdoch arises out of experience. Its value, again like philosophy, derives from its making sense of experience. Where philosophy provides a discursive overview of the nature of experience, art represents it in images. Art is connected to philosophy, but it is not to be reduced to it. In presenting reality art sharpens our awareness of what is beyond the self just as philosophy locates the self in a wider understanding of experience. Moral life is about recognizing the reality of others and responding lovingly to them and art and philosophy can contribute to our moral development. Art can enable us to see others and so prepare us for being responsive to them while metaphysics in providing an overall vision of experience can guide our moral development. The relations between art, philosophy and morality are intensified in modern times. In the context of the modern erosion of traditional myths that have supported morality, art can function as a means to enhance a moral sensibility. Likewise a revived and modified metaphysics can support morality.

The modern novel, like art in general and modern philosophy, has responded to the demythologization of modern life in ways that reflect modern tendencies to embrace a concentrated individualism that excludes a wider vision of things. Hence the existential novel, which examines an individual's consciousness intensively matches a modern moral philosophy that reduces morality to an individual's subjective choices. Murdoch's philosophy aims to widen our sense of the individual to include their alignment with truth and goodness while her novels show a modern individual's susceptibility to fantasy and delusion if they see the world entirely from their own egoistic perspective. Murdoch's novels work with her philosophy in showing the modern world, its dangers and its moral possibilities.

CHAPTER FOUR

Murdoch and morality

Murdoch: Moral theory, history and dialectic

Murdoch's moral theory is remarkable in many ways. It is radical. It critiques prevailing moral theory and the cultural moral mood. It sets out a perfectionist morality that is demanding in that individuals are not to do what is convenient or accommodating to their desires but are to strive for a Platonic form of moral perfection. This standpoint was radical when it was proposed, most notably in the three essays within *The Sovereignty of Good* (1970), and it remains so today. Broackes, in his thoughtful Introduction to *Iris Murdoch: Philosopher – A Collection of Essays*, highlights Murdoch's achievement in articulating a plausible, accessible conception of this departure from standard forms of post-war moral theory. Yet he also criticizes Murdoch for what he terms an unhistorical and undialectical perspective. He remarks,

> Even if it is an achievement of *The Sovereignty of Good* to show how a form of moral realism might be thinkable which talks of moral perception and virtue, and even if it is a strength to show that such ideas can be presented as very much in harmony with everyday appearances and ordinarily reflective thought, still a Hegelian might say that it was very undialectical of Murdoch not to have talked how *we ever got to a point* where it seemed such things could be said at all.[1]

He goes on to cite Cornford's comment to the effect that Murdoch's account of human nature and the good isn't apparently historical.[2] To the contrary, the strength of Murdoch's account of morality is that it *is* dialectical and this feature of her thinking is brought out in her reading of the historically constituted nature of moral experience and of reflection upon moral experience.

Murdoch's moral theory is historical in that it emerges out of her critique of the present by which she criticizes modern moral theory for taking on board uncritically, what is currently presumed but insufficiently considered in the practice. Her critical reading of present moral practice informs her critique of standard moral theory, which neither perceives the historicity of what it theorizes nor is attuned to what is being lost in current practice. Her historical reading of a loss of weight in our conceptualization of moral life has been observed by commentators, notably by Forsberg and Taylor.[3] Modern times celebrate choice over reflection on what is to be chosen and on a vision of how choice fits with a vision of others and with a wider scheme of things. The prospects for a morality that goes beyond a set of rules for accommodating individual preferences are correspondingly slim. Historic processes of demythologizing affecting all aspects of modern culture, exert an impact upon morality. Metaphysics is routinely dismissed, and metaphysical orientation of moral life is abandoned. Religion, or at least its supernatural components, is undermined by scientific and materialistic developments and a decline in religious faith removes a traditional support for morality. In Christianity the life of Christ has long been a source of moral motivation and the attachment of morality to a transcendent God, who is to be accessed by prayer, provides ballast for moral conduct. To undertake morality without divine assistance or sanction is to divest it of a traditional source of energy. Likewise art no longer imagines itself to be enhancing our perception of reality but rather serves as a vehicle for intensive introspection or as a means to deconstruct the very nature of artistic creativity.

The rise of an abstracted individualism and the correlative reduction of morality to the role of a sideshow underlie the devaluation of moral currency in contemporary theories that eschew perfectionism. Yet reliance on the isolated individual and the moment of choice are insufficient to support the continuing claims of morality. There is a persisting if muffled demand for a perfectionist commitment to do the right thing irrespective of immediate individual preferences. Murdoch perceives the current situation to call for an historical and dialectical response. The present poses particular historical problems that have to be resolved in theory and practice. We cannot move forward without knowing where we are, and where we are shapes how we are to understand what is to be done. She contends with historic cultural forces in a number of spheres that conspire to narrow the focus attention upon the individual and his or her choices rather than attending to wider visions of the world, and the reality of others. Her task is dialectical because it reacts to related movements in philosophy, religion, art, politics and moral practice. More specifically she critiques contemporary moral theory and offers an alternative conception of morality that goes beyond subjectivism. Hence she sees her moral theory as intimately connected to her related critical theorizing of the present in philosophy, religion, art and politics. Instead of reducing morality to minimal assumptions of agency and choice, she opens it up to a wider dialectical vision of experience that encompasses its historical identity and its connections with other forms of experience. Her perfectionist moral theory demands an individual's commitment to embrace a loving attention to others. It does not make things easy. It takes reflective and loving energy to orient oneself to the good and to counter a mechanical concentration upon satisfying the ego or an uncritical immersion in conventions. The obstacles to moral development are shown in particular ways in her novels. A novel such as *The Good Apprentice* (1985) is not an abstract piece of philosophy prescribing a set of rules for an apprenticeship in virtue. The virtue of pursuing the good is to be undertaken in multiple ways and this novel shows distinct pathways to the good. Murdoch's moral philosophy is dialectical and historical in that it involves reflection upon the present and the present's relationship to the past and it situates morality in relation to other aspects of experience.

Dialectic is at the heart of Murdoch's metaphysical reading of the interrelations of experience. In her journal for 1947 Murdoch declares that the spirit's capacities are organically connected – there is a dialectical relationship between religion, aesthetics and ethics.[4] Morality is at the heart of this dialectical interplay between areas of experience. It is what stirs her thinking and makes waves in her literary and philosophical writings. It animates her life. She wants to be good, yet it is hard and the project is complicated by our cultural history. In some sense morality is universal and absolute and yet it is also changeable and historical in at least two senses. Things have changed and morality, like the rest of experience, appears different in the modern world from how it has been conducted previously. If moral action is different, then so is moral theory, for theory and practice go together. This insight is at the heart of the essays on morality that are collected together in *The Sovereignty of Good*.[5] Standardly modern moral theory adopts the prevailing assumptions of individualism but takes them to be universal and so rehearses them uncritically. Murdoch's dialectical approach exposes the historicity of present assumptions and then offers an alternative moral theory, which draws upon recessive beliefs that have not disappeared entirely from the horizon. Murdoch was not alone in noticing what was happening. At the same time and for similar reasons, MacIntyre critiques contemporary moral theory for its failure to recognize its individualistic perspective as an historical rather than an absolute phenomenon. In *A Short History of Ethics*, which was published shortly before *The Sovereignty of Good*, he observes,

> Like Sartre the prescriptivist and emotivist do not trace the source of the necessity of choice or of taking up one's own attitudes to the moral history of our society. They ascribe it to the nature of moral concepts as such. And in so doing like Sartre they try to absolutize their own individualist morality and that of their age ... But these attempts could only succeed if moral concepts were indeed timeless and unhistorical.[6]

Plato, Murdoch and morality

The three celebrated essays on moral philosophy that are collected in *The Sovereignty of Good* focus upon critiquing present moral theory and aspects of contemporary culture that sustain the theory. They also propose an alternative moral theory that is historical, in that it draws upon past theory and cultural practice, but reframes what is taken from the past so as to render it amenable to the present historical conditions. Murdoch invokes Plato in framing a perfectionist morality in which individuals cultivate virtue by aligning the self with the good, and adopting a truthful and loving perspective on things.[7] In invoking Plato, however, Murdoch does not presume that morality is to be otherworldly. There are many interpretations of Plato, and as she makes explicit in her later *Metaphysics as a Guide to Morals* (1992), her Platonism is justified by its consonance with lived experience.[8] Murdoch's Plato differs from the Platonism that is ascribed to her by Nussbaum in her interpretation of the Platonism of Bradley Pearson in *The Black Prince* (1975), in which she critiques Murdoch's Platonic unworldliness and contrasts her literary attitude to the earthiness of Joyce.[9] Murdoch's Plato is not an advocate of supernaturalism. She invokes Plato's concept of the good to serve a timely metaphysical purpose, namely the task of replacing a personal and supernatural God with a metaphysical conception that fits with lived experience. In so doing she interprets Plato as a this-worldly philosopher, who can be assimilated to a post-Kantian philosophical context in which the operations of reason are limited by the bounds of experience. This revived Platonism also harmonizes with a modern cultural agenda that has abandoned aspects of a theistic religion, such as belief in an afterlife and the resurrection. In an age of sceptical rationalism, religion's supernaturalism is a sign of its redundancy. It is Murdoch's contention that a this-worldly Platonism can serve as an alternative to God and supernaturalism.

In his analysis of Murdoch's notion of the transcendence of the Good, Broackes concludes justly that Murdoch maintains a view of transcendence, which is compatible with a realistic account of experience. He observes, 'It is, Murdoch believes, integral to our conception of the good that it is in some sense a conception of something transcendent. But in which sense? Murdoch gives us a modest answer, something a naturalist (though perhaps not a simple scientific naturalist) would have no trouble acknowledging. Her conception could be described, I think, as both realist and deflationary.'[10] Murdoch's care to make her Platonic ethics compatible with naturalism is motivated precisely by an appreciation of the historical situation, which, she sees as integral to her intellectual strategy. It might be said that Plato's notion of the good plays a dual role in Murdoch's moral theory. On the one hand, Plato's austere moral perfectionism offers a radical alternative to contemporary moral theory and practice, which is enhanced by his philosophical authority and allusive artistry in presenting his core moral vision. On the other hand, Murdoch takes care to render her vision of Plato compatible with demythologizing modern attitudes. Where Murdoch's use of Plato might jar with her historical and dialectical sense of the development of morality is that the resort to Platonic language tends to play down or even undermine the identification of morality with an individual's development of their freedom. In following Plato, Murdoch resists the modern reduction of freedom to mere individual choice, but she is not deprecating the significance of individual freedom itself. For Murdoch, freedom depends upon the individual aligning their conduct with a perfectionist notion of the good, but it does not entail that individuals are to be coerced into doing the right thing. Freedom in the modern world is rightly seen to be integral to moral development. Murdoch critiques the submersion of individuals into merely conventional attitudes as much as she criticizes a reliance on mere choice as the sign of freedom. The repression of homosexuality for instance represents an unwarranted suppression of an individual's freedom to express their sexuality and Murdoch was a persuasive advocate for its legalization.[11] The conventional hostility to homosexuality represents a fear of freedom rather than a moral truth. Moral truths do not exist outside of mutual respect by individuals for the free development of one another.[12] Murdoch's novels testify to her commitment to personal freedom in that they incorporate a multitude of individuals, who interact freely in pursuing their purposes. Some strive to be morally good whereas others misperceive things in their egoistic pursuit of their own interests, but their freedom is common ground. Plato's moral theory was not couched in terms of freedom and Murdoch's Platonism is not distinguished sufficiently from Plato's actual theory to render its attitude to freedom unambiguous.

Morality in modern times

The essays in *The Sovereignty of Good* combine advocacy of a Platonic perfectionist moral theory with a focus upon the hollow and skewed nature of contemporary schemes of moral theory. The schemes that she reviews share deflationary expectations of moral demands. Their overall tenor can be summarized as reducing morality to a form of individualism in which subjective interests and inclinations are prominent features of a deracinated modern culture. Its most significant variants are its Continental and Anglo-American forms. Murdoch is uniquely equipped to recognize affinities between these variants as she had what was and remains, a rare expertise in the two fields. The Continental form outlines a heroic vision of the individual and is cast in existentialist terms. The existentialist individual exists in a solitary hostile universe, and his authenticity is established by enduring its solitariness. He (and existentialism in most of its elaborations save that of Beauvoir is centred upon the male) denies defining ties with others and sets himself to achieve authentic freedom by concentrating upon his own choices to exempt himself from the bad faith that is associated with merely conventional beliefs and attitudes.[13] Freedom is his sole value and operations of the will assume pride of place in the repertoire of human attributes.[14] The will exercises choice and existential man enjoys freedom when choosing and acting upon his choices. Morality tends to be conducted in silos, where solitary individuals struggle to achieve freedom by repudiating social commitments that are not freely chosen. Anglo-American moral theory has a different style. It is less heroic. Individuals are not pictured as agonizing over decisions and they do not stake their authenticity against the conditions of the universe or against the numerous unreflected conventions of society. What distinguishes Anglo-American versions of individualist morality is that ordinary unspectacular subjective choices are valued at the expense of traditional or supposedly objective values. If values are related to the empirical world in which individuals are situated, then morality is taken to be what can be shown to facilitate individuals realizing their preferences. Preferences and desires are not to be challenged unless they undermine the possibilities of others realizing their ambitions. Alongside a priority that is assigned to individual agents and their choices, Anglo-American forms of moral theory frown upon elaborated accounts of the background conditions for the exercise of morality. Behaviourist accounts of individual conduct tend to supplement a concentration upon choice so as to furnish an economical way of explaining moral action. Speculation about the good, and a vision of the world and of other people as amounting to more than an aggregation of preferences is dismissed as fanciful just as inner thoughts and doubts are disparaged because they are deemed insusceptible of verification. Hence Anglo-American versions of morality join forces with Continental existentialism in ruling out theorizing that goes beyond a narrow focus on the individual, who, in turn, is viewed narrowly.

Murdoch's moral perfectionism differs from rival modern moral theories on many counts. Her moral theory looks outward and away from the individual, both from an easy acceptance of the self or from its own intensive examination. Existentialism savours an intensive examination of the self to guarantee its authenticity over the bad faith of social conformity. Death matters for Heidegger, but above all it is the self's death that matters, and it is one's own death, contemplated and faced up to, which marks out a properly human response to the question of being.[15] Anglo-American theories are relaxed in taking the individual at their word and do not seek to modify the self. In fact the common denominator of moral judgment is the ordinary unreflected subjective choice of an individual and reflective procedures tend to be recommended so as to facilitate the realization of preferences. Utilitarians look to maximize the preferences of the greatest number so individual preferences may be sacrificed for the greater happiness but the nature of preferences themselves is not to be evaluated. Even moral theorists who look to a notion of universalizability to regulate moral decision-making are not imagining a reconstitution of the self within this process. The upshot is that standard forms of morality, which Murdoch critiques, tend to favour abstract notions of the individual alongside abstract models of procedural decision-making. In contrast Murdoch's moral perfectionism demands a change in the attitude and orientation of individuals. The self is imagined standardly to be overly concerned with the self. This attitude tends to make the self privilege itself over selves. Yet equally problematic is its promotion of a distorted vision of reality. In 'The Idea of Perfection' (1964), she remarks, 'In the moral life the enemy is the fat relentless ego.'[16] The relentlessness of the ego prevents it from seeing reality accurately. Murdoch's moral philosophy argues against this misperception and her novels show many forms of the ego's distortive vision of itself and others.

Unselfing, attention and the novel

What Murdoch proposes in contrast to the theories that she opposes is a kind of unselfing, by which individuals withdraw from an obsessive 'fat' ego that demands continual satisfaction. This unselfing flows from and leads to attention being directed outside the self and to what is other. If loving attention is bestowed on others then the self is changed and there is a different social matrix within which morality is conducted.[17] It is not a matter of maximizing or facilitating preferences of a solitary and static self, but of the self altering its perception of the world and of others, and in the course of this transformation, it alters its understanding of itself. Within this perspective morality becomes something other than a set of abstract rules for individuals whose identity and relations to others is left unexamined. Murdoch's novels lend themselves to showing phenomenologically what is involved in her moral philosophy. Their phenomenological attention to imagined experience allows for a recognition of how individuals perceive or misperceive themselves and others and shows how insight can develop over time and in the light of circumstances. The experiential focus of a novel can show how an individual may respond lovingly and virtuously to others. Conversely it can demonstrate the baleful consequences of 'the big fat ego', when an individual's absorption in their own desires and fantasies blinds them to the needs and realities of others.

A standard way in which modern moral philosophy deals with life and death issues is to set up a general procedural scheme to prescribe what is to be done in standard cases. Hence in examining cases of abortion or euthanasia the rights of individuals, either born or unborn, might be prioritized or the overall welfare of those involved might be favoured.[18] These life and death issues frame the very nature of human existence, but it is only in modern times that they receive extensive public debate, occasioning interest because of the modern expansion of democracy and a culture of human rights. Murdoch's novels attend closely to life or death situations and highlight the importance and also the difficulty of perceiving them accurately and non-standardly. For instance, Monty, in *The Sacred and Profane Love Machine* (1974), is faced with an appalling situation. His wife is dying and she is taunting him relentlessly. He lashes out. In doing so does he kill her to put a stop to her taunting or is it more of a mercy killing that shows a real but disappearing tenderness for a loved one? In the particular situation he finds himself, he is at a loss to find the right words. And so are we. But this does not point to a failing on the part of Monty or of Murdoch or of us. Rather it points to the sheer difficulty in perceiving and experiencing a demanding situation.[19] Its insusceptibility to being processed under the rubric of a general procedure of decision-making points to the inappropriateness of abstract schemes of morality that classify what escapes unambiguous identification. Likewise a number of characters in Murdoch's novels have abortions, and though some of these occur in the run up to the legalization of abortion in 1967, Murdoch's novels do not present a definite line on the issue. What they do is to look at what happens when they occur. In *The Italian Girl* (1964), for instance, Edmund, the central protagonist, is appalled when his niece, Flora tells him that she has had an abortion. His visceral response means he does not stop and consider what has happened and how Flora feels about what she has done.[20] In *A Severed Head* (1961) the central character, Martin Lynch-Gibbon, reacts casually to the pregnancy of his girlfriend Georgie and immediately offers her money for an abortion. What he does not do is to stop and attend to her and her feelings. Later in the novel Georgie attempts suicide and the suffering that leads to the suicide attempt involves her experience of an abortion that she had to undergo on her own and without her partner listening to how she feels. Again in *The Book and the Brotherhood* (1987), Lily Boyne, a feminist, blithely commandeers the youthful Tamar Hernshaw to have an abortion, without encouraging her to speak and to talk about her emotions. In the aftermath of Tamar's abortion, when Tamar is herself confused and upset by what has happened, Lily recalls uncertainly her own abortion, which she had put out of her mind. Murdoch recognizes the emotional turmoil that is involved in an abortion.[21] Lovibond has concluded that Murdoch regards abortion as a 'tragic and traumatic experience'. This is so and yet in these novels Murdoch is not against abortion, but she does imagine what it is like and how it figures within experience.[22] She is concerned to attend to what happens. If a moral lesson can be derived from what she writes, it is that a right to abortion may be a significant aspect of a woman's freedom, but it is not the end of the story. A woman who undergoes an abortion requires love and attention to help her in dealing with a demanding experience.

Murdoch's novels are superb in conveying the ways in which the 'fat relentless ego' can overwhelm a person and destroy the possibilities of moral life. The reality of the ego and of selfishness is something that tends to be ignored or overlooked in modern theories of morality, though Freud's psychoanalysis presents a modern reckoning with the power and strategies of the ego.[23] Murdoch is unflinchingly realistic in assessing human propensities, and her novels are unstinting in their recognition of human selfishness and self-deception. In her journals, a number of entries testify to her sense of the power (and dangers) of the ego in herself and in others. In the early 1970s she records how 'one-making is the task of the ego' and subsequently how 'all unifying is an image of power'.[24] Charles Arrowby of *The Sea, The Sea* (1978) is one amongst a series of selfish and egoistic leading characters in Murdoch's fiction. For instance, Jake Donoghue in *Under the Net* (1954), Martin Lynch-Gibbon in *A Severed Head*, Henry Marshalson in *Henry and Cato* (1976), Hilary Burde in *A Word Child* (1975) and Austin Gibson Grey in *An Accidental Man* (1971) see things from their own point of view. Their restricted pattern of seeing things issues in a series of repetitions of moral neglect, including omissions, accidents and deaths. The continuing unreflected pattern means that forms of egoistic behaviour recur, as these individuals continue to misread others and themselves.

What are less evident in Murdoch's novels are representations of individuals progressing towards moral perfection. Her realism pervades her literary imagination and a succession of minor and major characters are depicted as falling short of their own ideals. Murdoch's perfectionist morality is compatible with a realistic reading of experiential imperfection. The standard of perfection is implied by our capacity to criticize our imperfections. There are one or two characters that approximate to the good in their development. *The Nice and the Good* (1968) sets a series of 'nice' conventional bourgeois attitudes against progress towards the good. The central character, John Ducane, moves from being immersed in the nice and modern world of well-to-do conventionality that is free from traditional restraints on behaviour, to aspiring towards the good. It is uncertain progress but after experiencing the trauma of being trapped in a cave while attempting to rescue from drowning Pierce, the son of Mary Clothier, he emerges with a clearer vision of things. He feels and expresses love for Mary and looks to help others. He moves away from the smooth world of Kate Gray, with whom he has been having a Platonic affair, and his self reorients towards embracing loving relations with others, and he gives assistance to Paula Biranne in reconstituting her life. In *A Fairly Honourable Defeat* (1970), we meet a genuinely good character in

Tallis Browne, who is on the face of things an unprepossessing social worker whose domestic arrangements are as chaotic as his house is disorganized and dirty. He proves to be the only character in the book, which is immune to the wiles of the Julius King, a malign trickster. Tallis is unpretentious and honest. His lack of egoism gives him strength in dealing with Julius. What Tallis and Ducane have in common is the virtuous attention that they give to others, and it is the loving focus of their attention which enables them to do good.

Murdoch's moral philosophy is historical and dialectical. It is expressed in a concentrated form in a set of essays that are contained in the collection entitled *The Sovereignty of Good*. It is composed of three essays 'The Idea of Perfection', 'On "God" and "Good"' and 'The Sovereignty of Good over Other Concepts', which were first published in 1964, 1969 and 1967, respectively.[25] Together they critique prevailing ethical theories, showing their historical identity and express a distinctive perfectionist morality that is continued in her later writings. They identify contemporary moral theories as historical in their replication of features of the particular historic culture of the West in modern times and they connect morality to a synoptic view of experience, a perspective that is reinforced by her later work, *Metaphysics as a Guide to Morals*. Her metaphysics allots a privileged position to the Good as the source of a transcendent truth and value, underlying experience. Her view of morality is not fixed upon a delimited sphere of individual decision-making, in which the individual is separated from a wider view of the world. The good is intimated by loving relations with others and it goes beyond any particular performance. The good is never truly enacted. Perfection is beyond complete consummation. The virtue of lovingly pursuing the good is to be cultivated by many means. An appreciation of art is helpful, in that art imagines the world realistically in ways that demand concentrated and loving attention upon what is not the self. Likewise, religion, in its encompassing commitment to experience as a whole, continues to serve as a support for morality even if its magical aspects are no longer sustainable. In the succeeding sections of this chapter we will review the individual essays that make up *The Sovereignty of Good*. In so doing we will point out the connections between Murdoch's moral philosophy and other strands of her thought, and Murdoch's novels will be invoked from time to time to show how their attention to imagined individuals and contemporary circumstances bears upon an understanding of moral life in the modern world.

'The Idea of Perfection'

In 'The Idea of Perfection' Murdoch sets out a moral philosophy of her own, and standard assumptions of contemporary moral philosophy are subjected to critique. Murdoch is at odds with several strands of contemporary philosophy, which converge upon misleading doctrines that undermine traditional morality and reflect back uneasily upon contemporary moral practice. She is wide-ranging in her condemnation of how things stand in current moral philosophy, taking Continental existentialism, differing strands of Anglo-American ordinary language philosophy and utilitarianism to be of a piece in downplaying a view of morality that calls for a vision of things. These contemporary strands of moral philosophy are at one in focusing upon the bare individual, whose conceptualization consists in the ascription of a will to undertake action and a determination to act freely by exercising choices. There are differences between these idioms but they share a common perspective. Utilitarians look to rules of conduct promoting the general welfare, to guide individual behaviour, whereas rival versions point to the universalizability of preferences or else take preferences to be the ultimate arbiters of conduct. There is general agreement, however, that neither a critical examination of how others are perceived nor a critique of how an individual sees the world is required. A focus upon the act of choosing or a reliance upon abstract rules of ranking preferences are at one in dismissing the need for a more concrete engagement with how individuals perceive the world. Elaborations on how individuals perceive things are seen as muddying the waters. Murdoch takes this general approach to be epitomized by two of Hampshire's texts on the philosophy of mind, *Thought and Action* and *Disposition and Memory*. These texts discount any account of an individual's capacity to introspect and reflect upon their motives and situation that is removed from a genetic and public account of how their views have been acquired.[26] The upshot is that a stripped-down notion of the individual and their situation is presumed.

Modern philosophy in its various guises reduces moral life to the bare choices that an individual is inclined to make. The choices are not related to wider corrigible visions of the world. They are presented as if they are commodities available in a shop, and packaged in easily intelligible and publicly available ways. Moral theory abstracts from an individual's lived experience with others and fine-grained readings of their situations. Instead of assuming human conduct to be a series of price sensitive transactions, Murdoch takes moral life to require a critical perception of things and a rethinking of situations, so that decisions on action are the product of a sensitive reading of what particular circumstances require. The prevailing image of moral choice as accessing moral goods like a customer decides upon buying items in a shop, or as cars are purchased from a showroom and latest fashions are determined by the look of models on a catwalk, links morality to a modern world of atomistic liberalism and proliferating commodification. Murdoch imagines modern moral philosophy and its current practice as exhibiting rifts in shared practices and an absence of commitment to interpersonal ties. She observes how contemporary moral practice, in its objectification of value lends itself to Marxist critique.[27] Individuals are severed from their actual engagement with others and are pictured as atomistic rational decision-makers. She traces the severance of the good from the world of experience to Moore's idea of a mysterious and indefinable notion of the Good that is distinct from individuals. But she also notes how the contemporary critique of Moore reveals a poverty of moral imagination. The baby is thrown out with the bathwater. The very idea of goodness as lying beyond individual choice is shunned. Moral convictions now appear as so many subjective choices, whereas Murdoch imagines the subjective to be interwoven with a sense of objective goodness in its constitutive role in shaping subjective striving.[28]

The prevailing rhetoric of moral philosophy imagines morality to be enacted by individuals choosing between courses of action, which can be presented abstractly. Choices are to be facilitated by the adoption of general criteria covering a multiplicity of situations. The rhetoric ignores a sense of the fine-grained world in which distinct individuals actually live, where judgments are particular and things are imagined in specific ways that undermine generalization. In the actual world of experience moral particularism makes sense.

Judgments are made by expressions that pick out particular features of the moral landscape. Hence someone might be condemned for being boorish or praised for their openness rather described in abstract terms as nice or good. In countering the reigning orthodoxies, Murdoch invokes what has become a celebrated example to show what she means by an actual person considering and developing moral judgments. She imagines a mother (M), who is devoted to her son. He marries and the mother is disappointed in the outcome as the daughter-in-law (D) is a disappointment. Her son appears to have married beneath himself. She loves her son dearly and wants what is best for him, but his partner appears loud, brash and common. The mother's opinions reflect her status and her love for her son and yet she is also intelligent and loving. She wants to do the right thing. Murdoch invites us to imagine the mother rethinking her attitude as she aims to be fair-minded in her judgments. Hence she reconsiders how she has perceived her daughter-in-law so as to do justice to her. On thinking things over in a spirit of love and generosity she comes to believe that she has misrecognized her. Whereas previously she has figured her as vulgar, now she takes her to be refreshingly simple, and she no longer appears as undignified but rather as spontaneous, not noisy but gay, and youthful rather than juvenile.[29] Murdoch offers this imaginary episode as a paradigm of what might be achieved in moral thinking. Moral development is a product of moral reflection on concrete matters that does not necessarily spring from or lead to the use of general rules of conduct. Moral work and progress has been achieved by the mother attending closely to what is at hand and by altering her perceptions of another person. Morality for Murdoch depends upon moral vision, attention to others and moral progress is a matter of reviewing how we see things. She observes, 'M looks at D, she attends to D, she focuses her attention on D.'[30]

In Murdoch's language, the mother (M) asks questions of herself so as to perfect her moral attitude. The mother is pursuing perfection through focused and sensitive self-criticism. Murdoch's idea of perfection should not be misunderstood. It does not operate as an ideal external to the world of lived experience. It is not presuming another world of perfection. Her Platonism is not otherworldly. Rather the pursuit of perfection is the cultivation of the virtue of loving attention to others, which takes place in a common world of experience. Realizing the good is an endlessly critical and demanding ideal, which involves looking closely at others and ourselves. We are to resist the temptation to act in egoistic terms. As the example of the mother's attitude to her daughter-in-law reveals, however, it relates to our experience of trying to refine our responses to others rather than in imagining a perfection that is unrelated to actual experience. Clarke in an article on Murdoch's moral philosophy, 'The Prospects for Critical Moral Perception', highlights the critical spirit of Murdoch's perfectionism. She observes,

> Whether one is trying to understand another language or another person, on her [Murdoch's] account, one is guided by the sense that there is something *beyond* what one's current lights reveal to one, that there is more to be understood. With a nod to Plato, as well as to G. E. Moore, Murdoch identifies this sense of perfection with a principle of Good that is both elemental and indefinable.[31]

Murdoch notes how M's development is akin to what novelists focus upon in showing character development and this feature of fiction informs her sense of how her own novels deal with moral questions without conveying a precise moral doctrine.[32] In her journal for 1975–8 she observes, 'There must be moral clues in a novel, as in a detective story.'[33] The clues relate to how circumstances, experience and reflection can lead to moral progress, where progress is not to be assimilated to schematic judgements on courses of action that can be separated from a wider web of circumstances and perceptions of others. Moral progress depends on judgments, informed by experience, in which individuals get closer to appreciating the nature of situations and what is required. In effect it appears as a commitment to achieve an ideal of perfection. The ideal of perfection is not to be misconstrued. It is not otherworldly and does not depend on sophisticated forms of reasoning, and as is the case with the mother (M) in her change of attitude to her daughter-in-law, it might not require an overt change in actions to be performed. The novel *Bruno's Dream* provides an example of moral progress. On the face of things the situation is not conducive to moral progress on the part of Bruno. He is old and dying. He is physically revolting and as Gerstenberger observes, he has come 'to resemble the spiders which inhabit his old mansion'.[34] He is troubled about the past, most notably over his betrayal of his wife Janie in taking a mistress and by his racist remark on the occasion of his son Miles's marriage to the now dead Indian woman, Parvati. He asks to see his son, but their meeting does not go well. In his rambling disconnected thoughts Bruno tries to excuse himself for his conduct, focusing on the isolated nature of his racist remark and on his general loyalty to his wife. The flooding of the Thames into the Battersea house where he lives and the consequent loss of his valuable stamp collection adds to the dismal atmosphere in which Bruno ekes out his last days. Yet he receives loving kindness from Nigel, his male nurse and then from Lisa, the sister of the second wife of his son Miles and finally from Diana, Miles's wife. At the end, comforted by Diana, he reviews his life in a new light, refusing alibis and reflecting, 'He had loved only a few people and loved them so badly, so selfishly. He had made a muddle of everything. Was it only in the presence of death that one could see so clearly what love ought to be like?'[35] He reflects about his wife Janie, whom he had avoided at her death out of shame over his betrayal of her. He realizes that she too would have felt the kind of love that he was feeling now at the end of his life and that if he had seen her at that moment she would have forgiven and not cursed him. He concludes his thinking by murmuring, 'Janie, I am so sorry', and his tears flow, but he is glad that he now knows how Janie felt at the end.[36]

Murdoch's novels, however, do tend to deal in defeat and imperfection rather than in perfection and clear progress towards goodness, reflecting the realism of her moral psychology and her recognition of the relentless power of the ego to project its fantasies and to operate selfishly. *A Severed Head* deals with a group of characters, whose rapid turnaround of partners reflects the romantic and sexual freedom of modernity and the difficulties of giving and maintaining love. Its protagonist and narrator Martin Lynch-Gibbon is married to Antonia and has an adulterous relationship with Georgie. He is egoistic and selfish. At the outset he appears satisfied with himself and his situation. But his egoism prevents him from giving to others or even from seeing what is happening. He does not realize that his wife is having an affair with his brother Alexander and that she is also developing an affair with her psychoanalyst Palmer Anderson. Likewise his adulterous relationship with Georgie Hands is limited. He does not recognize her situation or her needs. He does not love her. A promised trip to

New York means a lot to her but never materializes. He allows her to suffer alone the emotional burden of an abortion. In an intoxicating atmosphere of emotional and sexual freedom, the characters are unable to sustain stable and meaningful emotional relationships. Couples form and reform; partners switch but the suffering continues. Georgie attempts suicide and Palmer, the psychoanalyst, lacks the moral authority to heal the wounds of the actors. He himself has an incestuous relationship with his half-sister, Honor Klein. Martin is left increasingly bewildered. Honor Klein has a power, truthfulness and primitiveness that is associated with the severed heads with which she is familiar in her anthropological studies. Martin senses the truthfulness of Honor and is drawn to her and it is only in his more equal and truthful burgeoning relationship with her that his development as a person is intimated. He is shocked out of his comfortable moral lethargy. Shortly after their first meeting Martin says to her prophetically, 'I don't imagine that you ever let people off, do you Dr. Klein'[37] In his literary commentary, *Murdoch*, Baldanza offers a tentative summary of the theme of the novel, 'The novel concerns Martin's difficult lesson in coming to accept and to love the otherness of other people.'[38] It is a summary that captures how Murdoch's novels show the nature of morality and the difficulties in making moral progress. *A Severed Head* is devastating in its revelation of the hurt and misery that are delivered by relationships that are not underpinned by love and which suffer from the misperceptions and indifference of an egoism that is not restrained by traditional institutions and beliefs. The freedom of modernity can easily turn into a nightmare. At the close of the novel, the glimmerings of Martin's moral development depend upon his readiness to see the world in a more truthful light and a willingness to accept the otherness of another person.

'On "God" and "Good"'

The essay 'On "God" and "Good"' expands upon the themes that are set out in 'The Idea of Perfection'. It combines a critique of current moral philosophy with a more sustained argument for an alternative moral theory that anchors morality to a conception of the Good. The positive argument is connected to the negative one. Murdoch rehearses how contemporary forms of moral theory exalt the individual over a relational view of morality, in which an individual's perception of reality and relations with others are to be prioritized. Murdoch sees the variety of forms of contemporary moral philosophy as existentialist insofar as they promote an abstracted individual and sheer choice over a more relational view of how an individual fits into a wider scheme of things. She complains that Marx and Freud are ignored along with the psychological and sociological background conditions that are constitutive of individuality. She remarks, 'Moral philosophy of an existentialist type is still Cartesian and egocentric. Briefly put, our picture of ourselves has become too grand, we have isolated, and identified ourselves with an unrealistic conception of will we have lost the vision of a reality separate from ourselves, and we have no adequate conception of original sin.'[39] Her moral philosophy is in part a lament for what has been lost. Original sin, for instance, is a concept that answered to our sense of requiring a notion of and explanation for substantive wrong-doing that is absent from modern culture. She notes how Kant and Hegel invoke a substantive notion of reason and a correlative sense of historical development to anchor moral conduct. Yet she maintains that these conceptions have been abandoned. Substitutes have not been put in their place. Sin, guilt, evil, repentance and moral progress do not get a mention in supposed ordinary language philosophy of the present, even though ordinary people still think in such terms. Murdoch's critique of the present highlights the loss of religious concepts and practices. Belief in God and in the efficacy of prayer enabled individuals to repent and reorient their conduct, whereas nowadays morality is about aligning the changeable preferences of individuals with one another. She wonders if something akin to a transcendent and perfect God can be invoked to inspire moral goodness in an age of waning religious belief. In this context she considers the prospect of imagining the Good as a transcendent and inspirational force for morality. Her positive moral theory, focusing upon the magnetic power of the Good arises out of her critique of the present.

In considering the prospects for aligning morality to a notion of the Good, Murdoch reviews the role of art in representing beauty in a way that goes beyond the personal and particular manifestations. Art identifies a sense of beauty existing beyond imperfect representations. Beautiful objects and paintings do not exhaust the beauty that they intimate and an ideal of perfection underlies the practice of genuine art. Art is a metaphor for moral achievement. The very imperfection of our efforts to be good intimate and inspire a sense of a perfection that can be said to inhere in the idea of the Good. The good operates as a metaphor in drawing upon experience and practice in the sphere of art and in ordinary life. Moreover, as Plato observed the idea of the unifying sense of the Good, relates to our understanding of the virtues as composing a unity.[40] Murdoch holds that in considering a single virtue such as courage we distinguish it from raw physical spirit. The courage of a concentration camp survivor is attributed to a range of interlocking virtues. The Good provides the unifying notion that holds the virtues together. Murdoch is aware that her metaphysical standpoint is contestable. Murdoch's Platonism is not held dogmatically. Her version of Platonism is a modern one, which accepts its contestability. In *Metaphysics as a Guide to Morals* she recognizes that metaphysics is a precarious undertaking and acknowledges that nowadays religious dogma is obsolete. In 'On "God" and "Good"' she recognizes how belief in a transcendent God is waning, and accepts the possibility that the idea of the Good is vulnerable to modern critique. Yet she sees positive reasons for maintaining it. She observes,

> There is, however, something in the serious attempt to look compassionately at human things which automatically suggest that 'there is more than this' a very tiny spark of insight ... the machinery of salvation is essentially the same for all. The 'there is more than this', if it is not to be corrupted by some sort of quasi-theological finality must remain a very tiny spark of insight, something with, as it were, a metaphysical position but no metaphysical form.[41] She goes on to muse, 'Do you then believe that the idea of the Good exists?' I reply, 'No, not as people used to think that God existed.' All one can do is to appeal to certain areas of experience, pointing out certain features and using suitable metaphors, and inventing suitable concepts where necessary to make these features visible.[42]

Just as *Metaphysics as a Guide to Morals* looks to justify its metaphysical standpoint by reference to ordinary lived experience rather than purporting to provide dogmatic truths, so the essay 'On "God" and "Good"' is wary of laying down supposed truths.

Metaphysics as a Guide to Morals appeals to a revised form of the ontological argument which derives its force from experiential beliefs, and likewise Murdoch in 'On "God" and "Good"' looks for no more than contingent experiential insight. Murdoch's Platonic metaphysics is very much of this world, deriving its support from experience and in turn supporting moral beliefs by its metaphorical vision of order and goodness. Her novels are set in a modern world in which former religious values are fading, and yet they show ways in which the language of good and even evil appears to be warranted. In *Nuns and Soldiers* (1980) the action of the novel takes place after the death of Guy, who has presided over his wife Gertrude and sundry friends, who have been drawn to their household. Guy's presence has held all the characters together and restrained their egoism. His death replicates what happens in the event of the death of god. It releases disorder and unruly forces that cannot be trammelled. However, just as in the case of God, the release of control also brings out qualities that have hitherto been repressed. The death of God is not merely loss. In *Nuns and Soldiers* glimmerings of spirituality in the various characters are to be seen along with naïve goodness, artfulness, and developing self-awareness. In Anne's continued spiritual quest, Daisy's insight and frankness, the Count's dutifulness and Tim's ingenuousness we witness awkward moral development in a world without God. Reflecting back on the death of Guy, Gertrude considers, 'Guy had overshadowed them all. His evident superiority must have irked them. Why had Gertrude imagined that they loved and revered him so much? They had envied him and his evident distinction had made them feel inferior.'[43]

If Murdoch's novels feature characters, notably priests, whose aspirations to virtuous conduct are complicated by their doubts over belief in God and the supernatural claims of religion, they also contain characters that are malign and perpetrate significant wrong-doing. In a world without God evil is not erased. Its power is retained even when, in the aftermath of a slackening of moral language and the modern turn against traditional images of God and the devil, contemporary moral theory is bereft of the words to identify it. *A Fairly Honourable Defeat* (1970) deals squarely with evil and our continuing susceptibility to it. Indeed the propensity for individuals in the contemporary world to be submerged in fantasy and conceits tends to make them vulnerable to its sway. The main action of the novel is a confrontation between good and evil as Julius King clashes with Tallis Browne, with the former arguably incarnating the devil and the latter Christ. The other characters are all more or less egoistic human beings. Julius contrives to make a bet with Morgan, his ex-lover, that he can divide the gay couple, Simon and Axel, and he takes things further by contriving to disturb the apparently secure relationship of Hilda and Rupert, by employing old love letters to make it appear to Rupert and Morgan that each loves the other. Vanity plays its inevitable role as they both relish the prospect of being loved. Rupert cherishes his status as the beloved, while apparently dispensing sage advice to Morgan. The upshot is that Rupert's marriage to Hilda is rattled and Simon is coerced into little lies that disturb his relationship with Axel. Meanwhile Peter, the emotionally highly wrought son of Hilda and Rupert, is anguished and Morgan becomes unhappy at the turn of events. Rupert's recently completed Platonic text on truth is torn to pieces by Julius and Peter. It is a reflection of Rupert's vanity and his inattentiveness to others and their feelings that, in the wake of see-sawing emotions unleashed by the trick played by Julius, he drowns in the swimming pool. The pool itself is a token of a commodified society that rates the purchase of luxury goods over attention to people and things.[44] Julius is evidently a malevolent character and one that readers are likely to be repelled by even if the devil on this, like other occasions, is in the detail. Julius is evil but he is also focused upon reality. He sees the vanity and egoism of individuals, which renders them vulnerable when events appear to confirm their egoistic desires. Even the likeable Simon resorts to lies. If Julius is evil, then Tallis is good and perhaps more evidently good than any other Murdochian character. On the surface he is unattractive in that he is disorganized and his flat is squalid and untidy. But his humility and lack of egoism enable him to respond decisively to Julius's malevolence. He is helpful to Peter, caring to his father and patient with Morgan. He is also decisive when the situation demands action. On hearing of Julius's deception he insists that Julius must confess what he has done to the parties concerned. Goodness does not win out in the novel. After all Rupert dies and a shocked Hilda departs with Morgan and Peter, who continues to be troubled. Murdoch's realistic novel on the moral life does not admit of a triumph for goodness. One should not expect goodness to be triumphant. To be good is a difficult endeavour and it is asking a lot to contend with the self's entanglement with fantasy and egoism. Perhaps the most that can be asked for is a fairly honourable defeat.[45]

In the wake of the mayhem that is inspired by the demonic plots of Julius in *A Fairly Honourable Defeat*, Simon and Axel, who have become mutually suspicious, talk honestly to one another and appear to recognize their previous mutual mistrust. They are open with one another and perceive each other justly, and so prepare the ground for a more honest relationship. In the light of the susceptibility of goodness to the wiles of the evil that is concocted by Julius this development in their relationship cannot be portrayed as a triumph but again it supports the idea that goodness does not suffer a dishonourable defeat. Murdoch's portrayal of this moral development in the relationship between Axel and Simon is noteworthy as it shows her treating a homosexual couple as living together and having some success in developing their relationship. Their capacity to pursue a relationship, notwithstanding that Axel does not disclose the relationship to his civil service colleagues reflects a change in the status of a homosexual couple after the legalization of homosexuality. The couple here is treated as capable of developing their relationship productively, and there is a background assumption of greater social acceptance of the rights of homosexuals even if Axel is cautious about advertising the relationship among colleagues in the civil service.[46] Murdoch's portrayal of the relationship lends cultural support to the idea of homosexuals having the right to develop sexual relations freely.

'The Sovereignty of Good over Other Concepts'

In 'The Sovereignty of Good over Other Concepts', Murdoch revisits the idea of the Good and highlights its role in providing a framework in which the virtues can operate. The Good serves as a metaphor attesting to virtue and of the unity between virtue and reality. Given that philosophy furnishes an overview of different forms of experience it relies on metaphor and the point, for Murdoch, is to scrutinize the metaphors to which one is committed to ensure that they can capture the character of human beings and the texture of experience. She holds a pessimistic view of human nature. Human beings are selfish deluded creatures, who are entranced by their own fantasies. They focus upon their own purposes and tend to misrecognize other persons. Moreover, there is no external end or telos to the drama of human life that may impel individuals to change their conduct. There is no extrinsic purpose to life either in God, or substitutes for God, such as History or Reason. Murdoch operates within a post-Kantian age and a priori truths cannot be proclaimed dogmatically.[47] She recognizes herself to be living in modern times and she takes on board its critical edge, its rationalism and its demythologization of former myths and traditions. It is a godless world. She remarks, 'There is no transcendent reality. The idea of the good remains indefinable and empty so that human choice may fill it. The sovereign moral concept is freedom, or possibly courage in a sense that identifies it with freedom, will, and power.'[48] The Enlightenment picture of the man of reason, who operates instrumentally to manipulate the world disinterestedly, is complicated by the impact of Romanticism, which imagines mankind as an isolated and courageous individual, who stands alone against an empty universe. The narrative of individuality might be complicated but it combines heterogeneous elements to make a powerful mixture; courageous rational individuals uphold freedom and operate with ingenuity to forestall a hostile universe. What is lacking is a reliable moral compass.

For Murdoch the abstractness and isolation of modern individuals render them relatively powerless to confront and combat the force of egoism. She is drawn to Simone Weil's notion of unselfing as a way in which individuals may be able to recognize what is other than self, even if she divests Weil's notion of its close association with a God that creates what is other than itself.[49] Formerly, religion has provided the doctrinal and ritual means to empower a human unselfing so as to mitigate the sheer egoism of the self. Prayer and confession serve a purpose in connecting a person with what is outside of them. In the wake of a decline in belief in God and associated supernatural doctrines, Murdoch imagines that the metaphor of the idea of the Good may serve as an acceptable substitute. She reviews ways in which the self can escape its preoccupation with itself and move towards a love of respect for the Good and exercise virtue in its light. She considers how contemplating beauty in nature or in art can transport the self away from its inward preoccupations to furnish a sense of reality outside of egoistic concerns. She invokes an image of how, when one is preoccupied, and perhaps nursing a grievance to one's status, one looks out of a window and catches sight of something moving and beautiful in nature. Selfish preoccupations are abated. 'Suddenly I observe a hovering kestrel. In a moment everything is altered.'[50] Likewise, in her journals, she mixes discussions of philosophical argument and reflections on her life with attentive appreciation of scenes in nature, such as rooks in flight.[51]

Murdoch's poems also express a delight in observing natural scenes that can divert and surprise in their reality. The close of her poem 'Fox' conveys this combination of surprise and rapt attention, 'My footstep creaks in grasses, Quietness makes me stare, While in a woodland space a sudden fox, Peers with his brilliant face, and passes.'[52] The untrammelled beauty of nature can remind us of form, of a reality that is beyond our immediate concerns and hence it can relieve our egoism. Art can do the same. Indeed art is an expression of significant human powers, but its human source also admits of the possibilities of corruption. She notes, 'The experience of art is more easily degraded than the experience of nature.'[53] Art is a human skill and it demands the exercise of virtue on the part of artist and audience if it is to succeed in superseding egoism. Painting and literature are to be prized because they can show us 'that absolute pointlessness of virtue while exhibiting its supreme importance'.[54] Art mixes content and form in a way that captures reality and disturbs mere immersion in the self. Art, though, must be true and cannot be consolatory; depiction of death, for instance, must be realistic rather than comforting if there is to be relief from fantasy and egoism. Murdoch in her own art took care to avoid distortion. Sudden deaths of Titus in *The Sea, The Sea* and of Harriet in *The Sacred and Profane Love Machine* come, as deaths sometimes do occur, without anticipation or explanations. The death of Bruno in *Bruno's Dream* is an extended account of a person slowly and painfully coming to terms with their death in life. It is accompanied by a variety of activities, some venal, and some touching, which again can occur. While Bruno lies dying there is a frenzied pursuit of his valuable stamp album, the frustration of his son Miles and the loving care that is offered by his nurses, his son-in-law and two women, Lisa and Diana, who are connected to Miles.[55] Accidental deaths in *An Accidental Man* are realistic in their arbitrary and unpredictable occurrence, while the suicides in *The Flight from the Enchanter*, *The Black Prince* and *The Bell* are more than plot devices, for they show credible individual deaths and forms of suffering.[56] Murdoch also discusses how intellectual disciplines of various kinds can serve as routes to goodness in the demands that they make on the self to be absorbed in their study. Learning a language, for instance, represents a task to which the self must devote itself wholeheartedly and the language itself always possesses more to be learnt than can be taken in by the skill of a learner at any point in the process.

Murdoch's novels all bear a moral weight if only to show the ways in which egoism and selfishness can frustrate moral intentions. They all deal with moral issues that are subtle and tend to show something more of what is involved in her conception of the Good. *An Accidental Man* poses questions that push the reader to consider the context in which moral action occurs. One major question involves how much moral responsibility we can expect an individual to assume for what they do and for what occurs. Murdoch's perfectionist morality presumes a context in which they operate and for which they are not completely responsible. How much responsibility are they to assume? Individuals control neither the incidents to which they react, nor the events in which they participate. How much can be asked of individuals in these circumstances? Murdoch's answer seems to be that we can expect more than is standardly given. The principal character in *An Accidental Man*, Austin Gibson Grey, is characterized by Baldanza in his literary study of Murdoch's novels, *Iris Murdoch*, as 'a spiteful wastrel, an abject whining failure'.[57] He is self-absorbed and neglects to attend to others. A series of accidents befall him. He imagines that an early accident in which his hand was injured is the fault of his brother, Matthew, on whom he places all the blame. Both his wives die in accidents after he has neglected them. He kills a young girl accidently in a motor accident and severely damages her blackmailing father in an argument. His responsibility for these events might be said to be limited, given their accidental nature, but his response to them is to be self-pitying and to deny responsibility. His abnegation of responsibility makes the situations worse and a reader tends to feel that things would work better if he were more responsive. Other more worthy characters in the book discuss the pros and cons of intervening in situations that that they did not initiate but which might have turned out differently if they had intervened. Garth, Austin's son, while in New York observes a gang of Puerto Ricans beating and killing a black man. He wonders about his non-intervention. Could he have made a difference? Was his non-intervention justified? Ludwig Leferrier, an American, who is a friend of Garth and who is set to marry Gracie Tisbourne whose family is friendly with Austin's, catches sight of Dorinda, the emotionally fragile second wide of Austin. She is looking troubled on a London street, but he is preoccupied and he does not talk to her. She dies, accidently, shortly afterwards, leaving Ludwig to wonder about his inaction. Matthew, Austin's brother, witnesses a demonstration on a Moscow Street and sees a passer-by join in which will lead to his certain arrest and detention. Matthew, a diplomat at the time, did not join in for perfectly sound reasons, but the extent to which contingent events that we have not initiated nonetheless call upon us morally is a disconcerting theme of the novel. There are no definitive answers; they depend upon how we see things.

The Good Apprentice (1985) shows individuals pursuing the Good. For instance, one of the characters, Stuart Cuno, sets himself upon realizing goodness and his half-brother, Edward Baltram is intent on making amends for a past indiscretion. Harry Cuno, the father of Stuart and the stepfather of Edward, is a committed romantic and Thomas McCaskerville is a practising but sceptical psychiatrist, whose vocation involves him in trying to heal individuals that have lost their way. The narrative testifies to the difficulties in achieving goodness, that Murdoch acknowledges in her philosophy. Becoming good is an arduous process and one that is never complete, and Murdoch's perfectionist morality is exhibited in the intricacies of the narrative. *The Good Apprentice* shows multiple journeys towards the good, intimating that there is no single route to goodness. Real individuals who are situated in real situations do not follow a guidebook that prescribes what is to be done in particular circumstances, even a guidebook that is written by Murdoch herself. Goodness is an art, and its art is to be acquired and practised in multiple distinctive ways. Pilgrimages to the good are ever delayed, guided and disturbed by egoism, misperception, guilt, saintliness, artistry, discipline and love. The characters that search for the good travel on differing routes and confront differing obstacles.

The Good Apprentice begins with the death of a friend of Edward Baltram, Mark Wilsden, who has leapt out of a window while under the influence of a drug surreptitiously administered to him by Edward. Edward's guilt plunges him into what might be termed the void of which Murdoch speaks in *Metaphysics as a Guide to Morals*.[58] He is disturbed and guilt-ridden, and is driven to seek redemption at his father's house. Like the prodigal son he journeys to the house of his natural father, the artist Jesse Baltram, who abandoned his son to set up a magical artist's home, in which he lives with his lover and their daughters. In undertaking this journey Edward moves away from an unreflective egoism. Harry, his stepfather appears as a wanton philanderer but his pursuit of sexual favours is energized by a pursuit of romance that lies beyond mere desire and perhaps is a sign of goodness. There are many ways to the Good, and Stuart Cuno, Edward's stepbrother, is saintly, in that he quests for a saintly religious fulfilment without God. In conversation with Thomas McCaskerville, a psychiatrist friend of the family, he observes, 'Let's say that God is a permanent non-degradable love object. Must we not imagine something of the sort?'[59] His sense of God as an object of love appears to be of a piece with Murdoch's sense of how the metaphor of the Good might operate in a secularized society. By the end of the novel, Stuart's saintliness is tempered into a more practical disciplined mode of being just as Edward emerges from the trauma of remorse to begin to think of and act for others. These quests for goodness are set against a background of persisting egoism and distortive fantasy on the part of friends, family and themselves. Yet the close of the novel offers a vision of love and understanding between seekers who will never arrive at the Good but who will quest it in different ways and be energized by its transcendence. At the close, Stuart, Edward and Harry are pictured together with Harry suggesting that they drink to their common recognition of good things.

> 'Oh well, there are good things in the world', said Edward. 'Are there? Let's drink to them. Edward, Stuart –'
> 'But which things are they?' said Edward. 'We might all mean different ones.'
> 'Never mind, drink to them, Come.'
> They raised their glasses.[60]

Edward, Stuart and Harry have different conceptions of the good and pursue different goals and yet they are united by quests that will not be completed but which they can recognize as being worthwhile and going beyond mere subjective desire. They can be said to be pursuing the good.

Conclusion

Murdoch's moral philosophy is central to her work. She describes her metaphysics as a guide to morals and the three essays that composed *The Sovereignty of Good* stand out as remarkable contributions to a philosophical world that had turned its back on Plato and on an objectivist notion of the Good. Her novels deal with moral issues as characters are shown either to ignore the interests and perspectives of others with disastrous consequences or to struggle towards the Good. Murdoch's moral theory is not susceptible of being expressed in neat formulas that can apply to multiple situations. It highlights the character of morality, namely that it calls upon a perfectionism, whereby individuals strive to see things from the perspective of the good rather than from their own self-interested way. What it does not do is to specify how people are to act. Their actions will depend upon how they perceive situations and Murdoch's novels show how individuals in multiple situations handle things and readers can reflect upon the meaning of these actions. There is no single route for individuals to follow so there is much to reflect upon. Murdoch provides a famous example of how an individual might act morally in the case of the mother, who changes her attitude to her daughter-in-law after rethinking things in the light of a loving critical perspective on her own original attitude. In many ways it is an unremarkable example in that it is the sort of thing that can happen in everyday life, but it is useful in showing how Murdoch's moral perfectionism is compatible with an ordinary display of virtue.

If Murdoch's moral theory is not that extraordinary in practice, it certainly represented a radical intervention into moral debate and remains a powerful and challenging viewpoint. She critiqued standard contemporary moral theories, warned against prevailing cultural currents and invoked Plato. Her invoking of Plato was perhaps the most challenging feature of her moral theory. Given Plato's status as a moral theorist of the past, who had nothing to say to the contemporary world, which had assimilated scientific advances and a materialist outlook, Murdoch's advocacy of a Platonic conception of the Good represented a challenge to orthodoxies. The way in which Murdoch interprets Plato renders his moral theory plausible and compatible with the anti-metaphysical outlook of the time in that she refused any reliance upon supernatural assumptions. Her resort to Plato reflects her clarity on the poverty of moral subjectivism and an awareness that Plato's language captured something of importance of our moral sense. It did, however, leave somewhat ambiguous what she was taking from Plato and what she was rejecting.

CHAPTER FIVE

Murdoch and the political

Is Murdoch political?

A feature of this book is its perception of Murdoch as a dialectical thinker, who aims to be inclusive in her understanding of things. Philosophy is not a lifeless abstract activity that is unrelated to life. Lived experience is at the heart of her attitude to reflection. What matters is how reflection can bear upon moral questions and her turn to literature in part represents her awareness that the novel is an ideal medium for showing what is to be borne in experience. Yet questions have been posed about her engagement with the totality of experience. Experience is not merely personal even if Murdoch allows for the primacy of individual consciousness and recognizes that individuals are not to shirk their personal responsibilities in aiming for moral perfection. Commentators have lined up to criticize Murdoch for neglecting politics. A focus on the quality of consciousness and individual moral responsibility, as is exemplified in the case of the mother (M) changing her mind on her daughter-in-law (D), has been critiqued for overlooking the political and social dimensions of life. Lovibond, for instance, is alert to what she takes to be the dangers of Murdoch's personalization of morality. For Lovibond, personal moral development is not a substitute for collective political action. Notably, feminism demands that prevailing conventions are to be challenged politically. In analysing the political implications of the mother (M) and daughter-in-law (D) example, she comments, 'The kind of moral consciousness that Murdoch has undertaken to bring to life for us through M is not that of a woman convinced that her sex shares the burden of *Aufklärung*, "dare to be wise", and enter as fully as anyone into the common life, including ethics *qua* juridicial.'[1] Likewise Bagnoli in 'The Exploration of Moral Life' is critical of Murdoch's disengagement with the political.[2] Griffin in her study, *The Influence of the Writings of Simone Weil on the Fiction of Iris Murdoch* draws a contrast between the depth and significance of Weil's political writing and the absence of political writings on the part of Murdoch. In contrasting Murdoch to Weil, she remarks, 'Murdoch on the other hand tends to bypass issues of social and political change in favour of a discussion of the relationship between the personal and the political.'[3] Literary commentators tend to review Murdoch's fiction while ignoring or downplaying her treatment of the social and political world. Nicol, for instance, maintains that Murdoch's novels pursue themes that do not invoke society in its widest sense.[4]

In defence of the commentators, who either minimize or play down the extent of Murdoch's engagement with politics, they might be said to be following Murdoch's lead. For instance, Murdoch herself dismissed the idea that she was a political novelist. In her reflection on the novel in 'Against Dryness' (1961) she is critical of the modern novel insofar as it adheres to crystalline and journalistic forms.[5] In contrasting ways, both these forms admit the possibility of political novels. The journalistic political novel, such as Beauvoir's *The Mandarins*, saturates the story line with detailed reporting on political action.[6] The crystalline novel, such as Orwell's *1984*, Camus's *The Plague* and Koestler's *Darkness at Noon*, accommodates political myths or ideologies by identifying political commitments in allegorical codes. The politics of a crystalline novel may be powerful in registering the enormity of political crimes or the urgency of political resistance, yet for Murdoch this kind of political form is liable to distort the artistic imagination by sacrificing the interplay of events and characters upon the altar of a political formula or lesson. Similarly, a journalistic descent into the milieu of politics may evoke a political atmosphere, but only at the expense of ceding a more credible evocation of character and situation. Murdoch reacts against the political authors of her time such as Sartre, Beauvoir and even Camus, who operate as ventriloquists in foisting their own philosophical and political ideas upon characters in their novels. In an interview of 1976 Murdoch responds to a question concerning her apparent avoidance of political themes by recognizing how she was unqualified to provide a journalistic account of political life. She observed,

> In general I don't feel I can as an artist write about politics. I mean I write about politics to some extent, you know, just as a citizen, but I can't do it as an artist, you know, one's got to do what one can understand. I don't understand enough about politics, I suppose, I tried to write a novel once about MPs and parliament and so on, but I couldn't do it, it's a terribly specialized thing.[7]

In her Platonic dialogue, 'Art and Eros: A Dialogue about Art', Mantias's arguments for the political regulation of artistic content are undermined by Plato and Socrates.[8] Murdoch harboured misgivings about becoming a political novelist. Yet her disavowal of the political novel applies to writing a specialized novel documenting a specifically political arena. She does not disqualify herself entirely from politics, and as a citizen she takes politics seriously and it informs her philosophical and literary work.

Murdoch set artistic integrity against the political novel, if political ideas or journalistic accounts of political institutions and events were to supplant a more open and realistic evocation of experience. However, Murdoch is a serious political thinker and her philosophy and novels deal with political questions because politics is an integral aspect of experience. An entry for her journal for 1947 declares, 'Somehow I must integrate my political and philosophical outlooks.'[9] A later entry shows her to be attending closely and positively to events in Eastern Europe as the Soviet Empire crumbles.[10] In her writings on Heidegger and Sartre she critiques the exclusivity of their focus in side-lining the political, and her intermittent interest in Hegel is stirred by his recognition of mankind's political identity.[11] She also framed a theoretical conception of the status of politics in the post-war world in 'A House of Theory' (1958) and subsequently in 'Morals and Politics', a section of *Metaphysics as a Guide to Morals*.[12] In 'A House of Theory' she reflects upon the state of politics in the light of the diminishing appeal of socialism in the post-war world and in the wake of a reaction against ideological politics more generally. In 'Morals and Politics', her erstwhile belief in socialism and an interventionist form of politics recedes in the context of guarding against the manifest harm that has been inflicted upon individuals by twentieth-century tyrannies. In neither case, however, is politics to be dismissed. In 'A House of Theory' Murdoch looks to socialist renewal, recognizing the common good requires political action, and in 'Morals and Politics', she perceived politics to be integral in providing security and welfare for individuals so that they can develop freely and have the opportunity of pursuing a perfectionist personal morality.

Throughout her career Murdoch takes the public and the personal to be intertwined. Personal freedom depends upon public protection and the value of public order is revealed dialectically in the possibilities of personal development. In her later consideration of politics, Murdoch recognizes the frailty of human beings, acknowledging their insecurity and the propriety of establishing rules whereby they can be protected against harm and against the evils that might be inflicted by rulers, exerting unlimited power. At all times Murdoch appreciates the historical nature of politics. In 'A House of Theory' she recognizes how the late twentieth century witnesses a turn against radical ideology. Her plays of the early 1970s, *The Three Arrows* (1972) and *The Servants and the Snow* (1970), show an awareness of the force of political traditions in shaping the ongoing development of political life.[13] In 'Morals and Politics' she looks to the provision of axioms or rights to secure essential freedoms and the basic welfare of individuals, but she takes these basic rights to alter over time. Conceptions of life, underpinning the allocation of rights, are not fixed. They respond to developing cultural norms and hence the rights that are assigned to individuals will vary along with changing cultural expectations. In subsequent sections of this chapter, I focus upon her expressly political writings and draw upon her novels to exemplify her early and late thinking on the question of politics. Initially I deal with her essay 'A House of Theory' and the early novels and subsequently I focus upon 'Morals and Politics', and her later novels that incorporate themes from her later line of political thinking. This course of analysis, however, presumes that Murdoch's novels can be correlated to her philosophical thinking on politics. This presumption will be considered and justified before the development of her political thought will be reviewed in the rest of this chapter.

Politics and the novel

Murdoch evidently cares about politics and incorporates politics into her metaphysical perspective, but how, if at all, does she include the realm of politics within her novels? She is wary of novels making moral and ideological claims. An author, who is committed to making a point tends to restrict the narrative and interplay between characters and events. For Murdoch, a novel is to be more than a vehicle for her authorial beliefs. Yet her novels, like her philosophy, are directed towards what is real and the changing nature of the political world in the aftermath of the Second World War constitutes a significant dimension of the reality to which her fiction is oriented. Just as her philosophy questions the prevailing cultural climate, so her novels are constituted by their modern post-war setting. In the novels, God is either questioned or denied, individual freedom enlivens and undermines cultural traditions and the question of the meaning of politics in the modern world looms. Murdoch may not have been a novelist, who conveys a set of political doctrines, but she brought a reading of the current political atmosphere to bear upon the fictional interplay of imagined individual lives. As a philosopher she reviews the nature of politics and its relations to other forms of experience. Her novels are shaped by her reading of the peculiarities of politics, institutions and ideas in the post-war modern world. Her novels reflect contemporary society and its moral and political dilemmas and possibilities are reflected in her novels.

Murdoch's early novels are alive with a sense of the changing nature of society and the ways in which individuals relate to social institutions and practices. The social and cultural atmosphere in the post-war world is established in her first novel. The protagonist of *Under the Net* (1954), Jake Donoghue, is sceptical over political doctrines but he maintains an uneasy ideological commitment to socialism, while pursuing a maverick lifestyle that does not allow room for conventions and institutions that had hitherto been respected. He inhabits a hollowed out public world and he is symptomatic of his age. Likewise other early novels feature individuals whose pursuit of freedoms fits uneasily with hitherto prevailing social conventions and institutions. Marriages break up, abortions are undergone, homosexuality is expressed even if repressed, religious truths are questioned and new forms of community are explored. Refugees fleeing from tyrannies in the aftermath of the Second World War turn up in England and face the realities of exile and dislocation and are at the mercy of a political and social world in which they are not at home. *The Flight from the Enchanter* (1956), *The Sandcastle* (1957), *The Bell* (1958), *A Severed Head* (1961) and *An Unofficial Rose* (1962) depict an uncertain political and cultural world that is distinct from what has gone before. The mix of refugees seeking political and spiritual asylum, homosexuals tentatively expressing their sexuality within a repressive culture, heterosexuals exploring forms of love and sex that are no longer tightly constrained by conventions and spiritual truth seekers looking for salvation outside a church, contribute to the energy of Murdoch's novels. The narrative of *The Red and the Green* (1965) revolves around the Irish Rebellion of 1916 and deals empathetically with a number of characters who are involved in the rebellion. The novel does not take sides but presents contrasting political styles and outlooks, and demonstrates Murdoch's interest in the differing possibilities of the political sphere.

Murdoch's later novels reflect changing attitudes to politics in the West in the latter part of the twentieth century. Central to her own later political thought is a sense of the divide between a private world of personal perfectionist moral commitments and a public world in which order is to be prioritized over utopian ideals. *The Nice and the Good* (1968) imagines a world in which intersecting and overlapping relations between morality and politics are traced. Ducane, its central character, is charged with investigating the unsavoury circumstances surrounding a death in Whitehall. In the course of his investigations that cover events reflecting the unseemly sexual scandals rocking British politics in the early 1960s, he has to tread a path between protecting the lives of friends and exposing the truths that his public role demands. Likewise *An Accidental Man* (1971) rehearses the dilemma facing a young American who has been called up to fight in the Vietnam War, to which he is not morally committed, but who has the opportunity to pursue an attractive academic career in England. This marking of the troubled nature of a dividing line between personal and public demands reflects tensions in society and in Murdoch's own thought. Her late novel, *The Book and the Brotherhood* (1987), focuses upon the prospective publication of a major book on political theory that is to be written by David Crimmond. The charismatic revolutionary Crimmond has been financed by a group of Oxford graduates to write a radical text to shake up the political world. The project is conceived in the 1950s when the group or brotherhood was more sympathetic to the radical politics that continue to be embraced by Crimmond. A controversial theoretical text on political theory was also more in keeping with the cultural and political climate of the 1950s than in the contemporary world of the late twentieth century. The members of the brotherhood, who are led by Gerard Hernshaw, are troubled by their commitment to a project in which they have lost belief. It is a drain on their finances and drags on interminably. It is a metaphor for the contemporary world in which Murdoch was writing. Radicalism seems a distant memory and grand narratives on politics are as anachronistic as metaphysical systems. The novel's exploration of these political themes is timely in that Lyotard's declaration of the end of grand narratives, was announced in his *The Postmodern Condition – A Report on Knowledge*, which was published in English shortly before *The Book and the Brotherhood*.[14] Murdoch, like Lyotard, takes the temperature of her age and poses the question as to whether grand narratives are obsolete. Are they outdated by Western affluence and the record of Soviet oppression or do they continue to serve a political purpose? Characteristically, Murdoch provides no easy or even express answer in the novel, for she is intent upon imagining realistic characters and situations rather than offering formulaic solutions.

'A House of Theory' and early novels

At the outset of her career Murdoch recognizes that her success or failure turns upon her capacity to combine her interests in philosophy, politics and literature.[15] Her subsequent success is a tribute to her maintenance of these interests. Her interest in politics is an important dimension of her achievement in thinking through the conditions of her time. As a philosopher, novelist and political theorist Murdoch was sensitive to historical change, recognizing the specificity of the modern historical contexts of these activities. Politically, Murdoch was a member of the Communist Party and a committed socialist at the outset of the Second World War, and she passed on secret documents to the Communist Party while working at the Treasury from 1942.[16] She had given up membership of the CP shortly before joining the Treasury, probably to avoid suspicions of her clandestine activities, but in the aftermath of the war her faith in socialism was wavering.[17] In the 1950s she interprets the political scene in the light of a more general reading of the post-war development, according to which substantive religious beliefs are waning, and morals and politics become mechanisms promoting and responding to a burgeoning individualism. Her reading of this condition frames the political aspect of her novels. In the essay 'A House of Theory', Murdoch examines the nature of politics in the post-war age, revealing an attenuated commitment to socialism but recognizing how in the present post-war world full-blooded ideological commitment of any sort is receding. She notes, 'There is a certain moral void in the life of the country.'[18] She observes how the project of socialism is being undermined by a number of connected factors, including the material prosperity of the post-war economy and the entrenchment of a welfare state that relies upon bureaucratic procedures to deliver general welfare. The upshot is that the left lacks political fire, imagination and conviction. For Murdoch, this decline in political vitality works upon the enduring empirical cast of mind on the part of English people, which has been reinforced by the perceived success of science and by the manifest social and material progress that promotes and delivers individual consumerism.

In 'A House of Theory' Murdoch relates ideological disenchantment to other factors that mark contemporary culture, namely the elimination of metaphysics in philosophy, and a loss of religious faith. She diagnoses the situation as amounting to a contemporary void of faith and decline in political and moral conviction. She observes, 'This void is uneasily felt by society at large and is the more distressing since we are now for the first time in our history feeling the loss of religion as a consolation and guide; until recently various substitutes (socialism itself, later Communism, pacifism (internationalism) were available; now there seems to be a shortage even of substitutes.'[19] Murdoch maintains a commitment to socialism and imagines that its appeal might be enhanced by a drawing upon the guild socialism and Hegelian phenomenological traditions to elaborate motivating images of possible socialist futures that are compatible with empirical truths.[20]

In the essay Murdoch advocates transformative political action so as to promote the common good, but she realizes that her vision for the future cannot be predicated upon an indemonstrable theory of history or upon a 'scientific' blueprint of a good society. Rather what is demanded are imaginative visions of social possibilities and of what might be done.

Murdoch's analysis of the political condition of the Western post-war world is aligned to her moral philosophy, which she developed in the 1960s and expressed most notably in the essays contained in *The Sovereignty of Good* (1970). The modern liberal paradigm, in which the rights of individuals to make their own moral choices trump traditional notions of a substantive right and wrong, underpins an individualistic morality. Murdoch critiques the thinness of the freedom that is delivered in this form of society. Choice is extolled at the expense of reflection upon the choices that are made, and the negative freedom enjoyed by an isolated individual is not related to how freedom might contribute to the widening of an individual's perspective so that they appreciate their links with other individuals.[21] The post-war world is a consumer society, in which individuals appear as rootless atoms, conducting their lives in discrete liberal ways. Standard forms of contemporary morality and politics, for Murdoch, are little more than ideological smokescreens for varieties of egoism that ignore the moral urgency of attending to others and a political commitment to the common good.[22]

Murdoch's recognition of a changing political and moral landscape underlies *Under the Net*. Jake Donoghue, its protagonist, is always on the move physically and emotionally. His emotional mobility is representative of a more generic severing of enduring commitments. The values and conventions, which he casually rejects, appear fugitive and transitory, reflecting a contemporary loss of ordering frameworks. The bohemian Jake lacks a steady job, clear ambition, articulate political convictions and a fixed moral compass. He is drawn to the philosophical scepticism of his friend, Hugo Belfounder. He is not so much an angry as a directionless young man. His bohemianism is not simply marginal to the general picture of post-war London, for the times are changing and what was hitherto marginal is now symptomatic of a more general erosion of conventional values. Jake refuses intellectual alibis and accepts the lack of underlying values. The wandering cast of characters suggests neither the imminence nor the immanence of political and moral renewal. Jake is left-wing and sympathizes with socialism, but cannot adhere to Lefty Todd's revolutionary socialism, because he understands the post-war world to be one without revolutionary credentials and possibilities. The welfare state and a spiritless consumerism eviscerate the prospects for revolutionary socialism. Yet Jake's professed socialism is more than nostalgic lip service to a past ideal. It harmonizes with his distaste for commercialism and its subordination of authenticity to the pursuit of material advantage. He himself undertakes hack translation work and buries his own creativity in the process. The baleful effects of commodification can be seen throughout the novel, notably in its depiction of the movie industry. The collapse of the Roman Republic is being turned into celluloid images for voyeuristic commercial purposes, and its hollowness is represented in the novel by the literal collapse of the movie set for the projected film.[23]

Jake may be a marginal figure in society but his restlessness reflects a more general erosion of values and conventions, which Murdoch tracks in other writings. The novel marks the fluidity of contemporary life, the decay of traditional institutions and the contemporary turn to a materialistic individualism. Murdoch's novels demand critical engagement on the part of readers and Jake's narrative voice is undermined by his own evident failings to attend to others. By the close of *Under the Net*, Jake is a discredited narrator as it becomes clear that he is misled by an egoism, which puts his own feelings and attitudes above recognizing what others are actually feeling and experiencing. The novel raises questions about contemporary individualism and an associated egoism. Is a radical individualism sustainable if it involves misperceiving others and acquiescing in a spiritual and social void?[24] *Under the Net* does not convey a clear-cut political lesson. What the novel delivers is a picture of a social world in which moral, philosophical and political beliefs lack foundations. A deracinated society and an uncertain political environment that contains frustrated and insular individuals spawns here and there vague aspirations for spiritual and political renewal, which is tracked in Murdoch's subsequent early novels of Murdoch.

In Murdoch's second novel, *The Flight from the Enchanter*, society appears yet more troubled and individuals more vulnerable. Its focus is upon migrants, whose status as displaced persons heightens a sense of the rootlessness in contemporary society. The London setting of *The Flight from the Enchanter* lacks the defining detail of the preceding novel, reflecting the uncertain world of the migrants. As Martz suggests, 'Appropriately in this novel of rootless beings, the Dickensian details of a truly London setting do not emerge.'[25] The migrants in *The Flight from the Enchanter* are neither of a piece nor are they conceived uniformly and sympathetically as victims.[26] The Polish refugees, Jan & Stefan Lusiewicz, whom Rosa Keepe initially helps but later becomes entangled with sexually, are strange and threatening. Mischa Fox, whose origins are shrouded in mystery, has invented himself as a domineering and sinister figure. Nina, a migrant dressmaker, who serves a number of characters, is one of the many women, who are held captive to Mischa Fox's demonic personality. She lacks security and is frightened by the uncertainties surrounding her migrant status. In considering Murdoch's treatment of the theme of exile and displacement in this novel, White remarks, 'The Ur-text for this theme of exile and dispossession, in Murdoch's work is her second novel, *The Flight from the Enchanter* of 1956, which is at the heart of her conception and portrayal of the evil and suffering which diaspora causes in individual human lives. *The Flight from the Enchanter* is essentially about refugeeism.'[27]

The plot of *The Flight from the Enchanter* is multidimensional but a pivotal moment occurs when a question is asked in parliament by a Conservative MP on the status of refugees. It is raised at the instigation of Mischa Fox, who responds to the request of Rosa Keepe to do something about the sinister Poles whom she had befriended. The existing status of migrants depends upon SELIB (the Special European Labour Immigration Board), an agency that regulates immigrant permits, and, in theory, controls their right of residence in the UK. Theoretically immigrants born east of an arbitrary point in Eastern Europe were not allowed to work in the UK, but in practice the regulation of migrants was not pursued energetically if they were in work and not causing problems. Nina, however, is insecure over her status. She does not know how things work either formally or informally, and lacks confidence that political decisions will be supportive. She hears of the question in Parliament and is unnerved. She was born on the wrong side of an arbitrary line in Eastern Europe from which migration is permitted officially. She is instantly terrified at the prospect of having to return to an inhospitable homeland. She is at the mercy of institutions and regulations that are mysterious and beyond her control.[28] Her fate turns upon the arbitrary contingency of where she happened to be born. In desperation, Nina commits suicide. It is a personal and political tragedy. At the last, she was unsupported by her acquaintance, Rosa Keepe, who ignores Nina's plea to talk over her situation. On a larger scale the state is indifferent to her fate, and a migrant is left in a state of extreme vulnerability.

Nina's death highlights the uncertainties of being a migrant and indicates the moral and political failings of a society that cares insufficiently for a vulnerable individual and more generally ignores the plight of migrants. As White observes, 'But *The Flight from the Enchanter* is an indictment, not only of individual failures of attention, but also of the failure of English society as a whole to attend to the plight of the displaced.'[29] Throughout her career as a novelist Murdoch does not lose sight of the issues facing refugees. Among the cast of characters in her subsequent novels are refugees, who have fled from tyrannies and concentration camps. She herself worked for UNRRA (United Nations Relief and Rehabilitation Administration) at the end of the Second World War in Graz and witnessed at first hand the wretchedness of survivors of the war's calamities.[30] *The Time of the Angels* (1966) records the desperation and quiet stoicism of Eugene Peshkov, a Russian refugee who spent nine years in a camp in Austria, and lives precariously in a dismal London setting. Willy Kost, in *The Nice and the Good*, is a concentration camp survivor who has to go on living with the memories of what he had to do in Dachau in order to survive. In turn the malignity of Julius King in *A Fairly Honourable Defeat* (1970) intimates a connection to the dehumanizing atmosphere of the concentration camp that he has survived.

The Sandcastle, *An Unofficial Rose* and *A Severed Head*, in more spectacular fashion, explore the pressures on marriage in a modern world, where it is no longer regarded as an absolute commitment. Its sanctification by religious doctrine is eroding. *A Severed Head* explores the fragility of conventions. Even incest, perhaps the most entrenched of all taboos, forms part of its plot, and incest appears again in the later novels, *The Red and the Green* and *The Time of the Angels*. The protagonist of *The Sandcastle*, the schoolmaster Mor, opts to remain with his wife and family having had a romantic liaison with Rain, a visiting artist. He then decides somewhat uncertainly to stand as an MP for the Labour Party. His motivations are not explored but it indicates a sense of diffuse political commitment and vague possibilities of political renewal. Likewise *The Bell* follows characters who have committed to spiritual and political renewal. At Imber Court in Gloucestershire, a spiritual community renounces life in the outside world, in favour of living within a spiritual ascetic and self-sufficing community in forsaking the consumerist liberalism of the post-war world. Work is undertaken for its intrinsic worth and to supply the needs of the community rather than for money. The community, however, fractures under the strain of events surrounding its leader and shows the fragility of spiritual renewal in contemporary circumstances. Its leader, Michael Meade, is undone by the pressures arising out of his homosexuality and the suicide of an adolescent, Nick Fawley, with whom he had been involved previously.

Murdoch's incorporation of homosexuality into her early novels performs a political role. At the time *The Bell* was published, homosexuality was outlawed and it was not until 1967 that it was made legal. The Wolfenden Committee's report recommending its legalization was published in 1957 and Murdoch's novel in showing sympathetically the devastating consequences of the legal and cultural repression of homosexuality contributes to a more open recognition of the situation. In her essay 'The Moral Decision about Homosexuality' (1964), Murdoch argues in favour of the liberalization of the law on homosexuality. She urges that the lifting of the legal restriction on homosexuality requires no special argument in its justification, because it relies upon a mere conventional prejudice against homosexuality. Murdoch is willing to critique conventions and to support reform to enable a more liberal attitude to sexual freedom.[31] In *A Severed Head* the only couple whose partnership remains intact is a lesbian relationship between two members of the office staff in Austin Lynch-Gibbon's business. Throughout her career Murdoch's novels include non-heterosexual relationships, and her willingness to treat homosexuality as a normal relationship that does not require special forms of explanation is a distinguishing feature of her liberalism.[32] Her commitment to sexual freedom and the rights of homosexuals is evident in a letter to Philippa Foot, in which she describes a conversation with a Party guide in Communist China. She relates how she asks questions about homosexuality and is incredulous when she is told of its non-existence in China.[33] Murdoch also frequently shows intergenerational relationships that go against the grain of conventionality. Michael Meade is older than Nick Fawley, Bradley Pearson is considerably older than Julian Baffin in *The Black Prince* (1973), and Theo in *The Nice and the Good* is haunted by a scandal involving his relationship with a boy.

Murdoch's early novels appeared at a time before abortion was legalized in 1967 and before survivors of suicide attempts were not made subject to prosecution in 1961. Her empathetic portrayal of Georgie Hands's abortion and attempted suicide in *A Severed Head* and her sympathetic portrayal of Nina's suicide in *The Flight from the Enchanter* show her sensitivity to those who face life and death issues. It is true that Georgie Hands suffers following her abortion and Nina's suicide is desperately sad and might have been avoided if friends and the state had provided a more reassuring context. However, Murdoch's very portrayal of these matters contributes to rendering them less shocking and more acceptable. Lovibond is right to indicate that Murdoch invariably describes the aftermath of abortions as exerting a strain on the women concerned, but this does not entail that she is against abortion.[34] Acceptance of the right to abortion does not preclude recognition that the experience of having an abortion is a demanding one that should elicit loving support. The legalization of abortion in 1967 and the decriminalization of suicide in 1961 are symptomatic of the gathering climate of liberal opinion on this and related social and moral matters to which Murdoch contributed.

Murdoch's early novels reflect a contemporary movement away from an ideological radical politics, and show how the cultural climate of liberalism allows for valuable freedoms but also involve an atomization of society that threatens the vulnerable, and inhibits the project of socialist renewal. In *The Red and the Green*, Murdoch provides a different historical context for a novel, which admits of a radical form of politics. The action of the novel takes place in the days leading up to the Easter Rising in 1916 when the Irish Volunteers took to arms in occupying the Dublin Post Office to declare an Irish Republic. In his Introduction to the novel in 2001 Declan Kiberd identifies its leading protagonists Pat and Cathal Dumay as being existentialist.[35] However, they are only to be termed existentialist if a very loose sense of the term is applied. What the novel does convey is the energy and passion of a political commitment to nationalism on the part of these characters. The ardour of Pat and Cathal Dumay sets them apart from the Anglo Irish liberal sentiments of Hilda Chase-White and her son Andrew, who is an officer in the British army, expecting to marry Frances Bellman. All of the characters are connected by intricate family ties. Pat and Cathal are willing to fight for their cause and their excitement and commitment is shared by Millie Kinnard, the aunt of Pat and Cathal and to some extent by Christopher Bellman, Frances's father, and Barnabas Drumm, the stepfather of Pat and Cathal. The novel, however, does not take sides and the risks involved in the violence of the rising are keenly felt by Kathleen, the mother of Pat and Cathal, who is horrified at the prospect of losing her sons and are recognized also by the sober assessment of the situation by the Anglo-Irish soldier, Andrew Chase-White. The novel runs together romance, sexual passions and the nationalist rising and some of its potential power is perhaps dissipated by the complexity of its plotting. But it stands out from other novels in dealing with a political revolt and with the passion of violent conflict. Murdoch treads a path between the various actors and sentiments and the novel is notable for its empathetic treatment of individuals who espouse a radical political cause. Murdoch herself was moving away from support for radical forms of utopianism but in a balanced treatment of the events of 1916 she portrays empathetically what it feels like to take up arms for a political cause. Her portrayal of Millie Kinnard is complex in that she manages to convey convincingly and sympathetically Millie's feminist resentment at her restricted opportunities including her exclusion from political action, while showing her to be willing to resort to blackmail to serve her own interests.

Murdoch's later political thought

In the early 1970s Murdoch published two plays, 'The Servants and the Snow' and 'The Three Arrows', that present a realistic reading of politics in which the roles of power and tradition rather than that of ideals are highlighted.[36] In 'The Servants and the Snow', Basil, a young liberal-minded heir takes his sophisticated urban wife, Oriane, to a remote country estate, which he has inherited from his tyrannical father. The servants have resented but not questioned the cruelty and injustices of the previous regime. The projected reforms and liberal spirit of the youthful Basil set in train a spirit of rebellion that threatens to undermine his power. In the ensuing disorder, Oriane observes to Basil, 'I'm a realist Basil. We do much less harm than you do in the end.'[37] To reclaim his authority, and in compliance with an ancient custom, Basil agrees to sleep with Marina, a mistress of his father's on the night before her wedding to Peter Jack a servant and childhood friend of Basil's. Growing resentment among the servants comes to a head at the wedding ceremony and in the confusion of a revolt Peter Jack is shot, and Oriane kills her husband, the would-be reformer, Basil. The play explores the difficulties of introducing political reforms in a traditional community that is attuned to the assertion of power.

Again, in 'The Three Arrows' power and tradition are to the fore as rivals for political power jostle for position in medieval Japan. The action of the play takes place at a time when political power is balanced between the Imperial family and the Shogun, a war lord. The hero, Prince Yorimitsu who, like Basil, is a would be reformer, leads a strong northern faction. Yorimitsu is currently being held prisoner by the Imperial family. Both the Shogun and the Emperor want the death of Yorimitsu but neither side can be seen to be responsible for it as that would transfer the allegiance of his supporters to the rival side. Yorimitsu maintains political ideals and ambitions, but is drawn to the Crown Princess, sister of the Emperor, who falls in love with him. Yorimitsu's enemies make him undertake the traditional ordeal of the thee arrows, whereupon his fate will be decided. He faces the prospect of either death or a marriage that will strip him of political power. After receiving a sentence of death, he is given another chance and he then has to choose between love while remaining a prisoner in the Imperial Palace and freedom that denies him the Princess. He muses, 'So, I have to choose between my love, my honour and my cause.'[38] He elects for freedom so as to maintain his political ambitions. The play like 'The Servants and the Snow' signals how politics involves a brutal power play, in which idealism is often to be subordinated the realities of the political situation.

If her plays of the 1970s intimate a hard-headed recognition of the realities of political power, Murdoch's account of the political sphere in 'Morals and Politics', a section of her *Metaphysics as a Guide to Morals* (1992) attends to the limits of what can be expected of the political. Whereas in 'A House of Theory' and in her early novels, she entertains diffuse hopes for a socialist renewal, in her later reading of the political she is sceptical of utopianism. She is mindful of the imperfections to which the public realm is liable and alert to the dangers of misguided Utopianism. The repressiveness of current and recent socialist regimes, for instance, the brutality of the Chinese cultural revolution, underpins her respect for the protection of the rights of the individual.[39] This suspicion of totalitarianism is reflected in her novel *The Nice and the Good*, where the presence of Willy Kost, a concentration camp survivor, serves as a reminder of its dangers. It is also a feature of her letters and journals, in which she writes of witnessing the wreckage of human life that had been scarred by the brutality of regimes before and during the Second World War.[40] In an essay on Murdoch and Arendt, 'Two Women in Dark Times', White recognizes the impact of the war and the Holocaust. She writes, 'The most obvious events which shaped their lives and thought were the Second World War and with that the Holocaust.'[41]

In turning away from radicalism and the lure of Utopian projects Murdoch recognizes the merits of British empiricists such as Hume and Hobbes in focusing upon the limited but important task of the state in providing security.[42] She moves towards acknowledging a distinction between the private and the public, which is the cornerstone of classic liberal thought. She observes, 'Liberal political thought posits a certain fundamental distinction between the person as citizen and the person as moral-spiritual individual.'[43] While accepting that there are problems over identifying the precise terms of the distinction, she is willing to accept its limitation on the power of the state as important for political philosophy. She remarks, 'political philosophy is about "advice to princes", or politicians, or citizens, whereas moral philosophy is aimed at each particular thinker or agent'.[44] The distinction between the private and the public and the prioritization of individual freedom are held by Murdoch to be significant and to be distinctively modern phenomena. Hence she does not look to Plato for guidance on politics, though she is concerned to excuse Plato for his apparent political authoritarianism. She recognizes that individual freedom was unknown to Plato and that Plato and the Greeks in general accepted the institution of slavery. She also notes that Plato's ideal commonwealth as set out in the *Republic*, values the common good above that of individual satisfaction. Murdoch adopts two strategies to mitigate any censure that might be directed towards Plato. On the one hand, past thinkers at some distance from the present are entitled to a charitable interpretation that is not condemnatory of aspects of their thought, such as slavery, that are repugnant to a modern reader. She notes, 'We "forgive" people in the remote past because we can (we think) see more clearly the limitations of their situations.'[45] On the other hand, she also remarks that Plato's *Republic* was never intended to be implemented. It functioned as a standard by which to asses practice, but was not itself a practical project.

Murdoch's observation that the distinction between the private and the public is both relatively new and less than clear cut is accurate and is rehearsed by many political theorists.[46] In *On Liberty* J. S. Mill identifies the rationale for governmental restriction of individual liberty to consist in its duty to prevent harm to other individuals.[47] For Mill governmental regulation of an individual's conduct is not justified when their conduct does not affect another. Hence Mill distinguishes between self-regarding and other-regarding actions as determining the sphere of liberty to which individuals are entitled. The distinction is notoriously tricky to specify. All actions can be seen as in some sense affecting others, just as their inspiration is not merely private.[48] Murdoch recognizes the indeterminacy involved in distinguishing a private sphere from a public one but considers that it is worth maintaining a distinction so as to protect the individual from violence, coercion and the dangers of an over mighty state. In protecting the individual she urges that politics must be regulated by moral norms and that this mode of regulation is distinct from personal morality even if regulatory norms are affected by personal morality. She inclines towards accepting a distinction that is suggested by experience, between a public political world that is to be governed by highly general axioms prescribing rights and rules and a personal sphere of moral aspiration affecting an individual's life. Personal moral life is perfectionist and is likened to a spiritual journey, where the self develops via its moral encounters with others and aims for perfection in its actions. Public regulation attends to the imperfect political world where individuals are liable to suffer and protects the basic requirements for a decent life.[49]

Murdoch's distinction between private and public morality does not amount to an absolute separation between two spheres and is not sanctioned by unassailable philosophical argument. It is a pragmatic way of drawing a line that is of service in working to protect individuals and to guard against the excesses of state intrusion into individual lives. It is a product of reflection upon modern political history. She is critical, however, of the Hegelian project of identifying an overall pattern to the development of history, and of Hegel's Marxist successors who posit an end to history and justify interim political actions in terms of this endgame. Murdoch is against any totalizing political judgments that abstract from a messy contingent world in which rights supersede any projected end state and the priority is to protect individual rights. She argues, 'The idea of Utopia is a danger in politics, it hints at a rectification of a primal fault, a perfect unity, it is impatient of contingency. The assertion of contingency, the rights of the object, the rights of the individual, these are connected.'[50]

In establishing the limits that have to be respected in theorizing politics and in her critique of Hegel and Marx, Murdoch respects Adorno's neo-Hegelian reworking of Marx. Adorno reacts against the Hegelian tradition by critiquing totalizing forms of thought. In contrast to Hegel himself, Adorno allows for the independence of the object, which is not to be subsumed by the subject in a dialectic that is to yield a final solution to the exigencies of experience. Adorno allows for a negative and continuing dialectical interplay between subject and object. Murdoch comments approvingly, 'This dialectical give-and-take mutually necessary relation between subject and object is not to be understood in a Hegelian manner as taking place within any sovereign determining totality, whether Hegel's absolute, or a Marxist idea of history as a story with a happy ending.'[51] Adorno's approach recognizes contingent events that cannot be encapsulated in a tight theoretical scheme. Yet he also allows for interrelations between the elements that are to be theorized. Murdoch avoids totalizing political thought by recognizing a distinction between the personal and the public. The public sphere is not to assimilate all experience into its own province. In taking her cue from Adorno, however, Murdoch allows for an interaction between the public and the private. Public laws are to protect and serve the individual, while personal moral thinking can contribute to the public agenda by framing ideas on how the welfare of individuals can be best secured by public provision. She envisages a dialectic between the public and the private but insists on securing rights protecting individuals and on limiting the power of the state to determine the conduct of individuals.

While personal morality is perfectionist, the public sphere is not set on achieving the ideal. It has to be flexible and accommodate to the needs of the moment and is alert to imperfections and deficiencies that require practical remedies. Murdoch acknowledges the problematic nature of establishing and developing norms for the public world. The dangers to individual welfare that follow from lax or ill-conceived regulation prioritize the maintenance of fundamental axioms that establish clear and firm rules that facilitate the transactions of individuals. The rules of the game require to be set so as to protect fundamental needs. Murdoch urges that the public sphere should be regulated by axioms securing basic requirements for a decent life, for example the human rights of life and liberty. These rights require to be protected from interference by governments as well by individuals. The rights are to be derived from experience, reflecting what has proven to be fundamental to the ordinary pursuit of individual purposes. They demand recognition that is unconditional and unmediated, so these axioms are not to be put into a system that would detract from their immediacy. Public awareness of their unconditionality is dissipated if they are made to fit within an overarching philosophical formula. Murdoch observes, 'They are barriers of principle which are not reducible to a system.'[52] They also issue from considered reflection upon a changing world. They specify what is thought to be necessary in the public realm from time to time. Hence they are contestable, and they will vary across time and space, even if many of them such as the right to life will persist. Their historical piecemeal articulation entails that they are not to be construed as the positive enactments of a supervening and universal natural law. Rather they evolve as political experience deepens and throws up issues that demand attention in the light of changing events and cultural moods. There is no precise specification of the ways in which they will evolve. According to Oakeshott, a friend of Murdoch, 'In political activity, then, men sail a boundless and bottomless sea; there is neither harbour for shelter nor floor for anchorage, neither starting-place nor appointed destination.'[53] Moral commitments and interests respond to changing forms of social interaction and to an evolving public sense of what is fundamental to the effective organization of the public sphere. Murdoch recounts a variety of ways in which the agenda for politics develops, noting the activities of feminist movements, and single issue groups canvassing the rights of animals and the planet.[54] Deeply felt personal moral beliefs, for instance, ecological concern for the planet, and animal rights might at one time seem eccentric but, at another point in time are absorbed into the norms of the public culture. Murdoch is light on detail in specifying how issues are to be handled by political institutions and more specifically on how substantive aspects of socioeconomic policy will be negotiated. Her highly generic account of how axioms are put on to the political agenda by assorted groups, however, intimates that she envisages a plural and democratic process of sifting norms and issues.

Murdoch's account of the framing of basic axioms in the public sphere is relatively thin on specifying how the political agenda is to be determined. Its lack of a clear reference to an agenda for collective action has been critiqued by Lovibond for betraying the Enlightenment principles of equality and freedom in regard to women. Lovibond takes Murdoch's novels to portray women as being subordinate to men, and she also bemoans Murdoch's lack of express support in any of her writings for collective action on the part of women to remedy their unequal conditions.[55] It is true that in Murdoch's novels there is a differential treatment of men and women. Men have higher social status and dominate women routinely in the course of the narratives. This privileging of the social position of men goes along with a political philosophy that prioritizes individual liberty over collective action. The issue of Murdoch's attitude to women and the dominance of men in society, however, is not as clear-cut as Lovibond suggests. Murdoch's first person male narrators are far from paradigms of goodness, and the bourgeois family structure is subject to critique within the narratives. In a carefully balanced review of the role of women in Murdoch's fiction Johnson observes, 'Iris Murdoch's novels pose in new and tantalising ways the question of what it means to write as a woman, to read as a woman. They disconcert and fascinate both female and male readers by continually questioning gender identity and transgressing gender boundaries.'[56] The attitudes towards women of Charles Arrowby in *The Sea, The Sea* (1978) and Hilary Burde in *A Word Child* (1975) are patronizing and controlling, but as Johnson signals, these attitudes are treated ironically in self-subverting first person narratives.[57] Murdoch's deconstruction of male domination is of a piece with her critique of bourgeois family structures that are shown to exert sustained damage to children in novels such as *The Sacred and Profane Love Machine* (1974) and *A Fairly Honourable Defeat*. Lovibond is right to perceive the relative lack of a determinate focus upon the inequalities between men and women in Murdoch's political thought. Murdoch, however, does recognize that axioms establishing equalities have been enacted and are likely to be further developed in the future, while her novels pose questions for the prevalent inequalities between men and women.

Murdoch provides no clear cut recipe for determining axioms on the political agenda and she recognizes the contestable nature of public axioms. Their contestability, however, does not imply that obedience to them is optional. Public order and security depends upon their command of widespread support. Their efficacy turns upon their capacity to elicit obedience, and obedience derives from their moral approval on the part of citizens. The public and the personal are linked dialectically by the formation and effective operation of axioms, Personal moral commitments inspire the adoption of axioms and reinforce community solidarity and the maintenance of laws and rights. There are, however, tensions between the public and the personal. While the axioms underpinning the operation of the public sphere demand respect and obedience from citizens, on occasions the personal moral commitments of individuals will clash with public rules. Murdoch imagines moral commitments to be more than merely subjective preferences that can be put aside easily; they form part of an individual's spiritual life. A clash between personal principle and public law raises the prospect of civil disobedience on the part of an individual to register their disagreement with the law and to canvas its overthrow. For Murdoch, civil disobedience is acceptable, even necessary, but should be practised sparingly, because there is value in the maintenance of a law insofar as it provides order. Murdoch endorses civil disobedience but she takes it to be exceptional and problematic. In undertaking civil disobedience in a democratic society where laws and policies reflect public opinion, an individual must be prepared to argue the case in public debate. If the debate does not lead to a change in the law then disobedience may be legitimate but the individual who refuses to obey the law must accept punishment for an offence. Disobedience is not to be generalized because it may weaken the force of public order, which allows for the very development of personal wide-ranging moral commitments that lie behind the civil disobedience.

Murdoch's later more avowedly realistic reading of politics, and her understanding of a distinction between personal and public forms of morality inform one of her most expressly political novel, *The Nice and the Good*. At the outset of the novel, its main protagonist, John Ducane, a legal advisor to a government department, is requested by his head of department, Octavian Gray, and the prime minister to head up an inquiry into the death of one of its members, Radeechy. Ducane is concurrently embarking upon a platonic relationship with Kate, Octavian's wife, who presides over Grays's Trescombe estate in Dorset. Ducane enjoys the warmth and expansiveness of Kate, which counterpoints his uneasiness towards Jessica, whose needy desperate attachment deters him from acting on his resolution to end their affair. Kate has opened her household to her friends, Mary Clothier and Paula Biranne, and their children, and she enjoys her relationship with Ducane, while basking in the charms of Trescombe. Her generosity is limited neither by a close observation of others nor by an appreciation of demanding emotions. Her attraction to Ducane is exemplary of her attitude. 'How lovely it is, thought Kate, to be able to fall in love with one's old friends. It's one of the pleasures of being middle-aged. Not that I'm really in love, but it's just like being in love with all the pain taken way.'[58]

Kate's self-absorption counterpoints Ducane's fastidious attention to things and people. While he is attracted to Kate and the warmth of her household, he attends to the lives of others. He is prepared to give and receive love. His investigation into Radeechy's death brings him into contact with depraved forces contaminating the political world, which reflect the corrupt and sexually charged atmosphere on the edges of the political world that was revealed by the Profumo scandal of the early 1960s. Ducane's own moral sensitivity is heightened in risking his life to save Pierce, Mary's son. He realizes that he is in love with Mary and he recognizes his love for Mary to contrast with the ersatz painless 'nice' love that is imagined by Kate. He takes his love for Mary to indicate a fundamental goodness in the world, to which he should devote himself, and his state of mind is captured in the following observation within the novel.

> Her [Mary's] mode of being gave him a moral, even a metaphysical, confidence in the world, in the reality of goodness. No love is entirely without worth, even when the frivolous calls to the frivolous and the base to the base. But it is in the nature of love to discern good, and the best love is in some part at any rate, a love of what is good.[59]

Ducane's insight into goodness inspires him to facilitate the reunion of Paula and her husband, Richard Biranne, who is implicated in the death of Radeechy. Due to his moral commitment to help Paula, he refrains from including any damaging reference to Biranne's entanglement in its occurrence in his official report on the death.

Ducane's selfless assistance to Paula is a token of a personal perfectionist moral commitment. At the same time it is a dereliction of his political duty to his department and to the Prime Minister to produce a full and inclusive report, which might re-establish public confidence in the political establishment. His neglect of his political duty is justified by the virtue of his action, but his appreciation of the tension between his moral and political duties is reflected in his decision to resign from his post. His resignation over his failure to produce the full facts in his report contrasts with the relaxed attitude of his head of department, Octavian Gray. At the close of the novel the latter observes with equanimity the thinness of Ducane's report on the Radeechy affair, because the affair is of receding significance. Octavian like Kate is nice and bourgeois rather than committed to perfectionist ideals. He is temperamentally suited to being a political actor. He is concerned with what works rather than with the good. He is not overly troubled by the demands of morality and, as is characteristic of top civil servants, he can be economical with the political truth. With a similar ease he also conceals his affair with a secretary, just as Kate can renew her social life in the absence of Ducane and the disappearance of her friends from Trescombe. Ducane's uneasiness at his failure to discharge his political obligation reflects Murdoch's recognition of the delicate balance between political and personal moral obligations. Politics, in the later post-socialist thinking of 'Morals and Politics', is not a Utopian project, but performs a service in maintaining the rules of the game, for they provide order and security in the public world. Individuals are protected, and in their personal lives, like Ducane, they can be virtuous in pursuing the good. The value of these political rules, however, does not transcend the perfectionist obligation of cultivating goodness.

Personal morality, in Murdoch's later political thought, may depend upon the maintenance of political axioms, but its perfectionist spirit is not to be constrained by them. Nonetheless the tension between the two requires to be recognized and does not admit of easy answers. This tension surfaces in another Murdoch novel, *An Accidental Man*, when Ludwig Leferrier, a young American historian, opts to remain in England to take up a lecturing position at an Oxford college and to marry the English Gracie Tisbourne rather than to return to the United States to serve the state in the Vietnam War. If he returns home Ludwig faces arrest for avoiding the draft. During the course of the novel Ludwig's parents express their disapproval of their son's projected marriage and avoidance of the draft. They urge him to return home and not to behave dishonourably. Ludwig takes a different view. He is opposed to the Vietnam War, and considers his decision to remain in England to be morally justified. By the end of the novel, however, and in response to his changing thoughts on marriage and Grace, he decides to return to the USA and to face the consequences. Clearly there are opposing arguments about what Ludwig should do. The Vietnam War excited opposition on many grounds. A super power fighting for indeterminate reasons and in controversial and largely ineffective ways did not seem a cause that justified large-scale loss of life, and yet a state requires a commitment from its citizens to engage on its behalf. The novel does not take sides on the issue, but it records a tension between the personal and the political on a leading issue of the politics of the day.

Murdoch's novel *The Book and the Brotherhood* is expressly political in that the plot centres around a projected text in political theory that is supported financially by a group of friends. The plan is for David Crimmond, a radical Marxist, to write the book on behalf of the brotherhood. The members of the brotherhood, a group of Oxford intellectuals, who have gravitated to the civil service and teaching, however, have become progressively disillusioned with the project. At the outset, when they had recently left Oxford, they were committed to a project that matched their left-wing views. With the passage of time, the writing of the book drags on, and the members of the group grow older and less radical. One of their members, Sinclair Curtland has died. Their political views have shifted away from radicalism to supporting parliamentary democracy, whereas Crimmond remains a charismatic and demonic figure on the radical left, and is a fervent critic of the political present and suffers no bourgeois qualms about preserving parliamentary democracy. He is a Marxist, and on the left of the Labour Party. The group is concerned about continuing to finance a project with which it does not sympathize and which shows no sign of coming to an end. They resolve to monitor progress on the book. Meanwhile Crimmond behaves abominably. He cuckolds Duncan Cambus, a member of the brotherhood, enthralling Duncan's wife Jean by his brand of iconoclasm. Gerard Hernshaw, the elder statesman of the brotherhood, is appalled by Crimmond's behaviour and vexed over the group's continued support of the project. At first Gerard meets with Crimmond alone, but subsequently he and other members of the group talk with Crimmond. They discuss his ideas and are dismayed by his continuing radicalism, which flies in the face of their beliefs. On reading Crimmond's completed book, however, Gerard is impressed. The book is a root and branch critique of the present by way of a review of the past and the projected future. It is multidimensional and synoptic, incorporating philosophy, sociology and the political. Simultaneously Gerard is appalled by and attracted to the Crimmond's ideas. It ignites his own thinking. The utopianism of the book rides roughshod over the ordinary world of families and friends, who make their way in the world in unspectacular ways, but it has something striking to say.

When Gerard meets with Crimmond to discuss progress on the book, their contrasting political ideas are aired and debated. Crimmond pours scorn on what he disparages as the safe comfortable world of Gerard and the brotherhood. He proclaims that he is exposing the root causes of what is going on. He urges, 'I'm doing the history of our time, which you and your friends seem to be entirely unaware of.'[60] He adds, 'Of course I think this society, our so-called free society, is rotten to the core – it's oppressive and corrupt and unjust, it's materialistic and ruthless and immoral and soft, rotted with pornography and kitsch.'[61] In reply, Gerard puts the case for a form of anti-utopian political realism, to which Murdoch was to turn in *Metaphysics as a Guide to Morals*. He avers, 'There is no good society ... not like you think, society can't be perfected, the best we can hope for is a decent society, the best we can achieve is what we've achieved now, human rights, individual rights and trying to use technology to feed people.'[62] When Crimmond meets with the wider group he disparages Gerard's privileged standpoint. 'Your whole picture of western civilisation is a "theory"', said Crimmond to Gerard, 'your whole way of life supports poverty and injustice, behind your civilised relationships there's a hell of misery and violence.'[63] Pointedly, he adds, 'There's something called history.'[64] Following the publication of Crimmond's text, Gerard discusses his reaction to it with Rose Curtland, the sister of his beloved Sinclair. He reports on its merit and reveals how despite or perhaps because of its misguided nature, it has stirred his own thinking. While he is convinced of the wrong-headedness of Crimmond's argument, he is aware of its significance. He is appreciative of having his thinking shaken by such a provocative radical broadside. He observes, 'He [Crimmond] thinks liberal democracy is done for. He's a sort of pessimistic utopian. And of course we're right, all right I'm right and he's wrong – but my rightness – needs to be changed – shaken, uprooted, replanted, enlightened.'[65] To Rose's question of whether Crimmond purports to be on the side of history, Gerard replies, 'Yes. History as a slaughterhouse, history as a wolf that wanders outside in the dark, an idea of history as something that *has to be*, even if it's terrible, even if it's deadly.'[66]

   The Book and the Brotherhood was published shortly before an English translation of Lyotard's *The Postmodern Condition – A Report on Knowledge* appeared.[67] Paradoxically in declaring the end of grand narratives, that is large-scale philosophical or political perspectives that purport to capture historical development or the essence of things, Lyotard himself was presenting a dramatic reflection on a supposed turning point in history. Postmodernism represented a repudiation of large-scale theorizing and in particular a critique of Hegel and Marx's assimilation of history to a single line of development. Murdoch's *The Book and the Brotherhood* is akin to Lyotard's *The Postmodern Condition* in highlighting and critiquing the role of grand narratives in theoretical and political debate. Gerard represents Murdoch's own ideas in protesting against the totalizing character of Crimmond's politics and the utopianism of his political theory. For Crimmond, everything is explained and political action is justified in terms of the overall directionality of history. The political present is subordinated to a schematic vision of the future. In the meantime a piecemeal commitment to human rights and the provisions of a decent society are forgotten. As in Murdoch's own analysis of politics in *Metaphysics as a Guide to Morals* Gerard accepts the imperfection of society and concentrates on pragmatic support for specific political measures, providing protection and welfare for individuals.

Murdoch's *The Book and the Brotherhood* departs from Lyotard's *The Postmodern Condition*, however, because Crimmond's grand narrative does not appear to be simply wrong-headed or without value. Gerard attests to Rose on its value as 'an extraordinary book'.[68] He recognizes that one should be inspired by 'something good even if one disagrees'.[69] The abiding sense of *The Book and the Brotherhood* is that grand ideas, large-scale theories of politics retain their significance even if their role is to stimulate defences of the status quo. Murdoch herself in arguing for a limited style of politics that focuses upon protecting the rights of individuals does not ignore large scale theories of politics that imagine alternative futures and see history as possessing a directionality. She argues her position by confronting opposing ideas, such as those developed by Hegel and Marx. Her own philosophical standpoint returns to the origins of grand philosophical schemes in embracing Plato. Murdoch maintains that politics is best served by concentrating upon the attainable and what can be delivered to help ordinary individuals but the processes of political debate should not be limited and should include grand narratives, even if as Lyotard detected they were going out of fashion towards the end of the century. If they were to end, as Lyotard envisaged, then the quality of debate and the liveliness of political argument would suffer.

Conclusion

Murdoch's philosophy and her novels possess a political dimension that has been overlooked or underrated by commentators. In the 1950s she was committed to socialism but she recognized the problematic condition of the socialist project. Her politics reflected her wider critique of a liberal individualism that put individual choices ahead of a commitment to the common good. It harmonized with her moral philosophy, which critiqued an over reliance upon mere choice. Her subsequent move to the right in politics led to her emphasis upon a politics that sought to protect individuals rather than aiming for a substantive common good. Her political theory continued to relate to her moral philosophy, in that her later attitude to politics took it to be a means whereby the pursuit of a perfectionist personal morality could be safeguarded. Her later reading of politics represents a way of connecting the public to the personal within a dialectical overview of experience. Her shift in political position can be identified by her increasing attention to the dangers of oppressive states and is related to her keen interest in the politics of her times.[70] Murdoch's prioritizing of individual rights over a collective good lends credence to Lovibond's view that she does not support collective action on the part of women to counteract their subordination to men. However, the subversion of male standpoints in many of Murdoch's novels shows her awareness of gender imbalances and her admittedly abstract account of the development of axioms to secure basic rights of citizens allows for reform to remedy continuing gender inequalities.

An enduring feature of her political thinking is her drawing upon eclectic traditions of thought. A student of her political theory class at St. Anne's College, Jenny Hinton (Jennifer Dawson 1949–52) has recorded the intellectually exciting spirit of Murdoch's classes. She comments, 'We roamed over philosophical and literary ideas from Plato to Arthur Koestler.'[71] Hinton evidently enjoyed the classes and the richness of Murdoch's thinking. She remembers how Murdoch referred to Oakeshott's image of politics as a ship's voyage that has no fixed destination and questioned his image by suggesting, 'Doesn't one want and need to get somewhere?'[72] Equally she recalls Murdoch's warnings against the idea that men and women could be forced to be free that she identified in Karl Marx and the *Communist Manifesto*.[73] In *Metaphysics as a Guide to Morals* Murdoch continues to discuss a range of theorists and the influence of Oakeshott can be seen more positively, and while she is critical of the record of communist regimes she is drawn to Adorno's post-Marxist ideas. Her recognition of the continuing need to open up to a range of political ideas, including those to which one is opposed, is suggested in her sympathetic treatment of the publication of Crimmond's radical text on political theory in *The Book and the Brotherhood*. Another feature of her late and early consideration of politics is her international perspective. Her sympathy for the displaced persons that she came across in her work at the end of the Second World War stayed with her and informs the sensitivity with which she deals with migrants in her novels. In *Metaphysics as a Guide to Morals* she expressly observes that the nation state does not represent the end of political development and her advocacy of the provision of basic rights for individuals is compatible with their international implementation. The international implications of her political theory, along with her Europeanism, and her progressive tolerance of divergent sexual attitudes mark her political thought as continuing to be of relevance in an uncertain world.

CHAPTER SIX

Murdoch: Her life and times

Introduction: The personal and the public

Why, if at all, does the life of an artist or a philosopher matter? If we attend to a philosopher's academic work so as to reconstruct their thinking on, say, the nature of rights or we reflect upon a novelist's style, we don't automatically think we need to refer to the life of the philosopher or artist. Indeed, it is tricky enough dealing with a philosophical argument or a passage in a novel. Why bother with the bits and pieces and messiness of an actual life. There is a difference between the public and the personal. Maybe it's difficult to draw a line, but Murdoch herself did so, and it's useful to recognize a distinction.[1] A personal life is lived in the moment and allows for experimentation and a relaxed persona outside of the public gaze. It is not offered for public examination. It is extemporized so as to make the most of opportunities and relations that are on offer, and it leaves the future open. Texts in the public world are written to be read and considered and they are intended to possess an argumentative or imaginative coherence to which a life does not aspire. Commentators have tied themselves up in knots chasing the shadows of Shakespeare's life, but rarely connect his art to a life. Hegel and Marx had illegitimate children, but this seems to have had little impact on their public texts, even when they wrote about the family. Perhaps Edie Sidgwick appeared 'just like a woman', but broke 'just like a little girl' and Joan Baez may have approximated to 'Queen Jane', but conjecture is idle and biography does not enhance our understanding of Bob Dylan's songs.[2] To come to the point, why should we be interested in the life of Murdoch? She took care to protect her private life and denied its relevance to her novels. She destroyed letters and so we only have her side of a correspondence. In any event it might be thought that we have more than enough to be going on with in Murdoch's published writings. We have access to multiple philosophical essays and books, and twenty-six novels. And yet her life is explored.

Murdoch's life has generated a range of differing interests, from a variety of perspectives. There is a fascination with her work and with her as an author that has led to a preoccupation with her personal life. Osborn in '"How Can One Describe Real People?" Iris Murdoch's Literary Afterlife' identifies the tone of memoirs and biographical studies in the immediate aftermath of Murdoch's death as testifying, at least in part, to the work of mourning in reviving an image or reconciliatory memory. She observes, 'These authors form a community of survivors into which Iris Murdoch is incorporated. While the biographical attempts to capture Murdoch after her death has been described as the battle for her memory, they are an inevitable part of a re-positioning of Murdoch in the lives of the survivors, which includes her reading public.'[3] Certainly it is true that those who knew Murdoch appear to have been keen to commit their views to print so as to memorialize their own perspective on her life. Conradi, who was commissioned to write the official biography, combined discretion with a conscientiousness of loyal friendship in framing a truthful and considerate reading of her life. When he confessed to Philippa Foot that he was finding it burdensome to deal with Murdoch's early and confused love life, she replied wittily, 'Write the biography without curiosity.'[4] She also said, 'Leave the philosophy to us. We can deal with that.'[5] Conradi appreciated her comments, and yet they invite questions. A biography of Murdoch in which the philosophy is left out seems incomplete and awkward. Her philosophy was a big part of her life. It lent a sharpness to her thinking and an edge to her reflections on her experiences. Likewise the identity of the 'us' to whom Murdoch's philosophy is being left is worrying. It presumes that she shared a philosophical perspective with others, when she appears to have followed a singular line of philosophical development. Murdoch was virtually alone among Oxford philosophers in taking Continental philosophy seriously and her thinking about the history of philosophy and its relation to the present was idiosyncratic. Murdoch's letters to Foot contain precious little philosophy, and hence do not suggest a common philosophical position.[6]

Murdoch's life has been looked at from multiple angles, and different aspects of Murdoch have been accentuated by succeeding biographical viewpoints. She has been proclaimed to be saintly. Towards the end of Murdoch's life Muroya rehearses the impressions of many interviewers of Murdoch in concluding that her life is 'one characterised by regularity and unassuming gentleness'.[7] The onset of Alzheimer disease, and the slippage from acute intelligence to distracted distress, allowed a poignant revisiting of her life. Her dementia is captured movingly by Bayley in his *Iris – A Memoir of Iris Murdoch*, which juxtaposes memories of their unworldly courtship with scenes of her final abjection.[8] Bayley's narrative was selective. The multiple relationships that Murdoch maintained with friends and lovers were glossed over, and her lesbian relationships were denied. His emotional concentration upon the innocence of their relationship and the pathos of her final days feature prominently in the film of her life, *Iris*, which drew inspiration from his memoir.[9] The film and the memoir threatened to turn the image of Murdoch into a sentimentalized portrait of an abject figure. Conradi's biography was painstaking and compassionate. Though it was sensitive in its detailing of her complex emotional relationships with both men and women, it raised questions about her saintliness. The image of Murdoch's saintliness was flattened by A. N. Wilson's provocative memoir, *Iris: As I Knew Her*, which shows Murdoch to be sexually promiscuous and utterly disorganized domestically. It aims to undermine the image of Bayley as a selfless carer, intimating that he relished the control over Murdoch that he was able to exert in her last years. Where Murdoch's prowess as a philosopher is neglected in Bayley's memoir, it is disparaged by Wilson, who dismisses it as 'just secular sermonising based on Plato and Weil'.[10]

Wilson and Bayley construct contrasting images of Murdoch, yet they share a concentration upon the personal and the domestic. Along with the film *Iris*, their portraits of Murdoch combine in shifting attention away from Murdoch's philosophical and literary work. Interest in Murdoch's personal life has been heightened by the publication of a selection of her letters in *Living on Paper – Letters from Iris Murdoch 1934–1995*, a volume that is edited by Horner and Rowe.[11] It represents a wide-ranging selection of her letters to a number of friends and lovers. These recipients include, among others, Brigid Brophy, the novelist and radical thinker, Philippa Foot, the philosopher, David Morgan, a student at the RCA, Frank Thompson, an Oxford friend, David Hicks, an Oxford University friend, Rachel Fenner, an RCA student, Michael Oakeshott, the political philosopher, Elias Canetti, the Nobel Prize winning author and Raymond Queneau, the experimental French novelist. Her letters reveal a variety of interests as she discusses her concerns over the bits and pieces of life and express a range of emotions that take in love, empathy, distress, guilt and courage. They tend not to comment directly upon her work, though they reveal moral concern for herself and for others, and reflect upon political events and moral conundrums. Notably in her letters to Queneau, in the 1940s she reviews the direction that her philosophical studies were taking and her engagement with Sartre and other philosophers. The editors of *Living on Paper – Letters from Iris Murdoch 1934–1995*, Horner and Rowe, provide letters covering the breadth of Murdoch's life and friendships. In contrast to biographies, they claim, with some justice, that 'letters provide a kaleidoscopic picture, their authors sometimes responding in remarkably different ways to different correspondents, even on the same day'.[12]

Critical reception of the publication of these letters has recognized the conscientious work of the editors. Osborn notes, 'Praise was universal for the "meticulous" editors whose comprehensive footnotes and illuminating introductions were roundly commended.'[13] Many reviews appreciated the widening perspective on Murdoch's life and style that the letters offer. Friegel in the *Daily Telegraph* concluded, 'Few books leave the reader with as dizzying sense of the need to question absolutely everything.'[14] But some reviews fixed upon Murdoch's sexual promiscuity and what were taken to be her moral failings. In *The Guardian* D. J. Taylor observed,

> The anatomist of Murdoch's complicated love life probably needs a private detective rather than a biographer. Grand obsessions burn on; old flames flicker brightly in the background. The early 60s, for example, find her married – to all intents and purposes, happily – to Bayley, conducting a highly charged relationship with the novelist Brigid Brophy while assuring her in a morata that 'I'm not in love with you, and don't want to be. When I am in love I am INSANE' … and sending endless wistful notes to her former lover, Elias Canetti.[15]

In *The Times* Roger Lewis was unrestrained in his debunking of Murdoch, opining, 'In her prime she was a nymphomaniac … from the moment she left school and arrived at university in 1938 she seemed to have felt obliged to sleep with everyone she met, particularly dreary ugly foreign intellectuals like Elias Canetti.'[16]

Publication of Murdoch's letters extends our knowledge of her private life, allowing us access to a kaleidoscopic array of friends and thoughts, but the letters have also been seized upon to condemn her sexual and emotional promiscuity and to shift attention away from her philosophy and literary achievements.[17] What are we to do? Is it best to ignore the letters and biographical information and to concentrate upon her published texts of philosophy and literature, and thereby to avoid a fascination with the energy and messiness of her complex relations with a circle of friends? It is an irony that Murdoch herself was aware of how letters can complicate rather than reveal truths, and distort rather than enable perception. In *A Fairly Honourable Defeat* (1970) the demonic Julius King contrives to undermine the seemingly stable and loving relationship of Hilda and Rupert Foster by despatching fabricated love letters to Rupert and Morgan, Hilda's sister, which purport to reveal the love each of them feels for the other. Rupert puts on a show of helping Morgan deal with her seeming infatuation, but basks in what he takes to be her adulation. Soon cracks appear in his apparently secure marriage to Hilda, and the culmination of the ensuing misunderstandings is the tragedy of Rupert's death. Julius declares to the saintly Tallis Browne, 'Yes. Human beings should be awfully careful about letters. They are such powerful tools. Yet people will write them in moments of emotion too, and other people will fail to destroy them.'[18] So why are we to read the letters of Murdoch? She destroyed the letters that she received. Are there compelling reasons to read them? On the face of it, their multiple expressions of love and tenderness tend to distract readers from the novels and from her philosophy. Certainly, they are readable. Other people's lives can draw us in. Her letters contain heartfelt sentiment, sexual confessions, gossip, arrangements and rearrangements, and the sorting out of responsibilities for what went wrong when arrangements to meet went awry. Yet the question remains, are we justified in using them to make judgments about her?

One clear reason to read them is that they enable us to find out more about Murdoch. In spite of the passage of time she remains a magnetic figure. We are naturally interested in what makes her tick. To whom is she drawn? What does she feel? What does she say? How does she respond to this or that remark? We are drawn to the letters as we are drawn to an affecting friend or acquaintance in the course of life. Still, in the light of the ways in which letters can be misused, the question of why we should read the letters remains. What are we doing when we consult her letters? We need to be clear on the matters in which we are interested and if those interests are justified? Moreover, even if there may be a legitimate interest in her life, caution is required to ensure that her privacy is afforded some protection from a prurient voyeurism of a subsequent age, which is likely to misperceive the emotional and sexual vitality of a person, contending with historic cultural constraints. Attention to her letters can be justified by focusing upon how Murdoch's personal life bears upon her public identity and public activities. This rationale begs the question of how we divide the personal from the public. Radical feminists have not been alone in maintaining that the personal, in some sense, is the political, and Murdoch herself in *Metaphysics as a Guide to Morals* (1992) points to the ways in which the private and the public spheres interrelate.[19] A relatively uncontroversial way of drawing a line between the personal and the public is to designate what Murdoch published in her engagement as a thinker and writer to represent the 'public' Murdoch and what she did not publish, or draw attention to publicly, to constitute the 'private' Murdoch. What Murdoch published is in the public domain and was intended for the public world, and her letters were intended for private communication. Scrutiny of Murdoch's letters and her private communication may be justified to the extent that it augments our understanding of her published work, her novels and philosophical writings. This view is promising but it demands interpretation. How might her private world and personal friendships relate to her published work? The answer to this resides in our reading of Murdoch as a philosopher and novelist. Murdoch's philosophy relates to experience, in that her metaphysics is not otherworldly but derives from questions that arise from our experience and its worth is shown in its capacity to guide our moral life. Likewise, her novels are not framed so as to convey an idiosyncratic philosophical or ideological standpoint but aim to portray the world and realistic characters. Insofar as Murdoch's published work stands or falls on its capacity to represent experience, then her personal experience as registered in her letters will bear upon her published work.

Philosophy, for Murdoch, attends to experience. Personal experience is to be worked upon in developing philosophical understanding and philosophy, in turn, can influence our lives. In her journal for 1947 Murdoch remarks, 'Philosophy is nothing to me if it is not my whole life.'[20] Murdoch conceived of philosophy as something to live by. She herself styled her metaphysics as a guide to morals. In a letter to Queneau she conveys her emotional involvement in reading Hegel's *Phenomenology of Spirit*, 'There is something just astounding and shattering in this great enterprise of thought.'[21] Murdoch takes a different view of philosophy and its relation to the flesh and blood world of experience than that of analytical philosophers in Oxford and Cambridge. Philosophy, for her, has something to say about feelings of despair, attending to someone else's pain, perfecting one's moral life and experiencing the void. Ordinary human morality is the stuff of philosophy, and she makes this very point in her critique of Heidegger.[22] In her letters, Murdoch deals with her own experience of suffering and her own efforts to scrutinize her actions. She reviews her life and tries to improve or perfect the way that she acts. In so doing she is showing how her philosophy can exert an impact upon moral life. Likewise when she intimates that she has known despair, she reveals how her philosophical description of such a state is related concretely to an experiential condition. Her empathy for friends who are suffering or misguided also shows the loving attitude of which her moral philosophy speaks. Murdoch's letters also testify to her first-hand experience of the suffering of refugees and they relate her awareness of the thwarted aspirations of socialism in Communist countries. These insights inform her philosophical probing of public political morality.

Murdoch's fiction, too, relates to her personal experience. This is not because we can look for blueprints of the novels in her own life or trace the identity of her novels' characters to herself or to her friends. Doubtless, friends might have served as inspirations for some of the novels' characters but unless Murdoch signposted the connections (and she does not do so) everything depends upon our interpretation of the fictional characters, and hence not much is gained by speculating on a link to one of Murdoch's friends. Murdoch in her novels, however, aims to be true to experience and so they reflect the honesty with which Murdoch's letters appraise her own experience. The letters also bear upon Murdoch's published work in that they disclose what philosophy she was reading and occasionally how she perceives philosophical issues that she would write about. This is particularly the case in regard to her letters shortly after the war when she writes to Queneau about existentialism and how she is finding her postgraduate studies in Cambridge. Here and there she also reveals her attitude to readings of her literary work. Of course, the letters neither give us direct access to the underlying nature of her philosophy, nor provide outlines for subsequent novels. What they do provide is evidence of how she experiences the world, which is refracted into her published writings just as her philosophical perspective informs the ways in which she responds to events.

In subsequent sections of this chapter a selection of Murdoch's letters will be analysed so as to show how they bear upon and, in turn, reflect themes of her published work. Her letters respond to the individuals to whom they are addressed. They reflect the particular character of the relationships that she had with different friends. The kind of thing that Murdoch shares with someone depends on the intimacy of their relations and the side of Murdoch that is evoked by the interests and sensibility of a particular friend. Conradi, in reflecting upon his experience of writing Murdoch's biography, refers to her 'negative capability', that is, her capacity to respond empathetically to a variety of individuals.[23] The content of the letters also reflect the times in which she lived. The spirit of Murdoch's letters during and immediately after the Second World War is more energized than in the later years. In commenting on Murdoch's early years before she had established her identity as a philosopher and then a novelist, White observes how Murdoch's life has a particular character. In those years Murdoch did not know the direction her career would take and hence there is an uncertainty but also a questing spirit to her attitude and letters of those years.[24] Murdoch is feeling her way and she lets out thoughts on a future career and on more aspirations for the future.

In the rest of this chapter her letters to Frank Thompson, David Hicks, Raymond Queneau, Michael Oakeshott, David Morgan, Brigid Brophy, and Philippa Foot will be reviewed. Chronologically the letters to these friends run from the war and its immediate aftermath until she stopped writing in the mid-1990s. In the letters to these friends Murdoch offers different things. They reflect the times when they were written and the persons to whom she was writing. The letters to Frank Thompson and David Hicks are romantic in contrasting ways. They disclose Murdoch's mood during the war years, her experience of Soho and a Bohemian set that opened her eyes to a certain style of freedom and her frustration at the limits that were placed on her own contribution to the course of the war. In the immediate aftermath of the war she shares with David Hicks her direct experience of working with displaced persons. Murdoch's letters to Raymond Queneau are distinctive. She opens up to him about the philosophical scene in the UK and her excitement at what was happening philosophically in France. She sets out her political hopes for the future and something of her experience in working for UNRRA (United Nations Relief and Rehabilitation Administration). Michael Oakeshott, the Conservative political philosopher, is a friend to whom she shows an empathetic side in comforting him on his troubled love life, while at times struggling to hold back her own romantic feelings for him. She was a teacher of David Morgan, and her letters to him reflect her status as a sort of authority figure, and she plays an important if equivocal role in his personal development. Her relationship with Brigid Brophy was fused with a spirited energy and loving feelings that resonate with Murdoch's capacity to be emotionally moved by friends, though she showed restraint in resisting some of Brophy's sexual advances. Philippa Foot was a friend from Oxford undergraduate days, and Murdoch's letters to Foot trace the ups and downs of their relationship. The downside involved Murdoch hurting Philippa Foot from which it took many years for their relationship to recover. The letters to Foot are revealing in indicating how much value Murdoch assigned to the depth of a long-term friendship that survives a serious disruption. They contain little on philosophy, however, apart from one or two asides by Murdoch, where she wonders about her own philosophical capacities.

In reviewing how these letters show the interrelations between the public and the private sides of Murdoch, for the most part, reference will be made to letters that are published in *Living on Paper: Letters from Iris Murdoch 1934–1995*. It represents a publicly available resource that can be consulted easily. Occasionally, though, reference will be made to letters that are not published in this volume but which are available in the Iris Murdoch Archive at

Kingston University, where these letters add to our understanding of Murdoch's published writings. Murdoch's journals will also be cited where they add to what is said in a letter. Hitherto only the diaries for the war period have been published in Conradi's edited collection of letters and diaries of the war period, though all the journals are available in the Iris Murdoch Archive, even if Murdoch erased some entries.[25] Here and there reference will also be made to the biographies and memoirs, which shed light on Murdoch's relationships with the friends to whom she wrote. For instance, David Morgan's memoir, *With Love and Rage: A Friendship with Iris Murdoch*, helps to contextualize her letters to him.[26]

Letters to Frank Thompson and David Hicks

The war dominates the horizon of her letters to Frank Thompson and David Hicks. It was a period of disrupted lives, in which things were thrown into confusion. Traditions and old loyalties were questioned, new perspectives were opened, men were thrown into danger, women were frustrated by their lack of first-hand engagement in the war. Murdoch felt a sense of the senselessness of the war and the imperative of action. Her concerns about the course of the war, about contributing to the war and to making a new political beginning after the war feature in her letters to Thompson. His chivalry and bravery are reflected in the warmth of her letters and would stay with her. In her letters to Thompson, she conveys her love, shares her political ideas and poetry and reports on her life. She discloses her recent acquaintance with a Bohemian set in London that opened her eyes to a kind of artistic freedom that she found attractive, if ultimately limited. Murdoch's politics, love and fascination with non-conformist attitudes comes to the fore. In a letter to Thompson of 1942 she shares her frustration at not being able to do something more positive for the war effort and reports on her acquaintance with Soho Bohemians. She writes,

> I get so damnably restless from time to time. I would volunteer for *anything* that would be certain to take me abroad. Unfortunately, there's no guarantee given when one joins the

women's forces! = and anyway the Treasury would never let me go; for inefficient as I am, I am filling a very necessary post in an semi-skilled sort of way. Sometimes I think it's quite bloody being a woman![27]

She goes on:

On the other hand, my Soho, Bloomsbury and Chelsea acquaintanceship is widening also. The Swiss in Old Crompton Street, the Wellington in Wardour Street and the Lord Nelson in King's Road are the clubs which I frequent in search of the Ultimate Human Beings – and knowledge and experience and freedom. A Strange society – composed of restless incomplete ambitious people who live in a chaotic and random way, never caring about the next five minutes, drunk every night without exception from six o'clock onwards, homeless and unfamilied, living in pubs and copulating on the floors of other people's flats. Poetry is perhaps the only thing taken seriously by them all.[28]

Her frustration at inaction and her determination to participate in developing things politically is expressed in a letter of 1943. She writes,

Oh I chafe at this inaction. I'd take on any job right now – any job – if it would get me out of England and into some part of the world where things are moving … People are getting awfully complacent about the war. I wish they wouldn't. We're hardly beginning to see the way out of the wood yet. Beveridge is a good thing – that's all right as long as people don't start relaxing with a sigh of relief.[29]

If her letters to Frank Thompson respond to his saintliness, then her letters to David Hicks reflect his more worldly personality. She is prepared to be candid, observing to him, 'Disasters I've met with lately make me mistrust relationships which go on from writing to meeting; but after all, you always were a casual cynical chap … One thing I liked about you was your straight male humanness underneath your horridness.'[30] She relates to Hicks her frustrations at her work for UNRRA, where she experienced a bureaucracy that inhibited action and she conveys to him something of her turbulent love life. She does not mince words in confessing, 'Shortly after I wrote to you last I tore myself away with agonies which I could not even have conceived of a year ago, from the utterly adorable but wicked Hungarian with whom I'd been living.'[31] She shows another side of herself in commenting on the incisiveness of Koestler's critique of contemporary morals,

> Am just reading [Arthur] Koestler's *the Yogi and the Commissar* ... how am I convinced Koestler is Satan? He's so well aware of so much that no one else notices or can comment on. He sees what are the real moral problems of now. He's a much better moralist than Sir David bloody Ross and all the Oxford and Cambridge chaps rolled together.[32]

When she writes to Hicks from Graz, where she is working with displaced persons for UNRRA, she shows an empathetic realism in appreciating their situation. In a letter of January 1946, she relates to Hicks her frustration at the treatment of a Yugoslav displaced person who after crashing a truck, had made a dash for the frontier and the French had arrested him at the frontier. She comments,

> I, being the only French speaker in the office when the crisis occurred, had to cope with complicated phone calls & eventually go up to investigate in a jeep ... hereafter, a great battle with the hard cynical swine at HQ whose only reaction was 'put him in the cooler' and a cynical laugh. God! All these dps are either apathetic or inclined to be thugs or crooks – they've had to be to survive. This boy – age 24 – a King Peter partisan – God knows how he's lived these past five years. And when he does something hysterical all our HQ gentlemen can think of is getting him the maximum penalty just because they're riled at the UNRRA truck being smashed. I haven't felt such misery& fury for a long time.[33]

Letters to Queneau

In letters to the intellectual Raymond Queneau, she shares many intellectual things. They contain her thoughts on philosophy, her enthusiasm for Continental philosophy, her political hopes for the post-war world, her appreciation of his novels and her experience of working directly with displaced persons in Graz. Her excitement at Continental philosophy is evidenced in the contrast that she draws between Continental adventure and the dry forms of analytic and language philosophy in Oxford and Cambridge. She expresses herself vivaciously, conveying to him how, above all, existentialism was the energizing philosophy of the moment. She describes how it was in the air of the post-war world. It promised a tougher response to the predicament of the age than a dry analytic philosophy. It was an expression of the emotional and intellectual texture of a post-war world, where illusions had been laid bare by the awfulness of the inhumanity of the Holocaust, and yet the exhilaration of freedom had also been unleashed. She remarks in a letter, 'When everything is broken our strength is reborn.'[34] She reflects on existentialism, 'At times it seems to me just the most explicit form of something which is generally in the air.'[35] What she responds to positively in existentialism is its anti-metaphysical phenomenalism; its engagement with the concrete puzzle of personal existence, rather than with general theories of human existence.[36] She is explicit in drawing a contrast between Sartre and English philosophy, observing how Sartre has set Oxford hairs on end.[37] Likewise she writes to Queneau of her excitement on reading Beauvoir's *Second Sex*, reflecting that she might well be the sole person doing so in Oxford. She recognizes how Beauvoir speaks directly to her experience even if she passes judgments in ways that would raise the hackles of Oxford philosophy. She observes, 'I am the only person in Oxford to have heard of this world ... splendid – tough, I like the fierce warlike manner.'[38] Her letters to Queneau express her passion for philosophy and her commitment to a political renewal that will depart radically from what has gone before. In this context she writes that she is aiming to pursue her intellectual career in a way that will do justice to her interest in philosophy, literature and politics.[39]

Murdoch also reports to Queneau on her experience of witnessing directly the suffering of displaced persons at first hand in her work with UNRRA. She notices and responds to the awfulness of the situation of those who had been displaced and disturbed by wartime events. It is a sobering experience. The displaced people whom she witnesses at close hand are not saints. They have been damaged and they behave in twisted, distorted ways. She recognizes suffering and its effects. She writes evocatively, 'True suffering is what we read on the face of others.'[40] Murdoch reveals her first-hand encounter with suffering, and human tragedy that will stay with her through her life and which lies behind her evocation of the stories of refugees in her novels. Murdoch is aware of the weight of this experience. She reflects, 'There is so much life here quite mysterious to me. Still, like fishes in a dark aquarium, but very moving and obviously significant.'[41] In her metaphysics, Murdoch discusses the void, which stands for an evacuation of the self when exposed to a harrowing experience. Extreme suffering or a witnessing of something shocking can demand a reckoning with experience that might disturb customary self-absorption and accentuate attention. Amidst attention to suffering, an 'unselfing' can occur. Witnessing men and women, 'like fishes in a dark aquarium', is an experience that challenges habitual routines of the self. The characters in Murdoch's novels include migrants who have been displaced from their homelands. Willy Kost in *The Nice and Good* (1968) is haunted by what he had to do to survive in Dachau. These figures in the novels are not mere translations of people in Murdoch's own past, as they are imagined in the context of an imaginary web of characters and events.[42] Yet they are framed in the light of Murdoch's own experience and they tend to be freighted with complex memories and ambivalent attitudes that cut across an uninformed and merely sentimental characterization.

Letters to Michael Oakeshott

In her letters to Michael Oakeshott Murdoch shows a capacity to empathize with a friend who is experiencing inner conflict and deep distress. She shows a delicacy of emotion. She still feels a lingering love for him after their brief relationship in 1950. Yet at the end of the 1950s, when they resumed contact, she was able to convey a deep sympathy for his troubled and hopeless love for another. Her writing shows a restraint on her part in her willingness to attend to his thoughts and to sympathize with his flow of feelings. Along the way she also reveals her respect for Oakeshott's unfashionable conservatism in its recognition of the primacy of traditions, and his critique of rationalism at a time when his traditionalism was frowned upon by the respectable liberal world to which Murdoch belonged. Oakeshott critiqued the post-war assumptions that society might be rebuilt anew according to first principles just as he rejected the idea that political thought in the abstract could provide rational foundations for action. Political development, for Oakeshott, was a matter of following intimations without supposing there was an end to the process or rational guidelines for the process of development. A cook, for Oakeshott, is more than the cookbook with which she might operate. A cook learns to cook by attending to others who have a practical expertise and there is no abstract essence of cooking. Similarly politics is learned by practice and by attending to a world of practice. Murdoch reveals how she is drawn to aspects of his political philosophy, even though they are sharply opposed to her own social democratic leanings.[43] In a letter of 1958 she relates, 'Yet I have very strong feeling about your mind – it's odd that something about your mind captivated me through your writing before we met – although I find your point of view politically speaking unsympathetic (indeed dearest one, pernicious) Yet somehow you were all *there* before I set eyes on you.'[44] She writes of how she makes use of his thought when she teaches political philosophy.[45] She admits that his theoretical standpoint influences her, noting 'I suspect that you are responsible, by reaction, for a lot of my political views.'[46] In her philosophy Murdoch was willing to draw upon a variety of sources, including Continental and Anglo-American forms of thought. Oakeshott's anti-rationalism was a continuing influence, which can be detected in her turn towards history rather than nature to support her political theory.[47]

Her intellectual respect for Oakeshott is combined with an emotional empathy for his despairing love for a married woman, who has broken off an affair. Murdoch combines close and loving attention to his desperate grief with tender expressions of feeling towards him. She confides, 'It is very hard to reach another person's grief'.[48] She goes on, 'This kind of Grief I know is pretty well incommunicable. The prospect of final partings is something one cannot bear to look at. What is so strange is that one survives.'[49] Yet in the act of sympathizing by identifying with the pain, she recognizes that she might well be conflating her own personal experience too hastily with that of another person. She adds, 'All this is really picturing myself, perhaps and not you. I reflected this morning, as I was walking down the road to St. Anne's how little in a way I knew you.'[50] She continues to support Oakeshott by drawing sensitively upon her own experience of hurt, but allows for differences between her own and his experience. In a letter at the beginning of 1959, she begins, 'Dear heart, I am so sorry that things are bad. I know how terrible such times are when one moves all the time between hope and despair and cannot kill hope and yet wants to be without it.'[51] While Murdoch is restrained about talking of herself overly in these letters to Oakeshott, in a letter of 1958 she discloses something about her unhappiness in the past and how her marriage has given her strength. She writes, 'When I got married I was determined to stop being unhappy and on the whole with John's help I have succeeded very well.'[52] Commentary on her marriage is rare in Murdoch's correspondence, and this comment rings true in relating how her marriage helped her to overcome the previous storms associated with falling in and out of love.

Letters to David Morgan

What stands out in reading Murdoch's letters to David Morgan, her student at the RCA, in conjunction with his moving memoir of their friendship, *With Love and Rage – A Friendship with Iris Murdoch*, is Murdoch's commitment to take on a demanding and difficult friend and to be open to him in attending to his troubles. She was willing to befriend Morgan, a needy and disturbed individual to whom she warmed and to whom, as a teacher and older person, she felt responsibility. Before the RCA Morgan had attended an approved school and had been sectioned. He lacked confidence and self-belief. Murdoch offered him friendship and along with her friendship came a validation of his own worth, intellectually and emotionally. Murdoch too drew from Morgan. She liked him and gained from the relationship. She was not dispensing charity. She felt for him and respected his candour. She empathized with him over the difficulties that he had experienced and respected the fact that he came from the wrong side of the tracks and that he was not respectable. They talked openly. In his book, *With Love and Rage – A Friendship with Iris Murdoch*, Morgan values her openness. He recalls, 'She wrote and said wonderful things – many forgotten – encompassing her views on love, obsession, control and final resignation to loss.'[53]

Murdoch served as a confessor figure to Morgan, listening to the pain of his troubled relationship with a girlfriend, Emma, and at times giving him reasonable advice.[54] In a letter of 1964 she shows her concern for Morgan and over his relationship with Emma:

> I was relieved to get your letter, though very sorry to hear about the Emma situation. I suddenly started worrying about you at the weekend ... thought too that you might be too deep in trouble or despair to be able to write. About Emma: you know you may just have to let go here. Only I know you can't envisage it. Anyway for God's sake stop the pursuit tactics ... Yes I know, I know about being insanely in love and I have pursued people long and with ingenuity, but never with your relentlessness in the face of a refusal.[55]

In turn she was fascinated by his life style, his edginess, his distance from bourgeois safety and taken by his honesty. In the same letter she says, 'But what mostly strikes me about you is that you are naturally, indeed involuntarily, honest.'[56] She was prepared to be honest with him. She was not afraid to rebuke him. She was appalled when he appeared to talk of the closeness of her relationship to a fellow student so as to undermine the respect that should be observed in relations between teacher and students. In a 1965 letter, she writes,

> I am terribly unhappy about this business, and I simply cannot understand how you can have behaved as you did. I was very reluctant to believe (even when you told me yourself) that you had told deliberate lies about me of a very damaging kind ... I simply cannot understand your motives here. As you said, you certainly have an instinct to estrange people you are fond of. But it seems you also have a kind of cruelty which I've never met before.[57]

Of course, she sailed close to the wind in allowing close physical and emotional relations with some students, but she tried to maintain a balance whereby she could still maintain authority and keep a sort of distance from them. Her support for Morgan was genuine even though at times relations were strained. In the letter that is cited above, she added a postscript in which she expressed how sorry she was about the whole thing and for the pain that he would feel. She remained friends with him despite this painful episode. Their relationship contributed to the progress that he made in maintaining a grip on himself and in undertaking a life of responsibility. Subsequently, he lectured at the Chelsea College of Fine Art. Their relationship shows how Murdoch was prepared to act in unconventional ways and to stay the course with someone who was trouble to himself and sometimes to her.

Letters to Brigid Brophy

In the 1950s Murdoch became close friends with Brigid Brophy. Like Murdoch, Brophy was a woman with many talents and interests. She was a political activist, and a public intellectual, espousing many diverse causes and a novelist, who had a passion for music and art. They shared cultural and intellectual interests, with Murdoch responding positively to Brophy's cultivated interests in opera and in Freud. Perhaps most importantly, Brophy brought out the fun and non-conformity within Murdoch's persona. They both mixed unconventional views on sexuality with settled married lives. They accepted bisexuality, and switched gender in imaginary games, though Murdoch resisted pressure to take on a full sexual relationship.[58] Murdoch was older than Brophy and assumed responsibility for keeping a lid on their relationship and she had to fend off a series of emotional as well as sexual demands. Nonetheless, Brophy's freewheeling personality answered to something in Murdoch's nature. Murdoch perceived sexuality to be more open and less fixed than was conventionally maintained and she welcomed Brophy's affirmation of sexual freedom and her transgression against social expectations. In a journal entry for 1970, Murdoch writes, 'Insofar as it is spirit intelligence is sexless. Insofar as intelligence is spirit it is bisexual.'[59] Sexuality for Murdoch was not to be limited and trammelled by the prevailing conventional dichotomy between male and female. She imagined sex as fluid between individuals of the same and different sexes and between styles. After all, in her novels she had written of same sex relations and had shown a variety of ways in which romantic and sexual relationships were enacted. Murdoch stood out against the conventional restrictions on sexual freedom, writing an article in favour of legalizing homosexuality in 1964.[60] The erotic, for Murdoch, was a significant aspect of the psyche and its energy reached into the moral and the philosophical and possessed the potential to waken a person from conventional lethargy, as well as having the capacity to hurt and to thwart moral progress. In her letters to Brophy Murdoch reveals a distinctive side of herself that is less evident elsewhere. Brophy is a confident younger woman, whose unconventionality attracts Murdoch and allows for sexual self-expression, fun and cultural enrichment. Brophy is assertive and demanding. She is prepared to be critical of Murdoch, and of Murdoch's work. She is upset by the limits Murdoch imposes on their relations and at times she does not hold back when she feels slighted. Murdoch is enlivened by Brophy, warms to her, and works with her even when Brophy is being contrary. Murdoch shows maturity in accepting gracefully Brophy's criticisms and in acting as a reliable and sensible friend.

In a letter of 1960 Murdoch responds directly and sensitively to Brophy's criticisms of her work. She writes,

> Dearest creature, your recently advertised efforts to amuse me certainly reached a new high in latest letter ... Until now I had taken the view that your odd attitude to my work was unimportant. Lots of my friends don't like what I write (e.g. Professor Frankel) but mostly they keep quiet about it, and it doesn't matter. I don't, by the way, dislike, or don't think I do, *interesting* criticism, if devoid of spite. Interesting criticism one practically never gets, of course ... I wonder why you so much *insist* on your feelings, instead of emulating the silence of Professor Fraenkel? You will speak here of 'honesty' etc. But I don't think honesty is the same as ruthless self-expression. You want to *do* something by insisting. I wonder if we shouldn't perhaps discuss the whole matter sometime.[61]

Murdoch was prepared to be clear in setting limits to the relationship. In March 1964 she replies directly to Brophy's pressure for full sexual relations,

> Darling so much thanks for your letter. I can't reply properly or argue now, just time-wise. Anyway I don't really know what to say. Alas we are not plants but a couple of ten stone (a little less in your case, and more in mine) incarnate girls. There would *have* to be decisions, actions, times, and I could not take this

calmly. It would be utterly frivolous for me to be persuaded by you here. I am terribly puritanical, and unable to be carefree about sex, even when I am in love. But I'm not in love with you and don't want to be.[62]

If Murdoch was careful to set limits to the relationship with Brophy she warmed to playful role playing and in doing so expressed her feeling for the fluidity of sexual identity that subverts a merely dichotomous ascription of female and male. In a letter to Brophy in May 1964 she imagines their sexual relations in unconventional terms,

My letter which crossed yours gave confirmation in writing of the point you make about lateral incest. In fact I don't want you to be my sister, I have little use for sisters. Your role is probably that of younger brother. (I am elder brother) I suspect my ideal relationship is that between two men. Usually I play the part of the younger man – but with you of course I am the older man. (Does this shew me to be homosexual I wonder?)[63]

Letters to Philippa Foot

Murdoch's discloses her sense of professional and personal responsibility in her relations with Morgan in assuming an advisory role and she shows calm and clarity in responding to Brophy. Her relations with Philippa Foot were different in that the two of them were on a footing of equality. She became friends with Foot as an undergraduate at Somerville and maintained the friendship for the rest of her life. The relationship was strained for a period after Philippa Bosenquet (as she was then called) had moved into Murdoch's Seaforth flat in London. Murdoch began a liaison with Philippa's partner, Thomas Balogh and in the process hurt her own current partner, M. R. D. Foot, to whom Philippa would turn and subsequently marry. Murdoch's affair with Balogh soon foundered but the marriage of Michael Foot and Philippa reinforced a frostiness between Iris and Philippa. Although Murdoch had lived with the Foots for a period when she took up her post at St. Anne's College, relations between Philippa and Iris remained somewhat awkward until M. R. D. Foot deserted Philippa in 1959. Murdoch's letters to Foot are plentiful throughout their friendship and cover a wealth of subjects taking in a variety of moods. Murdoch writes of everyday matters such as shopping in Summertown, suburban Oxford as well as politics in Europe, China and the UK, their brief sexual liaison and emotional trials, such as the death of her mother. On the decline of her mother into senility, Murdoch remarks in a letter of January 1985, 'I don't see much of Oxford. I go to London to see my mother. She is OK, still in that "home", getting more out of touch, but fairly quiet thank God. It's sad to see the person disappearing.'[64]

Perhaps what is most arresting is how Murdoch addresses her affair with Balogh. She admits guilt and accepts responsibility for how she has betrayed her friend. She acknowledges the emotional damage that she has inflicted upon herself and others. This admission of guilt and of her own suffering at what she has done is moving and shows how wretched personal experience can be. Murdoch neither ignores it, nor covers it up. It is dealt with and owned. In a letter of 1946 she writes,

> One doesn't – as I know you realise – get over an *histoire* like that of 1944 very quickly. When one has behaved as I then behaved to two people one loves the hurt and sense of guilt go very deep. In a way it's only since I came home from Austria that I've realised those events *fully* as things that I did, as apart from things I suffered. You understand I have lived through them again as my responsibility. This has not been pleasant, but was necessary.[65]

And in the light of Philippa Foot's continuing willingness to remain a friend, she replied, 'Darling – thank you – your letter gave me such joy. The fact that you do, after all that, still care for me, gives me great hope that the past will fall away ... Love can work miracles. Dear, there have been times when I have felt lacerated and broken beyond repair.'[66]

Murdoch letters to Foot share many things besides emotional disclosure, including her changing views on the political. Early letters offer wartime reflections. There is optimism over a socialist future and a sense that a war-torn and shattered Europe needs to be reconstituted. Her sympathy for Europe and memory of the war remain in later years, though there is a tone of weariness about European history. In 1981 she remarks, 'I Think I have stopped hating being in Germany. Dear old Europe, poor old Europe (Dear old Planet, poor old planet).'[67] In 1990 she writes to Foot enthusiastically on the heroism in the struggle for freedom in Eastern Europe, remarking, 'As you say, we can always think about Eastern Europe! I have had wonderful letters from friends in Czechoslovakia and Poland and Romania (one of then was actually fighting in Bucharest). *Dear* Europe.'[68] In advance of a trip to China by Foot, Murdoch recollects her own experience on a recent visit. She expresses profound reservations over the rigidity of Chinese Marxism and its restrictions on self-expression, which was highlighted by a denial of the very existence of homosexuality. She remarks,

> I am so pleased to hear of the China trip and look forward to talking with you about that marvellous, terrible country. I felt great sympathy, great interest, much enjoyed being there, but also it all *chilled* the blood very much. The power of the Communist Party in Russia is as nothing to its power in China. The 'Cultural Revolution' horrors not so long ago.[69]

In another letter she goes on to express her incredulity over the lack of freedom in China. She declares,

> Very interesting, very touching, *awful* too. My main impressions were the *absolute power* of the Party ... No religion (which is everywhere in India – but also no starvation! No-one lying in the street. Oh yes – and NO SEX! Sex abolished. Amazing. No holding hands in public. (may be changed now).Late marriages – one child – very sensible of course ... I asked about homosexuality. Our excellent interpreter didn't know the word. I explained. 'No, we don't have that!' Illegitimate children? 'Oh hardly ever' – but if so the *mother* and the *child* are persecuted.[70]

Murdoch's views on British politics swung to the Right in the late 1970s and early 1980s in the wake of a perceived radicalism on the part of trade unions and a sense that the Labour Party was out of touch with ordinary people. Her early socialism is a thing of the past. She is appalled by the violence of trade union pickets, and is exercised by the closed shop and by the permissive picketing

legislation of the Labour Government. With the prospect of a
general election, she muses to Foot on which way she might vote,

> The country is in a bad state. There may be an election soon, and
> about time. I hate the Labour Party and cannot love the Tories.
> The bullying tactics of the unions is an awful now forgettable
> fact. But what can be done? The closed shop is one of the villains
> of the piece, but what to do about it?[71]

In what would appear to be an ironic voice, she considers if the
time might be ripe for the assassination of Callaghan and Foot.
Murdoch's movement to the right in politics can be explained in
terms of an older person's natural tendency to conservatism that
is reinforced by a similar movement on the part of her friends.
Yet it also testifies to continuing reflection on political issues,
which was marked by Murdoch's heightened appreciation of the
state's capacity to do harm and in the light of historical events the
imperative to protect individual freedoms.

Conclusion

Why, if at all does the personal life of an artist or philosopher matter?
Is our understanding of their philosophy or artistry enhanced by
reading their letters? The answers to these questions require careful
consideration. If the letters of Murdoch are used as an alibi for
ignoring her work as a novelist and philosopher and for disdaining
what is taken to be a promiscuous love life, then they are not being
read in the right spirit. Murdoch is a holistic thinker, whose aim
was to make her philosophy relevant to life. Just as her philosophy
arises out of experience, so it can be used as a guide to a person's life.
Murdoch's life and letters can be read in terms of their connection
with Murdoch's published philosophy and fiction. Philosophy and
literature alike make sense out of experience, and experience in
turn forms the material for her thinking and imagining. Her novels
are imaginative formulations of experience, just as her philosophy
reviews the nature of experience as a whole. For Murdoch, a signal
ingredient of philosophy is that it can orient an individual to the
good and the nature of morality can be evidenced by the imagined
and realistic pathways to goodness or to fantasy on the part of

the individuals that feature in her novels. There is a reciprocal relationship between Murdoch's public writings and her personal life. They influence one another, though her public writings cannot be reduced to a transposition of her own personal circumstances and her personal life is full of contingencies, inconsequential bits and pieces and singularities that do not cohere with the carefully constructed novels and philosophical texts that Murdoch produced.

Can we detect Murdoch's philosophy in her life? Do her personal circumstances reflect key themes in her philosophy? One thing that is abundantly clear about her life is that she takes moral life seriously. Morality matters to Murdoch in her life in a way that goes beyond regarding it as a series of subjective choices. Just as Murdoch's philosophy takes goodness to be something that serves as a standard to which individuals should aspire by reviewing things in a way that takes into account the reality of other individuals, so Murdoch, in her life, takes on board the duty to look at things honestly and unselfishly. In reflecting upon what she takes to be her betrayal of Philippa Foot, and in her explanation of how it left her feeling, we can discern how profoundly morality and a loving friendship matter to her. Her sense of herself failing in her conduct is a token of her commitment to the perfectionist morality that is advocated in her moral philosophy. A perfectionist morality does not imagine perfect people. Far from it; the world is full of damaged, imperfect individuals. What it demands is that individuals set themselves high standards and that, in concert with a loving regard for others, they try to live up to them without deceptive self-regard distorting their vision of things. In owning up honestly to Philippa Foot over what she has done and in maintaining her friendship with her despite her shame, Murdoch is motivated by a moral sense of what is required. Her contrition testifies to her determination to be good. In letters to Michael Oakeshott and David Morgan she shows a compassionate concern for their welfare that reflects her capacity to get alongside individuals who are suffering. In both case she felt a love that sometimes threatened to overturn the terms of the friendships, but she kept her moral balance and supported both of them through demanding times. Her loving attitude reflects the love of others and of the good that she takes to be constitutive of morality.

Politics plays an important role in Murdoch's philosophy. At the outset she looks towards a socialist renewal to revivify the terms of political engagement in the wake of a burgeoning cultural disillusionment with grand political ideas in the aftermath of the Second World War. In her later political philosophy she envisages politics as playing the vital role of defending the rights of individuals without threatening their security by pursuing utopian schemes that prioritize an abstract future over the real lives of individuals in the present. Her letters express views on the political scene that are consonant with her published writings on philosophy. Her wartime letters to Frank Thompson and David Hicks look to the future and to the prospect of a socialist renewal, which mirrors the commitment to a renewal of socialism that she outlines in her essay, 'A House of Theory'. Subsequently she gives up on socialism and her letters to Philippa Foot show her disillusionment with socialism both in respect of UK politics and in relation to communist states. Her reading of politics in *Metaphysics as a Guide to Politics* highlights the priority that is to be assigned to the establishment of general axioms or rights to protect individuals that will guard against an over mighty state and also provide protection for vulnerable individuals, such as the displaced persons, whom she describes in letters to David Hicks and Raymond Queneau. Yet her lifelong engagement with ideas that is documented in her letters explains why she could envisage a positive role for the radical utopian ideas of David Crimmond in *The Book and the Brotherhood*. Just as she acknowledges the role of Oakeshott's pernicious doctrines in developing her own contrary political ideas, so she allows a positive role for opposing grand narratives towards the end of her life.

Murdoch's letters to Brigid Brophy show her willingness to entertain a fluidity in sexuality that is at odds with sexual stereotyping and disturbs the rigidities of a dichotomous sexual divide between male and female. Murdoch's attitude towards sexuality in these letters harmonizes with her long term support for the legalization of homosexuality. Murdoch's novels, of course, show a variety of sexual and romantic relations. In an early representation of homosexuality in *The Bell* (1958) Michael Meade's sexual problems stem at least in part from the prevailing atmosphere of legal and cultural repression of homosexuality, whereas a later representation of a homosexual relationship between Simon and Axel in *A Fairly Honourable Defeat* shows it to be capable of flourishing in a more tolerant atmosphere. In one of her letters to Michael Oakeshott,

Murdoch writes of the positive effects of her marriage to John Bayley in stabilizing her emotional life. It is a rare comment on her marriage but it rings true. Her fiction looks at marriage from a variety of perspectives. Some individuals, like Harriet in *The Sacred and Profane Love Machine* (1975) suffer from being absorbed uncritically into a marriage that they do not question. The marriage of Rupert and Hilda Foster in *A Fairly Honourable Defeat* appears to operate well but collapses under the weight of the pressures that are applied to it. Charles Arrowby in *The Sea, The Sea* (1978) in his quixotic pursuit of his childhood sweetheart Hartley fails utterly to understand her marriage. For the most part, this is due to his distorted vision of the world, but it also reflects the mystery of marriage. A relationship, such as a marriage, will be mysterious to someone who does not know the commitment from the inside. In *Something Special* (1999) Yvonne Geary has resisted the tide of marriage but then suddenly, she makes a leap of faith and commits herself.[72]

Murdoch's life and her letters relate to her philosophy and her novels because her life is a reflective life that takes notice of what is going on in the cultural and political world. She commits to a moral life in which she is self-critical and giving so as to align herself to the good that she discusses in her moral philosophy. Murdoch might not have been the saint that some commentators have suggested, but neither is her life to be dismissed as being entangled in torrid relationships. Murdoch was not perfect but a perfectionist morality does not assume perfection on the part of individuals. What it implies is a commitment to work for the good in loving relations with others. There is evidence that Murdoch endeavoured to do this in the relationships on which we have focused. Her life relates to her intellectual life in many ways. It helps us make sense of her thinking. Her philosophy aims to bring together the diverse strands of experience and her own life is both a resource for the experience that her philosophy and literary imagination work with and a translation of her ideas into practice. Murdoch always remained a philosopher who was different from the caricature of a dry as dust theorist, who is uninterested in the world. The excitement of her engagement with philosophy can be seen in the way she talks of her developing ideas in letters to Queneau and her engaged style of thinking is conveyed throughout her life. The letters and her life might be of interest for all sorts of reasons. The very multiplicity and diversity of her relationships is not something to sneer at but to see as contributing to her multidimensional talents and the range of her thinking and her literary imagination. Her life and letters can be understood in many ways but their greatest value lies in the way that they connect with the public Murdoch and her novels and philosophical writings.

CHAPTER SEVEN

Conclusion

Introduction

Integral to Murdoch's achievements in the several fields in which she flourished is her sense of the ambivalence of the times in which she lived. On the one hand, she is an exemplary modern, believing passionately in freedom and individuality that serve as hallmarks of the modern persona. As a woman, she did not believe in sitting back and playing a secondary role. From the outset she was driven to succeed in the areas to which she devoted her talents.[1] Her drive was accelerated by the experience of the Second World War and the prospect of further wars. In a letter to her friend Raymond Queneau of 1946, she explains how the atmosphere of uncertainty makes her want to do things rather than to sit back. She explains, 'In a year or two we may all be blown in some grand atomic experiment and then you would never know.'[2] The wartime Soho crowd of Bohemians fascinated her. They were not interested in staid conventions, but in their own artistic freedom. In her moral philosophy, commitments are to be undertaken freely by individuals. Stuart Cuno in *The Good Apprentice* (1985) and John Ducane in *The Nice and the Good* (1968) do not follow a metaphysical script in moving towards the good. They find their own individual pathways. For Murdoch, morals are not to be imposed upon others. In *The Sacred and Profane Love Machine* (1974) Harriet, the deceived wife of Blaise Gavender, realizes that her unreflective submission to conventions has been insufficient to sustain a good life. The individual must engage freely and critically with conventions.

Murdoch's life was conducted very much in a style of her own. She neither submitted to conventional constrictions on sexuality nor expected others to do so. She accepted bisexuality and in maintaining multiple loving relationships she was, what might now be termed polyamorous, though she was careful to avoid sexual relations where they might compromise enduring commitments.[3] She argued that homosexuals should enjoy the freedom that had been reserved conventionally for heterosexuals, and her novels portray homosexual relationships sympathetically. Her novels are truthful in their evocation of the situations that can emerge from the freely undertaken actions of intersecting and interrelating individuals. Paths are taken that lead to selfishness and misery, and occasionally to virtue and moral enlightenment. Her novels' characters are realistic creations, whose freedom to lose or find their way is never questioned. Characters have abortions, attempt suicide and undertake homosexual or heterosexual affairs, some of which are intergenerational and some of which break taboos. These actions are neither condemned nor supported, but the freedom of the actions and the actors is respected.

While Murdoch turns her back on past forms of authoritarianism in morality and politics, she recognizes the loss that accompanies the freedom that is achieved by breaking from preceding restraints and from traditional ways of operating. Processes of demythologization have undermined traditional religious beliefs, metaphysics and unquestioning attitudes to social and political institutions. Murdoch refuses to turn back to pre-modern beliefs and ways of thinking. History cannot be undone. At the same time, however, she recognizes how individuals require more than a degree of freedom that only registers the bare capacity to choose this, rather than that. What she proposes is to rework traditional forms of thinking so as to render them relevant to a modern world. Modernity's repudiation of supernatural beliefs and extra-experiential forms of knowledge must be acknowledged, while reflection upon how an individual is to orient themselves within the wide scheme of things requires revisiting. In the spheres of metaphysics, morality, politics, religion and art Murdoch admits that former dogmas cannot be rehearsed, but she continues to imagine that these forms of thought and action are more than forms of self-assertion.

Murdoch's metaphysics locates individuals on a general map of experience, which relates its messiness to a supervening goodness that can be accessed so as to guide moral life. Instead of submitting to a stripped-down version of philosophy that refrains from attending to values, Murdoch reworks metaphysics so as to provide a vision of an underlying meaning to experience. Her metaphysics is not a species of logical rationalism but, rather, relies upon and responds to experiential support. Its credentials are not unassailable. In 'On "God" and "Good"', she writes, 'On the status of the argument there is perhaps little, or else too much to say ... All one can do is to appeal to certain areas of experience, pointing out certain features, and using suitable metaphors and inventing suitable concepts where necessary to make these features visible.'[4] For Murdoch, a revived metaphysics that steers clear of an a priori approach can provide a wider vision of things to which individuals can orient themselves. Modern moral theory and practice have suffered from restricting unduly the terms of moral discourse. In differing idioms, Continental and Anglo-American moral theories have concentrated on the rational agency of individuals in making choices about their conduct to the exclusion of attending to ways of seeing the world that shape these choices. They disregard the imperative of adopting a critical perspective on the practice of making choices. Like other critics of mainstream modern moral philosophy, such as MacIntyre, Murdoch turns to a kind of virtue ethics. For Murdoch, the qualities that an individual possesses in attending to and caring for other individuals and the truth matter more in moral life than a mere capacity to make choices.[5]

Murdoch's moral philosophy favours a certain style of individuality, one that is attuned to what lies outside the self. The virtues that Murdoch values are a loving disposition towards others and a moral aspiration towards perfection rather than an inwardness that focuses upon the self. Murdoch's perfectionism judges experiential commitments in the light of an ideal standard but this standard does not represent an otherworldly attitude. In politics she settles for establishing a political order that would secure the safety of individuals, so that they can develop their personal lives and a perfectionist notion of the good. But if there are limits to politics and what it is to do, these limits are not fixed. The political world requires continual attention. Axioms of politics are to be set that protect individuals' rights and welfare, yet these axioms are not set in stone. Changing formulations of the good influence the ongoing framing of axioms. Ecological arguments, for instance, may serve in the formulation of new axioms covering the environment.[6] Unlike

Rawls's delimitation of the public sphere, Murdoch does not fix the sphere of the political and appropriate public reasoning in advance and she allows for general moral views to exert an ongoing impact on the public sphere.[7] For Murdoch there is a dialectical interaction between the personal and political, with the public arena protecting and responding to developments in personal moral viewpoints. *The Book and the Brotherhood* (1987) is a late novel that is focused upon a projected text in radical political theory. The projected text asks questions of the modern world, highlighting the complacency of the West and the human needs that have not been met by bourgeois Parliamentary democracy. The question that may be asked of the text itself concerns its own role as a grand narrative. Given the decline in radical ideological thinking and the need to safeguard the rights that individuals enjoy in liberal democracy, do we still need grand narratives that challenge prevailing presumptions and entertain radical futures? Notwithstanding Murdoch's own late inclination to adopt a cautious approach to politics, she appears to recognize that political debate requires the continuation of grand narratives to promote theoretical discussion of possibilities. Even caution in politics requires argument and its merits can be clarified by resisting the advocacy of reckless change.

Murdoch accepts that erstwhile religious beliefs in the supernatural powers of a personal God can no longer be maintained in a modern world that accepts the presumptions of science and the empirical limits of our understanding of the world. Yet she argues that the maintenance of religion conduces to a person's training in morality and to their recognition of the importance of adhering to the good and avoiding evil. Religious practice and a spiritual sensibility alert to world religions other than Christianity and to mysticism offer possibilities of religious support for morality in a sceptical age. Art, likewise, must retain something of its sense of being in touch with truth and of contributing to our appreciation of real things in the world. It is a failure of nerve to side with conceptual art's demolition of the identity of art and to go along with the deconstructionists, who undermine the creative role that has traditionally been assigned to the artist. Art must still be seen to play its creative role in enhancing our conception of experience. While modern novels are not to recapitulate former forms of literary realism, they should still create realistic characters, whose interactions stir our sense of what it means to be an individual.

Murdoch on Plato

The ambiguities of Murdoch's reading of modern times are captured in her interpretation of Plato. This is no accident as Murdoch read the Ancient Plato through modern eyes. Plato is invoked by Murdoch to provide a counter to those fissiparous tendencies in modernity that undermine a sense of the unity of experience. Plato symbolizes a commitment to take experience as exhibiting an underlying order. In *Metaphysics as a Guide to Morals* and in her unpublished 'Manuscript on Heidegger' Murdoch offers a metaphysical reading of experience in a cultural climate that is unsympathetic to the enterprise. The idea of philosophers providing a top-down set of principles to explain experience as a whole is out of fashion. Post-Kantian philosophy renounces a super-sensible role for reason that does not accommodate to sense experience. Murdoch's metaphysics draws upon experience in articulating a synoptic perspective on things. Murdoch looks to Plato as a paradigmatic predecessor, whose metaphysics provides a metaphorical way of understanding the unity of our experience. Reality consists in the forms that constitute paradigmatic objects of knowledge to which changeable experiential things are related. The Good is the ultimate metaphorical explanation of things and of values to which aspects of the experiential world are related. The Good might transcend things in the world but it is not otherworldly. It relates to and explains things in experience. Murdoch reads Plato as imagining the Good as a metaphor for an ultimate explanation of things and its metaphorical status is held to be an index of Plato's recognition that he is unable to provide a complete account of his metaphysics.

Murdoch understands the Platonic form of the Good as being able to play a credible and crucial role in moral philosophy. The good anchors a conception of morality as reaching out beyond merely individual choices to constitute a perfectionism to which individual moral actions are to be aligned. In 'The Sovereignty of Good over Other Concepts' (1967), Murdoch observes,

> Good is a concept about which, and not only in philosophical language, we naturally use a Platonic terminology, when we speak about seeking the Good, or loving the Good ... or all our frailty the command 'be perfect' has sense for us. The concept

Good resists collapse into the selfish empirical consciousness. It is not a mere value tag of the choosing will.[8]

For Murdoch, Plato's metaphor of the Good can be resumed because it can still perform an important role in moral philosophy. Moral decisions are not to be equated with what is conducive to the maximization of individual volitions. Our sense of what is required of us is not exhausted by aligning what is to be done merely with our choices. We have a sense that we can take wrong turnings. Some things matter in ways that suggest it is not enough simply to do what seems appropriate to us. What we choose should be aligned to what supersedes our interests. We should look outside ourselves to take into account the world as it appears to others. For Murdoch, it makes sense to see morality in the light of a goodness that goes beyond our individual interests and perspectives, though Plato's morality is not to be taken as a form of other-worldliness which lacks reference to our experiential world. Murdoch imagines our moral perspective is always provisional, and is to be subject to criticism so that we strive to realize a perfectionist goal of a transcendent goodness. Self-criticism is required. The work of the mother (M) in Murdoch's 'The Idea of Perfection' (1964) is exemplary in that her attitude to her daughter-in-law (D) was amended in the light of the critical work that she undertook upon her attitude.[9] The morality of the mother (M) is not remote but is one that looks more closely at the world to correct her initial standpoint. Likewise Bruno in *Bruno's Dream* (1969) does not look away from the world as he approaches his death. Rather he looks more closely at it and at the partiality of his own previous perspective so that at the last he opens to who he is and to what he has done.[10] Murdoch sees her own moral perfectionism to be foreshadowed in Plato's. It is a perfectionism of aspiration and our actual efforts to realize perfection are always provisional and imperfect. Murdoch recognizes her own sense of the provisional and corrigible character of philosophical and moral reasoning in Plato's acknowledgement that he has never resolved philosophical issues so as to furnish the certain knowledge to which he aspired.

Murdoch's reading of Plato serves as a way of reviving metaphysics and an objectivist morality, which at the same time conforms to modern demands. Hence philosophy is to be kept within the bounds of sense and morality is to presume the freedom of individuals in making their own fallible moral decisions. This is an interpretation of Plato that runs up against obstacles, because Plato appears to say things that run counter to Murdoch's modern reading. At times, Plato dismisses the phenomenal world and looks to a separate world of ideals. In the *Republic* the point of a philosophical education is to divert attention away from the phenomenal world.[11] Plato also maintains that art should be subject to political control, because the artist allows imagination rather than reason to dictate what is to feature in a work of art. Murdoch herself also recognizes that individual freedom is a modern phenomenon that was not conceptualized by Plato.[12] Plato's politics presumes rather than criticizes slavery. In the *Republic* he proposes a rigid class system that excludes classes of people from decision-making and allows the ruling class to make authoritarian decisions on art, and to exert control over the family life of the ruling class.

Murdoch's strategy in defending her view of Plato is twofold. On the one hand, she downplays those elements of Plato's philosophy that appear to conflict with her modern reading of his thought, and on the other hand she foregrounds those aspects of his thought that seem to fit with her own philosophizing in the present. In playing down the unacceptable, she suggests that Plato's politics should not be taken too seriously. The Ancient world was a long time ago and we should not expect to encounter modern political formulas in Plato's texts. Moreover, like Leo Strauss, she imagines that Plato's politics were never meant to be put into practice.[13] Again while she critiques Plato's view of art due to her respect for the credentials of art, she also complicates the picture by imagining Plato himself to be an artist as much as a philosopher. On this reading Plato resorts to metaphor rather than systematic dialectical analysis because of his artistry rather than due to his reservations over his own philosophizing. Murdoch's reading of Plato is ambiguous. She sidelines much of what he has to say and offers an interpretation that is not overburdened by scholarship. For instance, her dating of the dialogues was not informed by recent scholarly studies.[14] At times she runs together her own ideas with those of Plato's in presenting her critique of contemporary moral philosophy.[15] She herself discloses what she is up to by explaining that she is putting Plato's 'argument into a modern context'.[16] It is an interpretation that self-consciously relates Plato to a modern world and to the arguments that Murdoch wants to make against the philosophical assumptions of her time. The retreat from metaphysics and the moral subjectivism of her time are to be countered by drawing selectively on Plato. Moreover, as Tracy observes, Murdoch's use of Plato has a shock value in that Plato was radically out of favour among contemporary analytic philosophers.[17] Murdoch may be said to be offering a Gadamerian view of Plato in that Gadamer's hermeneutic view of intellectual history operates by fusing past horizons with those of the present. Gadamer himself admired Plato, and imputed to him a hermeneutical perspective that anticipates his own by his use of the dialogue form, whereby truth emerges from an exchange of views between dialogical participants.[18] What is not fully addressed in Murdoch's reading of Plato is Plato's deprecation of individual freedom and democracy. Murdoch herself accepts the modern ideal of freedom, even if she is a critic of the reduction of morality to that of freedom of choice. In her unpublished 'Manuscript on Heidegger', for instance, she critiques Heidegger precisely because he does not take into account the rights that have been granted to women in modern times that allow for a more general and equitable distribution of freedoms.[19]

Hegel on Plato

Plato's ambivalent reading of Plato is brought into focus by reviewing Hegel's opposed but equally ambivalent reading. Both Hegel and Murdoch address Plato in the light of their own readings of modernity. In his youth Hegel was a critic of modernity. His *Early Theological Writings* highlights the deficiencies of the modern world in that it critiques its lack of social and political community and its inflated and dislocating individualism.[20] Like many contemporary Germans, he looked back nostalgically upon Ancient Greece, admiring what he perceived to be its harmony and sense of community.[21] Hegel continued to perceive problems in the modern world throughout his career, but by the time he developed his mature philosophical system he had come to see the modern world as expressing a complex unity that included individual freedom. For the mature Hegel, the Ancient Greek world forms a stage in historical development that despite its beauty is superseded by the modern world.[22] The modern state, for Hegel possesses a depth that was not admitted in the Ancient Greek polis, because it allows for the freedom of individuals. The differences between Ancient and modern politics are brought out by Hegel in his *Philosophy of Right*. In its Preface, Hegel argues that philosophy relates to the historic cultures in which it is set, so that political philosophy does not innovate, but, rather rehearses the rationality of the historical form of politics that it reflects upon. He observes, 'When philosophy paints its grey on grey, then has a form of life grown old. By philosophy's grey on grey, a form of life cannot be rejuvenated but only understood. The owl of Minerva spreads its wings only with the falling of the dusk.'[23] Hegel identifies his own task to be that of articulating the rationality of the modern state, and in so doing to show its rational progress from preceding forms of political order. Subsequently, in the course of the text Hegel critiques Plato. He identifies the limits of Plato's political philosophy in its rehearsal of the features of the traditional Greek polis and in its omission of individual freedoms that distinguish the modern state. He remarks,

> In his *Republic* Plato displays the substance of ethical life in its ideal beauty and truth: but he could only cope with the principle of self-subsistent particularity, which in his day had forced its way into ethical life by setting it up in opposition to his purely substantial state. He absolutely excluded it from his state, even in its very beginning in private property and the family as well as in its more mature form as the subjective will, the choice of a social position and so forth.[24]

In contrast to Murdoch, Hegel aims to show that Plato does not provide a model for ethical life within the modern world, because the Ancient world lacked defining features of a modern world. The modern world, for Hegel, differs from what has gone before in allowing for moral and political freedom and notably for the freedom to participate in what Hegel terms civil society. For Hegel, modern individuals right demand the freedom of their moral conscience, which is to be satisfied within a political framework that establishes the legal rules that regulate social life. The modern development of civil society, which was unknown to the Ancient world, includes all the social activities that are not directly organized by the state. Central to those activities is the market, which allows for economic freedom even if its propensity to promote selfishness and to generate unemployment and structural poverty demands the intervention of a regulative state to counteract its antisocial tendencies. Hegel's rational state incorporates spheres of freedom for the individual, including those of civil society that he takes to be lacking in Plato's view of the world. Plato is not to be blamed for the shortcomings of his ethical and political perspective, that exclude a modern and Hegelian conception of freedom, because philosophy is intimately bound up with history. Hegel's *Lectures on the History of Philosophy* also review Plato at some length. At the outset he expresses his admiration for Plato as a teacher of the human race.[25] Plato is taken to be an objective idealist, who, like Hegel himself, imagines thought to be within the world. If he is positive about Plato's fundamental contribution to philosophy, Hegel is also critical of his inconsistent development of a systematic approach. Hegel reads Plato to be somewhat systematic in that he takes the *Timaeus*, the *Parmenides* and the *Republic* to form the three related strands of a system that resembles his own. He remarks, 'If the *Parmenides* be taken along with the *Republic* and the *Timaeus* the three together constitute the whole Platonic system of philosophy divided into three parts or sections – Logic, Mind and Nature.'[26] Yet Hegel considers Plato to be insufficiently systematic in that his resort to mere artistry and suggestiveness detract from the systematic nature of his writing. Hegel, then, sees Plato as an important contributor to the development of philosophy, but his contribution is limited by the context in which it appears. His thinking reflects the character of the Greek Polis, and his historical role as an early contributor to philosophy entails that his thought does not reach the systematic form of expression that it will assume in its latest guise.

Murdoch, Plato and Hegel

Murdoch and Hegel are ambivalent on Plato. They interpret him by reviewing his thought in the light of their own readings of the present, and in particular to their related but differing views on the modern world. However, they adopt opposing views of Plato and imagine that his thought relates to their own philosophies and worlds in contrary ways. They both perceive the modern world to be very different from Plato's world. For Hegel, Plato's relevance to the modern world is indirect and limited. According to Hegel, Plato stands for a way of viewing the world that precludes individual freedom and the rights of private property, the rule of law and the political representation of citizens. Plato's thought, for Hegel, is tied to his historical context and what comes later, namely the modern world, is more complex, and cannot be anticipated by Plato, a preceding thinker. The modern world is to be theorized in ways that postdate the assumptions of preceding thinkers. Murdoch agrees that the modern world is different from Plato's. She acknowledges that the distance in time between her age and Plato's exculpates Plato for his endorsement of slavery. Likewise she accepts Hegel's identification of the modern state with a novel recognition of individual freedom. Nonetheless, Plato's thought, for Murdoch, can contribute to modern moral philosophy and to modern moral agency. She sees Plato's conception of the good as representing a standard of perfection that individuals can continue to look to for guidance in their moral lives. Like Hegel, she admires Plato's philosophy as a whole, but unlike Hegel, she takes his unsystematic presentation of his views to serve as a continuing paradigm rather than serving as an index of its contribution to an embryonic stage of philosophical development. For Murdoch, Plato's use of metaphor remains exemplary and metaphysics is not to aspire to a watertight set of logical doctrines. Its role of connecting together aspects of experience persuasively requires the use of metaphor and allusion.

Murdoch's interpretation of Plato is insightful in its identification of Plato's continuous questing for truth and reality, which is intimated in his resort to art and metaphor. This aspect of Plato's thought is misrecognized by Hegel. To see Plato as advancing a system of Logic, Mind and Nature is to misread him as anticipating Hegel's own later philosophizing. Murdoch is also imaginative and insightful in construing Plato's theory of forms as allowing for a lack of closure on the part of epistemological and moral endeavour, due to the gap that is presumed between the forms and experiential theory and practice. Any particular action or thought will always be distinct from the form to which it is correlated, and so individuals can thereby be imagined as endlessly aiming to realize the good but without ever enacting or exhausting the good itself. Murdoch contrasts an open Plato with a closed Hegel, in that Hegel is taken to hold a teleological theory, which encapsulates individual activity within a deterministic historical process. Hegel has been interpreted variously and sophisticated interpretations of Hegel take him to have developed an open system. However, Murdoch's Platonic critique of Hegel is perceptive precisely because it is Hegel's highly contextual reading of Plato, which raises doubts about Hegel's enterprise. Hegel's interpretation of Plato indicates that he limits severely the freedom of historical thinkers and actors to think and act outside of contextual restraints that are set by an overly deterministic reading of history.

Hegel's Plato, however, raises questions for Murdoch's conception of Plato. Hegel shows how the freedom of the modern individual, in economic, moral and political life is different from the world of Plato. The idea of conscience and the freedoms to own property and exercise economic and political agency are not endorsed by Plato. In relating Plato's thought to contemporary morality Murdoch does not address the problem that arises from invoking a pre-modern thinker in a radically different context in which freedom is central. Modern moral theory and practice presumes the centrality of freedom and individual agency. Morality, on this modern view, is not to be seen in hierarchical or authoritarian terms, and depends upon the unconstrained agency of individuals for its enactment. In invoking Plato Murdoch tends to play down the role of freedom in her essays of moral theory that compose *The Sovereignty of Good* (1970). She is critical of contemporary theories that reduce morality to the bare notion of freedom and the choices of individuals. Of course, she is not denying the role of agency and deliberative reflection in moral life, but her use of Platonic concepts, and her criticisms of theories that extol inadequately formulated notions of agency, appears to minimize the positive role of deliberative reflective agency in her own moral philosophy.

In her novels, Murdoch shows multiple forms of individual agency and freedom as operating in modern moral life. She is critical of the selfishness and distorted perceptions of individual characters, but she assumes that the drama of modern life involves the exercise of agency. Her novels show the interactions of free individuals. Moreover, she is sympathetic to extending the range of agency to include sexual freedom. In her essay 'The Moral Choice about Homosexuality', she argues for extending sexual freedom to homosexuals and her novels show the ill-effects of the cultural and legal repression of homosexuals. She also deals with agents having abortions, attempting suicide and practising euthanasia in ways that at least display a sympathy with the exercise of agency in these areas. Plato's *Republic* is critical of the exercise of agency when it is not supervised by those that possess hierarchical authority. Art is to be censored, class roles are to be assigned and family life and property arrangements among the ruling class are to be tightly regulated. Murdoch responds to the authoritarianism of Plato by playing down the practicality of his political project and by pointing to his own artistic prowess. The authoritarian side of Plato's thought, however, is not removed altogether by these interpretive manoeuvres.

Plato is not a liberal and Murdoch's use of Plato to develop a critique of contemporary moral theory runs the risk of being misunderstood as being illiberal. In fact, Murdoch imagines individual freedom to be central to moral life in a way that Plato does not. Perhaps the danger of confusion is worth running as Murdoch values what Plato brings to moral discussion. In the modern world she is right to insist that the mere assertion of agency and choice is insufficient to explain moral life. A larger vision of things is required so that individuals can widen their perception to see more than the projections of their own desires and fantasies. Murdoch in interpreting Plato is going 'where the honey is' and she finds in Plato a discourse about morality that stirs modern assumptions and captures something important that is in danger of being lost.[27] Moreover, her use of Plato rightly assumes that the past is not insulated from the present and that past thought can bear upon present circumstances. There is no logical reason why a preceding thinker cannot be used to contribute to a subsequent discourse. Hegel is wrong to imagine past theory is encapsulated by a past context. Plato himself in the *Republic* advocated the equality of women for his ruling class, which conflicted with existing norms.[28]

Murdoch and Hegel, in considering Plato, relate his thought to modern life and in doing so highlight different features of modernity, which are instructive to compare. Hegel sees his own historical metaphysics as the culmination of philosophy in underpinning ethical, political and religious life. Rational foundations for social and political life are provided by reading history as culminating in a teleological outcome that explains the course of history and the development of the human activities of politics, art, religion and philosophy. Hegel imagines his teleology as responding positively to the challenge presented by Kant of working with a notion of reason that is limited by the bounds of sense. Murdoch's view of modernity comes after Hegel and she attends to the continuing processes of demythologization that have led to a further decline of metaphysics, the erosion of supernatural beliefs and a personal God in religion, the deprecation of artistic truth, the supersession of grand ideologies and the loss of an objective grounding of moral concepts. Hegel's historical metaphysics has not halted these ongoing processes. In her study of Heidegger, Murdoch praises Hegel as one of the two preceding metaphysicians that she aims to emulate.[29] However, she rejects Hegel's project of providing an absolutist reading of the process of historical development.[30] While accepting the impetus behind modern processes of demythologization, Murdoch revives Plato's moral and metaphysical vocabulary to contribute to her project of continuing metaphysics, and maintaining the integrity of moral life and the possibilities of art and religion. She shows an awareness of the acuteness of the dangers posed to these areas of life by the ongoing processes of modernity, which Hegel's confidence in his own metaphysics presumed to supersede.[31] Unlike Hegel, she also recognizes the indeterminacy of philosophical argument in supporting a modern form of metaphysics.

Hegel's confidence in his own capacity to frame a metaphysics that provides an absolute conception of the modern world is not shared by Murdoch.[32] She recognizes the insusceptibility of her own metaphysics to a form of decisive justification. In her 'Manuscript on Heidegger', in 'On "God" and "Good"', and in *Metaphysics as a Guide to Morals* she admits the indeterminacy of what she offers. Her experiential transposition of the ontological argument depends on our faith in things rather than on a logical proof. In *The Unicorn* (1963) the old and wise scholar, Max Lejour delivers what comes close to Murdoch's own viewpoint in observing,

> What we can *see* determines what we choose. Good is the distant source of light, it is the unimaginable object of our desire. Our fallen nature knows only its name and its perfection. That is the idea which is vulgarized by existentialists and linguistic philosophers when they make good into a mere matter of personal choice, It cannot be defined not because it is a function of our freedom, but because we do not know it ... All religions

are mystery religions. The only proof of God is the ontological proof, and that is a mystery. Only the spiritual man can give it to himself in secret.[33]

Murdoch's metaphysics is avowedly open and insusceptible of definitive proof. Its corroboration depends upon its sensitivity to experience, which is for each person to judge. Murdoch might have said more about how we are to discriminate between metaphysical accounts of experience, though her reading of Heidegger in her 'Manuscript on Heidegger' is instructive. It is a reading in which she develops her own countervailing thoughts and offers judgments on how well Heidegger's thought fits with notable aspects of our experience. She asks pertinent and down to earth questions of Heidegger and crucially she finds him lacking due to his omission of ordinary features of moral experience. A comparison of Murdoch with Hegel serves as a related means of assessing her metaphysics.

In contrast to Murdoch, Hegel points to the role of institutions and practices within civil society and the political state in shaping a distinctive modern social world. Hegel sees the market as an important element in modern society in its promotion of freedom and in its creation of problems, including structural unemployment and poverty, and a consequential alienation. He imagines the political state to play a role in maintaining representational institutions to alleviate these problems. The state's policies unite citizens in constituting a community that replicates and develops the unity of family life. While Hegel's proposed solutions to the problems of civil society are by no means convincing, they do ask further questions of Murdoch. As a political theorist she tends to ignore economic issues such as economic hardship, poverty and unemployment in the modern world. She has little to say about the workings of political institutions and their representativeness. Her novels also tend to focus upon the well-to-do and for the most part ignore socioeconomic issues. In reviewing Murdoch's novels in *Iris Murdoch – Work for the Spirit*, Dipple observes, 'Murdoch's ostensibly bourgeois mode has called out hostility from both conventional novel readers and critics.'[34] Dipple defends the art of Murdoch but recognizes the restricted social range of her characters, noting 'The world that Murdoch knows best is always her subject, and if this means a proliferation of civil servants and middle-class types, her uncanny achievement shows how little the contours of an original and varied series of novels are limited by such necessities.'[35]

Murdoch's relative neglect of socioeconomic issues is not to be denied, but she highlights the provision of basic rights or axioms, which are envisaged as changing over time in response to developing perceptions of welfare needs.[36] Where Hegel sees colonialism as contributing to the development of Western economies, Murdoch's cryptic reference to the possible demise of the Western nation state opens up a prospect of an internationalism that harmonizes with her appreciation of the plight of migrants throughout her life. In her critique of Heidegger's metaphysics, Murdoch also points out the significance of egalitarian political reforms in Western societies.[37] Moreover, Dipple is right to raise objections to any facile characterization of Murdoch's novels as supporting bourgeois privilege. Dipple observes, 'A patient study of Murdoch's work reveals how deceptive the bourgeois surface in fact is, and how ironic her deployment of its materials.'[38] Dipple is perceptive in recognizing Murdoch's critique of bourgeois moral smugness. Murdoch is acute in exposing bourgeois complacency and hypocrisy. At the outset of *A Fairly Honourable Defeat* (1970) the bourgeois couple Rupert and Hilda Foster appear secure and content. The novel opens with their installation of a swimming pool in the garden of their exclusive London house, a piece of conspicuous consumption to testify to their wealth and comfortable lifestyle. However, the action of the novel undermines the presumptions of their lives. Rupert's vanity and complacency is an easy target for Julius's malign plotting and their marriage is destroyed. Rupert ends up dead, in the swimming pool.

In his account of an ethical community in the modern world, Hegel provides a positive reading of the modern family as furnishing a loving context in which children can be nurtured. This notion of family life is expressly distinguished from Plato's plans for nurturing the children of his ideal ruling class of guardians. Yet Hegel's patriarchal family is restrictive and is liable, literally and figuratively, to abuse. Murdoch's openness to sexual freedom and to the lifting of legal restrictions on sexuality harmonizes with an increasing fluidity in sexual identity of more recent times. Murdoch see the possibilities of personal development as residing in exploring forms of friendship rather than relying on the family and organizations within civil society. Personal relationships for Murdoch furnish the loving context in which individuals can flourish and for many individuals in the modern Western world friendship is an important vehicle for spiritual growth. It is true that the personal is not entirely removed from public considerations and Lovibond has critiqued Murdoch for her failure to support a feminist agenda of collective action.[39] Murdoch, however, is aware of the interrelations between the public and the personal and she views the development of women's rights to be a significant historical development.[40] Likewise the voice and tone of male characters are deconstructed in her novels.

Reviewing Murdoch's reading of Plato in the light of Hegel's rival account of Plato and modernity, allows critical judgments to be made on Murdoch's use of Plato and on her reading of the modern world. There are pros and cons in her use of Plato. On the one hand, her reading of Plato is subtle and recognizes his reliance upon metaphor and his unsystematic style of philosophizing that never claims to provide definitive knowledge. She also deploys Plato to positive effect in critiquing contemporary forms of moral philosophy that identify morality with mere choice. Plato's perfectionism is invoked to telling effect in highlighting what is missing from modern accounts of moral life. Her reading of Plato, however, tends to gloss over his authoritarianism and his subordination of the individual to the requirements of philosophical truth and political power. Her use of Plato to critique modern moral philosophy also tends to underplay her commitment to the role of the free deliberation of individuals in moral reasoning. What stands out in Murdoch's reading of the modern world when contrasted with Hegel's is her emphasis upon processes of demythologization and upon sexual freedom. These aspects of modernity have retained their significance in the light of continuing modern developments. Her analysis of modern politics is alert to the dangers of repressive forms of utopianism, though it tends to neglect engagement with social and economic issues and the details of institutional arrangements. Murdoch uses Plato to understand modern times in a different way from Hegel. She uses Plato to criticize aspects of modernity, most notably its moral practice, whereas Hegel, for the most part, defends modernity against Plato's pre-modern standpoint.

Why Iris Murdoch matters

In considering how and why Murdoch matters it is worth rehearsing how Murdoch's use of Plato is striking and effective in critiquing problematic modern forms of theory and practice. Her critique continues to be relevant. Moral life, for Murdoch, is to be conceived neither as the mere calculation of interests nor as the manipulation of abstract procedures that minimizes attention to the specificities of situations. While experience is often muddled, the muddle does not preclude a Platonic aspiration to moral perfection. Perfectionism is an antidote to the queasy modern feeling that our uncritical acceptance of preferences can lead us to the wrong destination. Striving for perfection resists our tendency to subvert moral reflection by seeing the world only through our own distorting fantasies. Murdoch's revisionary practice of metaphysics might seem to hang on indeterminate means of support but reflection on experience and a comparison of metaphysical systems can establish critical means for its evaluation. Her novels may reflect a restricted range of characters and incorporate men as enjoying social advantages over women, but they raise questions about social structures and practices in simultaneously drawing us in and provoking us to consider the situations that they describe. Her politics may have lacked a focus upon economic circumstances and substantive issues of equality but she provides a dialectical reading of public and personal life that allows for political reform and personal freedom. Moreover, her life is a testimony to the possibilities of her philosophy notwithstanding the inevitable imperfections to which it was prone.

Iris Murdoch continues to matter for several reasons, and these reasons are appreciated by recognizing their interrelated character, which reflects the interdependencies between the various strands of her work. Murdoch developed a multidimensional understanding of the times in which she lived. Her pursuit of philosophy was framed by her reading of the peculiar modern circumstances in which it was to be undertaken. She was acutely aware of the post-Kantian situation, whereby metaphysics is no longer to operate dogmatically but is to respond to and reflect back upon experience. Is there a role for metaphysics in such a situation? Murdoch's answer was 'yes' and her answer continues to respond to our sense of wanting to explore experience by relating its several aspects to one another. To consider morality outside of its relations to politics is to limit our understanding of both and Murdoch's dialectical understanding of their relations shows her comprehensive approach to philosophy. Likewise her framing of a wider experiential context for morality appeals to our sense that the moral life involves more than a narrow focus upon accommodating conflicting subjective choices. Taylor is insightful in indicating how Murdoch turns a moral vocabulary of the rights of individuals into one that sets out the virtues that they require to achieve good or just ways of life, and also beyond that to one that imagines what commands unconditional commitment.[41] Murdoch's metaphysics is a guide to morals because it sets moral life in a wider setting, which encompasses a feeling of the void, of the reality of death and of loving and truthful relations with others. Her commitment to a metaphysics of experience that allows us to contextualize morality in a wider vision of things offers a continuing if indeterminate response to our sense of the interconnections between aspects of our experience.

Murdoch's moral philosophy remains as challenging today as when it was set out in the 1960s. Her summons of Plato to disturb a subjectivism that rests content with the choices that we habitually make continues to shock and stimulate in equal measure. It testifies to the awkwardness that we feel when we are tempted to deny that our moral decisions relate to matters that go beyond our own or everyone's choices. This awkwardness can be brought out by imaginative constructions of forms of life where there seems to be something at stake that goes beyond questions of our own welfare and preferences. Murdoch provides those imaginative fictional constructions. In *Bruno's Dream* the old and disintegrating Bruno lies in bed reflecting back on his life. He revisits the past and seeks to absolve himself from any wrong-doing. His racist remark was not really meant, his betrayal of his wife was not overly serious. But he continues to reflect on what has happened and, in the context of his own impending death, he moves to thinking beyond himself to embrace a loving perspective, where he does not set his own self apart from others so as to justify or excuse it. The need for justification recedes before a love that embraces others. Death is not sentimental in Murdoch's eyes but it can evoke an attitude that unsettles selfishness.[42] Murdoch's moral philosophy matters to us because what matters in morality goes beyond the self, and its choices, in ways that she has explored imaginatively and productively.

The example of the imaginative and realistic portrayal of death and redemption in *Bruno's Dream* reflects how Murdoch's novels are connected to her philosophy and yet retain an independence that renders them autonomous works of fiction rather than mouthpieces for an author's doctrines. Murdoch's novels are framed so as to present and testify to characters interacting freely so as to strain against the formal designs of their author. In so doing real characters exemplify aspects of experience that bear upon Murdoch's sense of how morality depends upon individuals looking outwards from themselves to notice and to love others, while for the most part they reduce things to their own egoistic agendas. Murdoch's philosophy does not dictate the content of a novel, for the freedom of individuals to pursue unspecified paths is presumed by her philosophical perspective. The novels, however, show how selfishness works itself out in specific situations and suggest here and there intimations of a moral perspective that supersedes egoism. In a letter to Conradi in which she comments on his reading of her novels, Murdoch observes, 'I like what you write, which seems to me on the right lines, only don't overdo the Platonism, dear boy.'[43] Murdoch's novels offer a richness of experience that is not to be condensed into a formula of Platonism. They are funny, playful, serious, sad and tragic. They are realistic and unsentimental. People die for no particular reasons and tend to leave no lasting legacy though occasionally, as with Bruno, they see things clearly before they expire. The sublime realism of her novels is what Murdoch intended them to achieve, and it might be said that this was a philosophical aim, albeit one that deliberately sets the novels apart from her philosophy. In their realism, they are imaginative constructions of life in the period after the Second World War, which incorporate the processes of demythologization that Murdoch identifies as shaping experience in the modern world, and to which Murdoch sees her philosophy as responding.

Murdoch's interest in politics continues to be underrated as an element of her work. Her metaphysics is discussed with minimal reference to its dialectical reading of the interrelations between morality and politics and her novels are taken to be absorbed by personal rather than public issues. Yet throughout her career Murdoch pointed to the interweaving of personal and public issues that remains of continuing relevance. Migration today assumes a centrality in a public discourse that appears to assume that it is a novel and previously unremarked phenomenon. Yet Murdoch's sensitive and realistic depiction of migrants is exemplary. The migrants to which she refers are not of a piece. Some are powerful, others are vulnerable; some are escaping persecution or the horrors of a concentration camp, others are carrying memories of what they have done to survive in such a camp. Above all Murdoch draws attention to the contingency and arbitrariness of relating a person's rights to their place of birth. Her sensitivity to the situation of migrants and the vividness of her description of their situation in, say, *The Flight from the Enchanter* speaks to us today and shows her capacity to imagine characters outside the bourgeois world. The impetus inspiring her call for a set of basic axioms or rights to protect individuals represents a recognition of the need to protect vulnerable individuals from social and political insecurities. Her openness to the possibility of a supra-state sphere of politics is perhaps directed towards resolving issues affecting migrants. Murdoch's warnings against schemes of utopian politics which subordinate individuals to projected forms of historical development continue to retain their force, as does her recognition of the continuing utility of grand narratives in articulating and testing our beliefs.

Murdoch continues to matter in all sorts of ways and her relevance is perhaps registered most clearly in the current interest in her personal life. The confused expression of this interest, which includes a fascination with her romantic attachments as well as with the sheer vitality of her friendships, suggests that we are not entirely clear about Murdoch's legacy. Above all, what her life reflects is not a random promiscuity but the practical relevance of her thought and published work. Murdoch was a wonderful novelist and insightful philosopher whose work constitutes an interconnected way of recognizing underlying patterns of unity and goodness to which we should respond. Her letters reveal the ways that she responds to experience and aims to conduct herself morally. She is far from perfect but her practical engagement with moral perfectionism renders her moral philosophy and her literary realism more intelligible. Her life represents a philosophy that she lived by, and which we too might live by.

NOTES

CHAPTER ONE

1 I. Murdoch, 'Letter to Raymond Queneau', 17 October 1947, in A. Horner and A. Rowe (eds), *Living on Paper – Letters from Iris Murdoch 1934–1995* (London: Chatto and Windus, 2015), p. 99.
2 I. Murdoch, 'Application for the Post of Tutor in Philosophy', St. Anne's College, St. Anne's College Library, p. 1.
3 Ibid.
4 Ibid., p. 2.
5 I. Murdoch, 'Dame Iris Murdoch's Address to Kingston University Humanities Graduates, the Barbican, London, 4 November, 1993', in Y. Moroya and P. Hullah (eds), *Occasional Essays by Iris Murdoch* (Okayama: University Education Press, 1998), pp. 49–53.
6 See I. Murdoch, *Metaphysics as a Guide to Morals* (London: Chatto and Windus, 1992), pp. 431–60.
7 I. Murdoch, 'Above the Gods: A Dialogue about Religion', in I. Murdoch (ed.), *Existentialists and Mystics – Writings on Philosophy and Literature* (London: Chatto and Windus, 1997).
8 Murdoch, *Metaphysics as a Guide to Morals*, p. 2.
9 The impetus behind Murdoch's metaphysics and moral philosophy lies in her revival of Plato for the modern world. It is a particular modernized Plato, and the character of her reading of Plato will be focused upon in later chapters. She draws upon Plato in most of her major philosophical texts. See, in particular, I. Murdoch, *The Fire and the Sun – Why Plato Banished the Artists* (Oxford: Oxford University Press, [1977] 1978); I. Murdoch, *The Sovereignty of Good* (London: Routledge, [1970] 1985); and Murdoch, *Metaphysics as a Guide to Morals*. In subsequent references to *The Fire and the Sun – Why Plato Banished the Artists* and *The Sovereignty of Good*, the reprinted versions of these texts, in Murdoch, *Existentialists and Mystics – Writings on Philosophy and Literature*, will be cited.

10 I. Murdoch, Journal 14, 1981–92, Iris Murdoch Archive, University
    of Kingston, p. 108. This phrase, and the attitude it represents, is
    important for Murdoch, and it occurs again in her 'Manuscript on
    Heidegger', Iris Murdoch Archive, University of Kingston, p. 19.

11 See I. Murdoch, 'Against Dryness', in Murdoch, *Existentialists and
    Mystics – Writings on Philosophy and Literature*, pp. 287–97; and
    Murdoch, 'The Fire and the Sun – Why Plato Banished the Artists'.

12 M. Antonaccio, *A Philosophy to Live By: Engaging Iris Murdoch*
    (Oxford: Oxford University Press, 2012), p. 4.

13 Murdoch, *Metaphysics as a Guide to Morals*, p. 7.

14 Murdoch witnessed the devastation of wartime lives in Europe at
    first-hand, and her thoughts on this and subsequent political events
    can be seen in her letters, her fiction and non-fictional writings. See,
    for instance, the selection of Murdoch's letters to Raymond Queneau
    and Philippa Foot that has been published in Rowe and Horner,
    Living on Paper – Letters from Iris Murdoch 1934–1995. See also
    I. Murdoch, Journals, Murdoch Archive, University of Kingston.
    Many of Murdoch's novels relate the experience of refugees from
    twentieth-century tyrannies. See, for instance, *The Time of the
    Angels* (Harmondsworth: Penguin, [1966] 1968), *The Flight from
    the Enchanter* (London: Vintage, [1956] 2000) and *The Nice and the
    Good* (London: Penguin Books, [1968] 2000).

15 I. Murdoch, 'Against Dryness', in Murdoch, *Existentialists and
    Mystics – Writings on Philosophy and Literature*, p. 291.

16 Murdoch, *The Time of the Angels*.

17 I. Murdoch, *The Philosopher's Pupil* (London: Vintage, [1983]
    2000), p. 187.

18 N. Forsberg, *Language Lost and Found – On Iris Murdoch and the
    Limits of Philosophical Discourse* (London: Bloomsbury, 2013),
    pp. 3–15.

19 'Iris Murdoch Talks to Stephen Glover', in G. Dooley (ed.), *From
    a Tiny Corner in the House of Fiction – Conversations with
    Iris Murdoch* (Columbia: University of South Carolina Press,
    2003), p. 36.

20 'Literature and Philosophy: A Conversation with Bryan Magee', in
    Murdoch, *Existentialists and Mystics – Writings on Philosophy and
    Literature*, p. 19.

21 See P. Conradi, *Iris Murdoch: The Saint and the Artist*
    (Basingstoke: Macmillan, 1986); A, N. Wilson, *Iris Murdoch: As
    I Knew Her* (London: Random House/Arrow, 2003). Wilson
    disparages her philosophy and Conradi tends to leave the philosophy
    to the commentaries of philosophers. See Chapter 6 for further
    discussion of this.

22 B. Heusel, *Patterned Aimlessness – Iris Murdoch's Novels of the 1970s and 1980s* (Athens: University of Georgia Press, 1995). See also M. Leeson, *Iris Murdoch: Philosophical Novelist* (London: Continuum, 2010); M. Antonaccio *Picturing the Human: The Moral Thought of Iris Murdoch* (Oxford: Oxford University Press, 2000).

23 Forsberg, *Language Lost and Found – On Iris Murdoch and the Limits of Philosophical Discourse*, pp. 15–57.

24 I. Murdoch, 'Against Dryness', in Murdoch, *Existentialists and Mystics – Writings on Philosophy and Literature*, p. 291.

25 See Murdoch, *Metaphysics as a Guide to Morals*, pp. 1–25.

26 Murdoch, 'The Fire and the Sun – Why Plato Banished the Artists'; Murdoch, *Existentialists and Mystics – Writings on Philosophy and Literature*, p. 456.

27 I. Murdoch, 'The Sublime and the Beautiful Revisited', in Murdoch, *Existentialists and Mystics – Writings on Philosophy and Literature*, p. 286.

28 See I. Murdoch, 'On God and Good', in Murdoch, *Existentialists and Mystics – Writings on Philosophy and Literature*, pp. 348–9.

29 Murdoch, *The Fire and the Sun – Why Plato Banished the Artists*; Murdoch, *Existentialists and Mystics – Writings on Philosophy and Literature*, p. 457.

30 Ibid., p. 461.

31 I. Murdoch, *The Nice and the Good.*

32 I. Murdoch, *A Fairly Honourable Defeat* (London: Chatto and Windus, 1970); Murdoch, *The Time of the Angels.*

33 I. Murdoch, *Sartre – Romantic Rationalist* (London: Fontana/Collins, 1976), p. 9.

34 S de Beauvoir, 'Literature and Metaphysics', in M. A. Simons with M. Timmerman and M. Mader (eds), *Philosophical Writings*, trans. V. Zayteff and F. Morrison (Urbana: University of Illinois Press, 2004), pp. 261–78.

35 Murdoch, *Sartre – Romantic Rationalist*, p. 10.

36 Murdoch, 'The Fire and the Sun – Why Plato Banished the Artists'.

37 See I. Murdoch, 'A House of Theory', in Murdoch, *Existentialists and Mystics – Writings on Philosophy and Literature.*

38 Forsberg, *Language Lost and Found – On Iris Murdoch and the Limits of Philosophical Discourse*, pp. 113–51.

39 I. Murdoch, 'Letter to Raymond Queneau', 2 June 1946, in Horner and Rowe, *Living on Paper – Letters from Iris Murdoch 1934–1995*, p. 72.

40 A. S. Byatt, *Degrees of Freedom – The Early Novels of Iris Murdoch* (London: Vintage, 1994), p. 31.

41 Ibid., pp. 9–40.

42 J.-P. Sartre, *Being and Nothingness*, trans. H. E. Barnes
    (New York: Washington Square Press, 1966).

43 I. Murdoch, 'Letter to Raymond Queneau', 7 August 1946, in
    Horner and Rowe, *Living on Paper – Letters from Iris Murdoch
    1934–1995*, p. 76.

44 Murdoch, *Sartre – Romantic Rationalist*, p. 32.

45 Ibid., p. 84.

46 I. Murdoch, 'On "God" and "Good"', in Murdoch, *Existentialists
    and Mystics – Writings on Philosophy and Literature*, pp. 341–2.

47 R. Moran, 'Iris Murdoch and Existentialism', in J. Broackes (ed.),
    Iris Murdoch Philosopher – A Collection of Essays (Oxford: Oxford
    University Press, 2012), p. 195.

48 Murdoch, *Metaphysics as a Guide to Morals*.

49 K. Ryan, 'Introduction', in I. Murdoch (ed.), *Under the Net*
    (London: Vintage, 2002), p. xvi.

50 H.D. Spear, *Iris Murdoch* (Basingstoke: Macmillan, 1995), p. 24.

51 I. Murdoch, *Under the Net* (London: Vintage, [1954] 2002),
    pp. 28–9.

52 Ibid., p. 65.

53 I. Murdoch, 'Manuscript on Heidegger', Iris Murdoch Archive,
    University of Kingston. The opening section of this manuscript has
    been published in J. Broackes (ed.), *Iris Murdoch, Philosopher –
    A Collection of Essays* (Oxford: Oxford University Press, 2012).

54 J. Bayley, *Iris – A Memoir of Iris Murdoch* (London: Duckworth,
    1998), pp. 17–19; and R. Eyre, *Iris* (West Hollywood: Paramount
    Pictures/Miramax, 2000).

55 'Introduction', in Horner and Rowe, *Living on Paper – Letters from
    Iris Murdoch 1934–1995*, p. xviii.

56 I. Murdoch, 'The Moral Decision about Homosexuality', in Muroya
    and Hullah, *Occasional Essays by Iris Murdoch*.

CHAPTER TWO

1 D. Tracy, 'Iris Murdoch and the Many Faces of Platonism', in M.
   Antonaccio and W. Schweiker (eds), *Iris Murdoch and the Search
   for Human Goodness* (Chicago: University of Chicago Press,
   1996), p. 58.

2 S. Rosen, Letter on the 'Manuscript on Heidegger', 2001, Iris
   Murdoch Archive, University of Kingston.

3 See H.-G. Gadamer, *Truth and Method*, trans. and rev. J.
   Weinscheiner and D. G. Marshall (London: Sheed and Ward, 1960).

For a wider discussion of the character of intellectual history, see G. Browning, *A History of Modern Political Thought – The Question of Interpretation* (Oxford: Oxford University Press, 2016).

4   See H.-G. Gadamer, 'Hermeneutics and Historicism', in Gadamer, *Truth and Method*; and R. G. Collingwood, *The Idea of History* (Oxford: Clarendon Press, 1946).

5   I. Murdoch, *Metaphysics as a Guide to Morals* (London: Chatto and Windus, 1992), pp. 185–217.

6   M. Antonaccio, 'Form and Contingency in Ethics', in Antonaccio and Schweiker, *Iris Murdoch and the Search for Human Goodness*, p. 112.

7   On the mirroring qualities of Murdoch's novels, see N. Forsberg, *Language Lost and Found – On Iris Murdoch and the Limits of Philosophical Discourse* (London: Bloomsbury, 2013), pp. 57–95.

8   Murdoch, *Metaphysics as a Guide to Morals*, p. 2.

9   Murdoch, Journal 4, 1947, Iris Murdoch Archive, p. 91.

10 Murdoch, *Metaphysics as a Guide to Morals*, p. 438.

11 Murdoch, Journal 4, 1947, Iris Murdoch Archive, p. 158.

12 Murdoch, *Metaphysics as a Guide to Morals*, pp. 185–217. For Derrida's classic deconstruction of traditional metaphysics, see J. Derrida, *Of Grammatology*, trans. G. C. Spivak (Baltimore: Johns Hopkins University Press, 1974).

13 Murdoch, *Metaphysics as a Guide to Morals*, p. 190.

14 Ibid., p. 510.

15 Ibid.

16 Ibid.

17 Ibid., p. 511.

18 I. Murdoch, 'The Fire and the Sun – Why Plato Banished the Artists', in I. Murdoch (ed.), *Existentialists and Mystics – Writings on Philosophy and Literature* (London: Chatto and Windus, 1997).

19 Tracy, 'Iris Murdoch and the Many Faces of Platonism', p. 54.

20 P. Conradi, *Murdoch – A Life* (London: HarperCollins, 2002), p. 547.

21 B. Williams, '*The Fire and the Sun – Why Plato Banished the Artists* by Iris Murdoch', in B. Williams (ed.), *Essays and Reviews 1959–2002* (Princeton and Oxford: Princeton University Press, 2014), p. 145.

22 Murdoch, *Metaphysics as a Guide to Morals*, pp. 226–7.

23 Ibid., p. 227.

24 For more open readings of Hegel, see G. Browning, *Hegel and the History of Political Philosophy* (Basingstoke and New York: Macmillan, 1999); S. Houlgate, *Hegel, Nietzsche and the Criticism of Metaphysics* (Cambridge: Cambridge University Press,

2004). A commentary that goes a long way in establishing Hegel as a theorist of freedom, whose philosophy of history is not constrictive of freedom and contingency, is J. McCarney, *Hegel on History* (London: Routledge, 2010).

25 See Murdoch, Journal 4, 1947, Iris Murdoch Archive, pp. 30–40.

26 For alternative readings of the Hegel–Plato relation, see Browning, *Hegel and the History of Political Philosophy*; G. Browning, 'Hegel's Plato: The Owl of Minerva and a Fading Political Tradition', 36, 1988, pp. 476–85; G. Browning, 'Plato and Hegel: Reason, Redemption and Political Theory', *History of Political Thought*, 8.3, 1987, pp. 377–93.

27 Murdoch, *Metaphysics as a Guide to Morals*, p. 227.

28 Ibid., pp. 20–24.

29 Ibid., p. 2.

30 M. Antonaccio, *A Philosophy to Live By – Engaging Iris Murdoch* (Oxford: Oxford University Press, 2012), p. 39.

31 Murdoch, *Metaphysics as a Guide to Morals*, p. 227.

32 Ibid., p. 79.

33 Ibid., p. 428.

34 See her remarks to Philippa Foot on the power of the Party, when visiting China. 'Letter to Philippa Foot', 30 May 1970, Iris Murdoch Archive.

35 I. Murdoch, *The Sacred and Profane Love Machine* (London: Vintage, 2003), p. 237.

36 Murdoch, *Metaphysics as a Guide to Morals*, p. 498.

37 S. Weil, *Gravity and Grace* (London: Routledge and Kegan Paul, 1952).

38 I. Murdoch, *A Word Child* (London: Vintage, 2002).

39 I. Murdoch, *The Good Apprentice* (London: Vintage, 2000).

40 Note the comment, 'But her protests is too harsh and her idea of the operation of truth too simple.' I. Murdoch, '"Waiting on God": A Radio Talk on Simone Weil (1951) with a Prefatory Note by Justin Broackes', *Iris Murdoch Review*, 8, 2017.

41 Murdoch, *Metaphysics as a Guide to Morals*, p. 487.

42 Ibid., p. 482.

43 Ibid., p. 419.

44 I. Murdoch, *Nuns and Soldiers* (London: Vintage, 2001).

45 I. Murdoch, *Henry and Cato* (London: Vintage, 2002).

46 I. Murdoch, *The Book and the Brotherhood* (London: Vintage, 2003).

47 I. Murdoch, *The Sea, The Sea* (London: Vintage, 1999).

48 I. Murdoch, *Jackson's Dilemma* (London: Penguin Books, 1993).

49 R. G. Collingwood, *An Essay on Philosophical Method*
(Oxford: Clarendon Press, 1933), pp. 24–5.

50 Ibid., p. 24.

51 Ibid., p. 121.

52 S. Mulhall, 'All the World Must Be "Religious": Iris Murdoch's
Ontological Arguments', in A. Rowe (ed.), *Iris Murdoch: A
Reassessment* (Basingstoke: London, 2007), p. 27.

53 I. Murdoch, *The Sovereignty of Good* (London: Routledge and
Kegan Paul, 1970); Murdoch, *Existentialists and Mystics – Writings
on Philosophy and Literature*.

54 I. Murdoch, 'Manuscript on Heidegger', Iris Murdoch Archive. She
prepared it for possible publication in 1993 but decided against
publishing. Subsequently only the first section of the manuscript
has been published in J. Boakes (ed.), *Iris Murdoch Philosopher –
A Collection of Essays* (Oxford: Oxford University Press, 2012).

55 S. Rosen, 'Letter on the "Manuscript on Heidegger"', Iris Murdoch
Archive.

56 Murdoch, 'Manuscript on Heidegger', p. 69.

57 Ibid., p. 35.

58 See I. Murdoch, Application for the Post of Tutor in Philosophy, St.
Anne's College, St. Anne's College Library.

59 Murdoch, 'Manuscript on Heidegger', p. 35.

60 Ibid., p. 68.

61 Ibid., p. 35.

62 Ibid., p. 36.

63 Ibid., p. 60.

64 Ibid., p. 66.

65 Ibid., p. 65.

66 Ibid., p. 140.

67 M. Heidegger, *Being and Time*, trans. J. Macquarrie and E. Robinson
(Oxford and Malden: Blackwell, 1962), p. 297.

68 Ibid.

69 Murdoch, 'Manuscript on Heidegger', p. 206.

70 I. Murdoch, *Sartre – Romantic Rationalist* (London: Fontana/Collins,
1976), p. 70.

71 Murdoch, 'Manuscript on Heidegger', p. 64.

72 Ibid., p. 134.

73 Ibid., p. 112.

74 Plato, *Parmenides*, trans. F. M. Cornford, in E. Hamilton and H.
Cairns (eds), *The Collected Dialogues of Plato Including the Letters*
(Princeton: Princeton University Press, 1961), pp. 920–56.

75 Murdoch, *Metaphysics as a Guide to Morals*, pp. 349–68.

76 I. Murdoch, *The Time of the Angels* (London: Vintage, 2002), p. 150.
77 See Murdoch, *Metaphysics as a Guide to Morals*, pp. 504–13; and the 'Manuscript on Heidegger'.
78 Murdoch, *Jackson's Dilemma*, pp. 46–7.
79 Murdoch, *The Time of the Angels*, pp. 51–85.
80 J. Broackes, 'Introduction', in J. Broackes (ed.), *Iris Murdoch, Philosopher* (Oxford: Oxford University Press, 2012), p. 45.
81 G. W. F. Hegel, *Hegel's Science of Logic*, trans. A. V. Miller (London and New York: Allen and Unwin, 1969).
82 Murdoch's engagement with Wittgenstein is dealt with in different ways in B. Heusel, *Patterned Aimlessness – Iris Murdoch's Novels of the 1970s and 1980s* (Athens: University of Georgia Press, 1995); N. Forsberg, *Language Lost and Found – The Limits of Philosophical Discourse* (London: Bloomsbury, 2013).
83 S. Lovibond, *Iris Murdoch, Gender and Philosophy* (Abingdon: Routledge, 2012) p. 9.

CHAPTER THREE

1 R. Monk, 'Introduction', in I. Murdoch (ed.), *A Word Child* (London: Vintage Books, 2002), p. vii.
2 See M. Antonaccio, *A Philosophy to Live By: Engaging Iris Murdoch* (Oxford: Oxford University Press, 2012).
3 I. Murdoch, 'The Novelist as Metaphysician', 'The Existentialist Hero', 'The Sublime and the Good', 'The Sublime and the Beautiful Revisited', 'Against Dryness', all in I. Murdoch (ed.), *Existentialists and Mystics – Writings on Philosophy and Literature* (London: Chatto and Windus, 1997).
4 Murdoch, 'The Novelist as Metaphysician', p. 107.
5 Ibid., p. 107.
6 Murdoch, 'The Existentialist Hero', p. 109.
7 Ibid., p. 114.
8 See A. S. Byatt, *Degrees of Freedom – The Early Novels of Iris Murdoch* (London: Vintage, 1994), pp. 36–8.
9 See H.D. Spear, *Iris Murdoch* (Basingstoke: Macmillan, 1995), pp, 26–7.
10 I. Kant, *Critique of Judgment*, trans. J. C. Meredith (Oxford: Oxford University Press, 1969), p. 54.
11 G. W. F. Hegel, *Phenomenology of Mind*, trans. J. B. Bailee (London: Allen and Unwin, 1971).
12 Murdoch, 'The Sublime and the Good', p. 218.
13 Ibid.

14 Murdoch, 'The Sublime and the Beautiful Revisited', p. 282.

15 J. Jordan, 'Mess, Contingency and Iris Murdoch', in J. Jordan (ed.), *Chance and the British Novel* (London and New York: Continuum, 2011), p. 119.

16 Murdoch, 'Against Dryness', p. 287.

17 Ibid.

18 Ibid., p. 290.

19 On Murdoch's identification of the significance of the conceptual loss in contemporary life and language, see N. Forsberg, *Language Lost and Found – On Iris Murdoch and the Limits of Philosophical Discourse* (London: Bloomsbury, 2013).

20 Murdoch, 'Against Dryness', p. 291.

21 Ibid.

22 Ibid.

23 Ibid., p. 293.

24 Ibid. See also Byatt, *Degrees of Freedom – The Early Novels of Iris Murdoch*.

25 Murdoch, 'Against Dryness', p. 293.

26 Ibid., p. 294.

27 I. Murdoch, *Metaphysics as a Guide to Morals* (London: Chatto and Windus, 1992), p. 491.

28 I. Murdoch, *The Good Apprentice* (London: Vintage, [1985] 2000).

29 I. Murdoch, *An Accidental Man* (London: Vintage, [1971] 2003). Conradi sees *An Accidental Man* as both serious and funny. See P. Conradi, *The Saint and the Artist – A Study of the Fiction of Iris Murdoch* (London: HarperCollins, 1986), pp. 90–94.

30 D. Gerstenberger, *Iris Murdoch* (New Jersey and London: Associated University Presses, 1975), p. 49.

31 Murdoch, *The Time of the Angels*; *A Fairly Honourable Defeat*; *The Flight from the Enchanter*; *The Sea, The Sea*.

32 A. Rowe and A. Horner (eds), *Iris Murdoch and Morality* (Basingstoke: Palgrave Macmillan, 2010).

33 P. Martin, 'Houses of Fiction: Iris Murdoch and Henry James', in A. Rowe (ed.), *Iris Murdoch: A Reassessment* (Basingstoke: Palgrave Macmillan, 2007).

34 Rowe and Horner, *Iris Murdoch and Morality*.

35 Murdoch, Journals, Iris Murdoch Archive, University of Kingston.

36 B. Heusel, *Patterned Aimlessness – Iris Murdoch's Novels of the 1970s and 1980s* (Athens: University of Georgia Press, 1995), p. 70.

37 I. Murdoch, *The Sea, The Sea* (London: Vintage, [1978] 1999).

38 See B. Nicol, *Iris Murdoch – The Retrospective Fiction* (Basingstoke: Palgrave Macmillan, 2004), p. 51.

39 B. Nicol, 'The Curse of the Bell: The Ethics and Aesthetics of Narrative', in Rowe, *Iris Murdoch: A Reassessment*, p. 106.

40 L. Sage, 'The Pursuit of Imperfection: *Henry and Cato*', in H. Bloom (ed.), *Iris Murdoch* (New York: Chelsea House, 1986), p. 113.

41 Rowe, *The Visual Arts and the Novels of Iris Murdoch*, p. 194.

42 Ibid., p. 196.

43 In a journal entry for 1968, she comments, 'The trouble is that the highest good reaches down into the lower and the lower sometimes to the higher so no clear distinctions are possible.' Murdoch, Journals, 10 February 1964–March 1970, Iris Murdoch Archive, p. 240.

44 Rowe, *The Visual Arts and the Novels of Iris Murdoch*, p. 194.

45 I. Murdoch, *The Bell* (London: Vintage, [1958] 2004).

46 I. Murdoch, 'Literature and Philosophy: A Conversation with Bryan Magee', in Murdoch, *Existentialists and Mystics – Writings on Philosophy and Literature*, p. 14.

47 I. Murdoch, *The Sandcastle* (London: Vintage, 1957), p. 19.

48 A. Byatt, *Portraits in Fiction* (London: Vintage, 2002), p. 86.

49 Murdoch, *Metaphysics as a Guide to Morals*, pp. 1–25.

50 I. Murdoch, 'The Fire and the Sun – Why Plato Banished the Artists', in Murdoch, *Existentialists and Mystics – Writings on Philosophy and Literature*.

51 P. J. Conradi, *Iris Murdoch – A Life* (London: HarperCollins, 2002), pp. 546–8.

52 B. Williams, '*The Fire and the Sun – Why Plato Banished the Artists* by Iris Murdoch', in B. Williams, *Essays and Reviews 1959–2002* (Princeton: Princeton University Press, 2014), p. 28.

53 Plato, *The Republic of Plato*, trans. with an introduction and notes by F. M. Cornford (Oxford: Clarendon Press, 1951).

54 Plato, *The Laws*, trans. A. E. Taylor, in E. Thomson and H. Cairns (eds), *The Collected Dialogues of Plato Including the Letters* (Princeton: Princeton University Press, 1961).

55 Murdoch, *Metaphysics as a Guide to Morals*, pp. 20–4.

56 I. Murdoch, 'The Fire and the Sun – Why Plato Banished the Artists', p. 442.

57 Williams, '*The Fire and the Sun – Why Plato Banished the Artists* by Iris Murdoch', p. 28.

58 Murdoch, 'The Fire and the Sun – Why Plato Banished the Artists', p. 443.

59 Ibid., p. 453.

60 Ibid., p. 455.

61 Murdoch, *Metaphysics as a Guide to Morals*.

62 Ibid.

63 I. Murdoch, 'Art and Eros: A Dialogue about Art', in Murdoch, *Existentialists and Mystics – Writings on Philosophy and Literature*, p. 481.

64 Ibid.
65 Ibid., p. 486.
66 Ibid., p. 487.
67 Ibid., p. 488.
68 Ibid., p. 493.
69 Ibid.
70 Murdoch, *Metaphysics as a Guide to Morals*, p. 8.

CHAPTER FOUR

1 J. Broackes, 'Introduction', in J. Broackes (ed.), *Iris Murdoch, Philosopher – A Collection of Essays* (Oxford: Oxford University Press, 2012), p. 78.
2 Ibid.
3 N. Forsberg, *Language Lost and Found – On Iris Murdoch and the Limits of Philosophical Discourse* (London: Bloomsbury, 2013); C. Taylor, 'Moral Philosophy', in M. Antonaccio and W. Schweiker (eds), *Iris Murdoch and the Search for Human Goodness* (Chicago: University of Chicago Press, 1996).
4 I. Murdoch, Journal, 1947, Iris Murdoch Archive, University of Kingston, p. 100.
5 I. Murdoch, *The Sovereignty of Good* (London: Routledge and Kegan Paul, 1970). The three essays of this book – 'The Idea of Perfection', 'The Sovereignty of Good over Other Concepts' and 'On "God" and "Good"' – are reprinted in I. Murdoch, *Existentialists and Mystics – Writings on Philosophy and Literature* (London: Chatto and Windus, 1992).
6 MacIntyre, *A Short History of Ethics*, p. 246.
7 Her notion of the transformation of the self draws upon the notion of unselfing in Simone Weil's work. See S. Weil, *Gravity and Grace*, trans. E. Crawford and M. von der Ruhr (Abingdon: Routledge, 2002).
8 I. Murdoch, *Metaphysics as a Guide to Morals* (London: Chatto and Windus, 1992).
9 M. Nussbaum, 'Love and Vision: Iris Murdoch on Eros and the Individual', in Antonaccio and Schweiker, *Iris Murdoch and the Search for Human Goodness*; M. Nussbaum, '"Faint with Secret Knowledge": Love and Vision in Murdoch's *The Black Prince*', in Broackes, *Iris Murdoch, Philosopher – A Collection of Essays*. See also the criticisms of Nussbaum in Forsberg, *Language Lost and Found – On Iris Murdoch and the Limits of Philosophical Discourse*
10 Broackes, 'Introduction', pp. 58–9.

11   See I. Murdoch, 'The Moral Decision about Homosexuality', *Man and Society* 7, 1964, reprinted in Y. Moroya and P. Hullah (eds), *Occasional Essays by Iris Murdoch* (Okayama: University Education Press, 1998).

12   See I. Murdoch, 'The Sublime and the Good', in Murdoch, *Existentialists and Mystics – Writings on Philosophy and Literature.*

13   See S. de Beauvoir, *The Second Sex*, trans. H. M. Parshley (London: Jonathan Cape, 1953).

14   Moran has argued that Murdoch is partial in this critique of existentialism and insists rightly that freedom must be involved in all aspects of moral thinking. See R. Moran, 'Murdoch and Existentialism', in Broackes, *Iris Murdoch, Philosopher – A Collection of Essays.*

15   M. Heidegger, *Being and Time*, trans. J. Macquarrie and E. Robinson (Oxford and New Malden: Blackwell, 1962).

16   Murdoch, 'The Idea of Perfection', p. 342.

17   With modifications, she is influenced by Simone Weil in highlighting the importance of attention and unselfing. See Weil, *Gravity and Grace.*

18   See, for instance, Glover's utilitarianism in J. Glover, *Causing Death and Saving Lives* (London and New York: Penguin Books, 1990).

19   See I. Murdoch, *The Sacred and Profane Love Machine* (London: Vintage, [1974] 2003).

20   Murdoch, *The Italian Girl.*

21   I. Murdoch, *The Book and the Brotherhood* (London: Vintage, 1988).

22   S. Lovibond, *Iris Murdoch, Gender and Philosophy* (Abingdon: Routledge, 2011), p. 127.

23   For Murdoch's views on Freud, see Murdoch, *Metaphysics as a Guide to Morals*, pp. 104–5 and 110–11.

24   Murdoch, Journal 11, 1970–72, Iris Murdoch Archive, pp. 180 and 182.

25   See n. 5.

26   Murdoch, 'The Idea of Perfection', p. 302.

27   Ibid., p. 305.

28   Ibid.

29   Ibid., p. 313.

30   Ibid., p. 317.

31   B. Clarke 'The Prospects for Critical Moral Perception', in Broackes, *Iris Murdoch, Philosopher – A Collection of Essays*, p. 242.

32   Murdoch, 'The Idea of Perfection', p. 317.

33   Murdoch, Journal 12, 1975–8, Iris Murdoch Archive, p. 150.

34   Gersternmebrger, *Iris Murdoch*, p. 46.

35   I. Murdoch, *Bruno's Dream* (London: Vintage, 2001), p. 284.

36 Ibid.
37 I. Murdoch, *A Severed Head* (London: Vintage, [1961] 2001), p. 66.
38 F. Baldanza, *Iris Murdoch* (New York: Twayne, 1974), p. 92.
39 Murdoch, 'On "God" and "Good"', p. 338.
40 See Plato, *The Republic of Plato*, trans. with an introduction and notes by F. M. Cornford (Oxford: Clarendon Press, 1961).
41 Murdoch, 'On "God" and "Good"', pp. 359–60.
42 Ibid., p. 361.
43 I. Murdoch, *Nuns and Soldiers* (London: Vintage), p. 179.
44 See the comments of Henscher on the swimming pool in P. Henscher, 'Introduction', in I. Murdoch, *A Fairly Honourable Defeat* (London: Vintage, 2002), p. xiii.
45 Murdoch, *A Fairly Honourable Defeat*.
46 Ibid.
47 See Murdoch, *Metaphysics as a Guide to Morals*.
48 Murdoch, 'The Sovereignty of Good over Other Concepts', p. 366.
49 Weil, *Gravity and Grace*.
50 Murdoch, 'The Sovereignty of Good over Other Concepts', p. 369.
51 Murdoch, Journals, Iris Murdoch Archive.
52 See I. Murdoch, *Poems by Iris Murdoch*, ed. Y. Muroya and P. Hullah (Okayama: University Education Press, 1997), p. 86.
53 Murdoch, 'The Sovereignty of Good over Other Concepts', p. 371.
54 Ibid.
55 Murdoch, *Bruno's Dream*.
56 I. Murdoch, *The Black Prince* (London: Vintage, [1973] 1993); *The Bell* (London: Vintage, [1958] 2004); *The Flight from the Enchanter* (London: Vintage, [1956] 2000).
57 Baldanza, *Iris Murdoch*, p. 164.
58 Murdoch, *Metaphysics as a Guide to Morals*, pp. 498–504.
59 I. Murdoch, *The Good Apprentice* (London: Vintage, 2000), p. 151.
60 Ibid., p. 561.

CHAPTER FIVE

1 S. Lovibond, *Iris Murdoch, Gender and Philosophy* (Abingdon: Routledge, 2011), p. 27.
2 C. Bagnoli, 'The Exploration of Moral Life', in J. Broackes (ed.), *Iris Murdoch, Philosopher – A Collection of Essays* (Oxford: Oxford University Press, 2012).
3 G. Griffin, *The Influence of the Writings of Simone Weil on the Fiction of Iris Murdoch* (San Francisco: Mellen Research University Press, 1993), p. 276.

4 See B. Nicol, *Iris Murdoch: The Retrospective Fiction* (Basingstoke: Palgrave, 2004), p. 24. For the omission of politics by a literary critic, see H. D. Spear, *Iris Murdoch* (Basingstoke: Palgrave, 2005).

5 I. Murdoch, 'Against Dryness', in I. Murdoch (ed.), *Existentialists and Mystics – Writings on Philosophy and Literature* (London: Chatto and Windus, 1992).

6 S. de Beauvoir, *The Mandarins*r (New York: W. W. Norton, 1954).

7 I. Murdoch, 'Interview with Stephanie de Pue', *Iris Murdoch Review*, 1, 2008, p. 6.

8 I. Murdoch, 'Art and Eros', in Murdoch, *Existentialists and Mystics – Writings on Philosophy and Literature*.

9 I. Murdoch, Journal, volume 4, 26 August, 1947, p. 45, Iris Murdoch Archive, University of Kingston.

10 I. Murdoch, Journal, volume 14, 1981–92, 1990, p. 116, Iris Murdoch Archive, University of Kingston.

11 I. Murdoch, Journal, volume 4, 1947, Iris Murdoch Archive, University of Kingston.

12 See I. Murdoch, 'A House of Theory', in Murdoch, *Existentialists and Mystics – Writings on Philosophy and Literature*; I. Murdoch, 'Morals and Politics', in I. Murdoch (ed.), *Metaphysics as a Guide to Morals* (London: Chatto and Windus, 1992).

13 I. Murdoch, *The Three Arrows and the Servants and the Snow* (New York: Viking Press, 1974).

14 J.-F. Lyotard, *The Postmodern Condition*, trans. G. Bennington and B. Massumi (Manchester: Manchester University Press, 1989). See also G. Browning, *Lyotard and the End of Grand Narratives* (Cardiff: University of Wales Press, 2000).

15 Murdoch, 'Letter to Queneau', 1947, Iris Murdoch Archive, University of Kingston.

16 P. Conradi, *Iris Murdoch – A Life* (London: HarperCollins, 2001), p. 145.

17 On the reasons why Murdoch left the Communist Party, see ibid., p. 144.

18 See I. Murdoch, 'A House of Theory', in Murdoch, *Existentialists and Mystics – Writings on Philosophy and Literature*, p. 172.

19 Ibid., p. 180.

20 Ibid., p. 179 and 185–6.

21 For an account of negative and positive liberty, see I. Berlin, 'Two Concepts of Liberty', in I. Berlin, *Four Essays on Liberty* (Oxford: Oxford University Press, 1969).

22 I. Murdoch, *The Sovereignty of Good* (London: Routledge and Kegan Paul, 1970).

23 I. Murdoch, *Under the Net* (London: Vintage Books, [1954] 2002).

24 For an extended commentary on Murdoch's politics and *Under the Net*, see G. Browning, 'Iris Murdoch and the Political: From Bohemia to the Nice and the Good', *Iris Murdoch Review*, 4, 2013.

25 L. L. Martz, 'The London Novels', in H. Bloom (ed.), *Iris Murdoch* (New York and New Haven: Chelsea House, 1986), p. 49.

26 In her comments on displaced persons in a letter to Raymond Queneau, she comments on differences between them and how some become tough to survive the experience. I. Murdoch, 'Letter to Raymond Queneau', Iris Murdoch Archive, University of Kingston.

27 F. White, '"The World Is Just a Transit Camp": Diaspora in the Fiction of Iris Murdoch', *Iris Murdoch Review*, 2, 2009.

28 Murdoch, *The Flight from the Enchanter*.

29 White, 'The World Is Just a Transit Camp'.

30 Murdoch, 'Letter to Raymond Queneau'.

31 I. Murdoch, 'The Moral Decision about Homosexuality', in Y. Moroya and P. Hullah (eds), *Occasional Essays by Iris Murdoch* (Okayama: University Education Press, 1998). This is a reprinted version of an article that was originally published in *Man and Society* in 1964.

32 See the relationship between Simon and Axel in I. Murdoch, *A Fairly Honourable Defeat* (London: Vintage, 2001).

33 Murdoch, 'Letter to Philippa Foot', Iris Murdoch Archive, University of Kingston.

34 Lovibond, *Iris Murdoch, Gender and Philosophy*.

35 D. Kiberd, 'Introduction', in D. Kiberd (ed.), *The Red and the Green* (London: Viking Press, 2001).

36 Murdoch, *The Three Arrows and the Servants and the Snow*.

37 I. Murdoch, 'The Servants and the Snow in Murdoch', in Murdoch, *The Three Arrows and the Servants and the Snow*, p. 51.

38 I. Murdoch, 'The Three Arrows', in Murdoch, *The Three Arrows and the Servants and the Snow*, p. 219.

39 Murdoch, 'Morals and Politics', pp. 354–7.

40 I. Murdoch, Letters.

41 F. White, 'Two Women in Dark Times', in M. F. Simone Roberts and A. Scott-Baumann (eds), *Iris Murdoch and the Moral Imagination* (Jefferson: McFarland, 2010).

42 See D. Hume, *Essays, Moral, Political and Literary* (Oxford: Oxford University Press, 1962); T. Hobbes, *Leviathan*, ed. R. Tuck (Cambridge: Cambridge University Press, 1990); J. Locke, *Two Treatises of Government*, ed. Peter Laslett (Cambridge: Cambridge University Press, 1960).

43 Murdoch, 'Morals and Politics', p. 350.

44 Ibid., p. 357.

45 Ibid., p. 389.
46 Ibid., p. 350.
47 J. S. Mill, 'On Liberty', in J. S. Mill (ed.), *Three Essays on Liberty, Representative Government, the Subjection of Women* (Oxford: Oxford University Press, 1976).
48 See G. Browning, *A History of Modern Political Thought: The Question of Interpretation* (Oxford: Oxford University Press, 2016). See also G. Browning, 'Contemporary Liberalism', in G. Browning, A. Halci and F. Webster (eds), *Understanding Contemporary Society: Theories of the Present* (London: Sage, 2000).
49 Murdoch, 'Morals and Politics'.
50 Ibid., p. 378.
51 Ibid., p. 370.
52 Ibid., p. 565.
53 M. Oakeshott, 'Political Education', in M. Oakeshott (ed.), *Rationalism in Politics and Other Essays* (London and New York: Methuen, 1962), p. 127. Murdoch was critical of Oakeshott's politics but his sense of the contingency of political developments is powerful, and Murdoch certainly took notice of it.
54 Murdoch, 'Morals and Politics', p. 369.
55 Lovibond, *Iris Murdoch, Gender and Philosophy*, pp. 3–7.
56 D. Johnson, *Iris Murdoch* (Brighton: Harvester Press, 1987), p. 1.
57 Ibid., especially pp. 97–114.
58 I. Murdoch, *The Nice and the Good* (London: Vintage, 1968).
59 Ibid., p. 332.
60 I. Murdoch, *The Book and the Brotherhood* (London: Vintage, [1987] 2003), p. 295.
61 Ibid., p. 296.
62 Ibid.
63 Ibid., p. 335.
64 Ibid., p. 336.
65 Ibid., p. 560.
66 Ibid., p. 563.
67 Lyotard, *The Postmodern Condition*.
68 Murdoch, *The Book and the Brotherhood*, p. 557.
69 Ibid.
70 See the discussion of her letters in Chapter 6.
71 Jenny Hinton (Jennifer Dawson 1949–52), 'Iris Murdoch's Political Theory Class', originally published in *The Ship* magazine, St. Anne's College Library.
72 Ibid.
73 Ibid.

CHAPTER SIX

1 See I. Murdoch, 'Morals and Politics', in I. Murdoch (ed.), *Metaphysics as a Guide to Morals* (London: Chatto and Windus, 1992), pp. 348–91.

2 Even if connections between these people and Dylan's songs were to be made, the songs would still have to be interpreted. Dylan himself is unimpressed with associations of this kind.

3 P. Osborn, '"How Can One Describe Real People?" Iris Murdoch's Literary Afterlife', *Iris Murdoch Review*, 5, 2014, p. 54.

4 P. Conradi, '"The Guises of Love": The Friendship of Professor Philippa Foot and Dame Iris Murdoch', *Iris Murdoch Review*, 5, 2014, p. 18.

5 Ibid.

6 Philippa Foot and Iris Murdoch were close friends and we know that they discussed philosophy and were part of a philosophical discussion group. Moreover, Murdoch's letters to Foot are valuable in interpreting Murdoch's philosophical perspective as well as in constituting an eloquent testimony. Yet Murdoch is a complex individual and it seems to me that she did not share or impart her philosophy to any single person. For Murdoch's relationship with Foot, see Conradi, 'The Guises of Love'; and *Iris Murdoch – A Life* (London: HarperCollins, 2001).

7 Y. Muroya, 'Introduction', in Y. Muroya and P. Hullah (eds), *Poems by Iris Murdoch* (Okayama: University Education Press, 1997).

8 J. Bayley, *Iris – A Memoir of Iris Murdoch* (London: Duckworth, 1998), pp. 17–19.

9 R. Eyre, *Iris* (Miramax, 2000).

10 A. N. Wilson, *Iris Murdoch – As I Knew Her* (London: Arrow, 1996), p. 28. It is worth remarking that at a Conference of the Iris Murdoch Society in Chichester in 2017, Wilson was most respectful about her philosophy.

11 A. Horner and A. Rowe (eds), *Living on Paper – Letters from Iris Murdoch 1934–1995* (London: Chatto and Windus, 2015).

12 Ibid., p. xi.

13 P. Osborn, 'Turning the Kaleidoscope: Critics' Responses to *Living on Paper: Letters from Iris Murdoch 1934–1995*, edited by Avril Horner and Anne Rowe', *Iris Murdoch Review*, 7, 2016, p. 50.

14 L. Friegel, '"Flirtatious": Review of *Living on Paper: Letters from Iris Murdoch 1934–1995*, edited by A. Horner and A. Rowe (London: Chatto and Windus, 2015), p. 54', *Iris Murdoch Review*, 7, 2016, p. 56, reprinted from *Daily Telegraph*, 14 November 2015.

15 D. J. Taylor, '*Living on Paper: Letters from Iris Murdoch 1934–1995*, edited by Avril Horner and Anne Rowe – Review', *The Guardian*, 22 October 2015.

16 R. Lewis, *Living on Paper: Letters from Iris Murdoch 1934–1995*, ed. A. Horner and A. Rowe (Princeton: Princeton University Press, 2016).

17 In her biography of Murdoch's early life, Frances White manages to combine a honest recognition of the bewildering plurality of Murdoch's relationships with a keen sense of Murdoch's intellectual interests and its development. She also reflects interestingly on what undertaking a biography means in terms of how it is driven by a biographer's interest but also stretches their conception of the subject. See F. White, *Becoming Iris Murdoch* (Kingston: Kingston University Press, 2014).

18 I. Murdoch, *A Fairly Honourable Defeat* (London: Vintage, [1970] 2001), p. 393.

19 See K. Millet, *Sexual Politics* (New York: Columbia University Press, [1970] 2016). For Murdoch's reading of the public and private, see Murdoch, *Metaphysics as a Guide to Morals*, pp. 348–91.

20 I. Murdoch, Journal 4, 1947, p. 100, Iris Murdoch Archive, Kingston University.

21 I. Murdoch, 'Letter to Raymond Queneau', 23 October 1946, Iris Murdoch Archive, Kingston University.

22 I. Murdoch, 'Manuscript on Heidegger', Iris Murdoch Archive, p. 206.

23 See P. Conradi, 'Oedipus, Peter Pan and Negative Capability: On Writing Iris Murdoch's Life', in A. Rowe (ed.), *Iris Murdoch: A Reassessment* (Basingstoke: Palgrave Macmillan, 2007), pp. 189–203.

24 F. White, *Becoming Iris Murdoch* (Kingston: Kingston University Press, 2014).

25 P. Conradi (ed.), *Iris Murdoch at War – Letters and Diaries 1939–45* (Exeter: Short Books, 2010).

26 D. Morgan, *With Love and Rage: A Friendship with Iris Murdoch* (Kingston: Kingston University Press, 2010).

27 I. Murdoch, 'Letter to Frank Thompson', 24 November 1942, in Horner and Rowe, *Living on Paper – Letters from Iris Murdoch 1934–1995*, p. 28.

28 Ibid., pp. 28–9.

29 Murdoch, 'Letter to Frank Thompson', p. 31.

30 I. Murdoch, 'Letter to D. Hicks', 4 September 1944, in Horner and Rowe *Living on Paper – Letters from Iris Murdoch 1934–1995*, p. 38.

31 Ibid., 4 September 1944, p. 38.

32 Murdoch, 'Letter to David Hicks', 1 June 1945, p. 44.

33 Ibid., 25 January 1946, p. 38.

34 I. Murdoch, 'Letter to Raymond Queneau', 1 June 1945, in Horner and Rowe, *Living on Paper – Letters from Iris Murdoch 1934–1995*.

35 Ibid., p. 44.

36 I. Murdoch, 'Letter to Raymond Queneau', 19 May 1946, Iris Murdoch Archive.

37 Ibid., 2 June 1946.

38 Ibid., 17 January 1950.

39 Ibid., 17 October 1947.

40 Ibid., 25 May 1946.

41 I. Murdoch, 'Letter to Raymond Queneau', 2 June 1946, in Horner and Rowe, *Living on Paper – Letters from Iris Murdoch 1934–1995*.

42 Anne Rowe makes a good case for David Morgan figuring in a number of Murdoch's novels, but it is informed speculation. See A. Rowe, 'Introduction', in Morgan, *With Love and Rage: A Friendship with Iris Murdoch*, pp. xvii–xxii.

43 M. Oakeshott, *Rationalism in Politics and Other Essays* (London and New York: Methuen, 1962).

44 I. Murdoch, 12 November, 1958, in Horner and Rowe, *Living on Paper – Letters from Iris Murdoch 1934–1995*, p. 186.

45 She draws upon Oakeshott's view of politics and tradition in her analysis of Sartre in p. 214 note 64.

46 I. Murdoch, 'Letter to Michael Oakeshott', 14 October 1958, in Horner and Rowe, *Living on Paper – Letters from Iris Murdoch 1934–1995*, p. 181.

47 Murdoch, *Metaphysics as a Guide to Morals*.

48 Murdoch, 'Letter to Michael Oakeshott', 28 November 1958, in Horner and Rowe, *Living on Paper – Letters from Iris Murdoch 1934–1995*, p. 189.

49 Ibid.

50 Ibid., p. 190.

51 I. Murdoch, 'Letter to Michael Oakeshott', January 1959, in Horner and Rowe, *Living on Paper – Letters from Iris Murdoch 1934–1995*, p. 192.

52 I. Murdoch, 'Letter to Michael Oakeshott', 4 November 1958 in Horner and Rowe, *Living on Paper – Letters from Iris Murdoch 1934–1995*, p. 182.

53 Morgan, *With Love and Rage: A Friendship with Iris Murdoch*, p. 7.

54 'Emma' seems to be the 'Magda' that Morgan talks about in his memoir, see ibid., pp. 4–10.

55 I. Murdoch, 'Letter to David Morgan', 30 June 1964, in Horner and Rowe, *Living on Paper – Letters from Iris Murdoch 1934–1995*, p. 268.

56 Ibid., p. 269.

57 Ibid., early July 1965.

58 His letters indicate this and Bayley makes this point quite firmly in *Iris – A Memoir of Iris Murdoch*.

59 I. Murdoch, Journal 11, 1970–72, Iris Murdoch Archive, p. 118.
60 I. Murdoch, 'The Moral Decision about Homosexuality', *Man and Society*, 7, 1964.
61 I. Murdoch, 'Letter to Brigid Brophy', 19 November 1960, in Horner and Rowe, *Living on Paper – Letters from Iris Murdoch 1934–1995*, pp. 215–16.
62 Ibid., 15 March 1964, p. 252.
63 Ibid., 10 May 1964, p. 260.
64 Ibid., 25 January, 1985, p. 521.
65 Ibid., 10 October 1946, p. 83.
66 Ibid., mid–late October 1946, p. 85.
67 Ibid., 25 January 1985, pp. 521–2.
68 Ibid., early February 1990, p. 562.
69 Ibid., 20 April 1982, p. 490.
70 Ibid., 30 May 1982, pp. 491–2.
71 Ibid., 24 March 1979, p. 473.
72 I. Murdoch, *Something Special* (London: Vintage, [1999] 2001).

CHAPTER SEVEN

1 F. White, *Becoming Iris Murdoch* (Kingston: Kingston University Press, 2014), p. 18.
2 I. Murdoch, 'Letter to Raymond Queneau', 2 June 1946, in A. Horner and A. Rowe (eds), *Living on Paper – Letters from Iris Murdoch 1934–1995* (London: Chatto and Windus, 2015), p. 73.
3 See the commentary in P. Osborn, 'Turning the Kaleidoscope: Critics' Responses to *Living on Paper – Letters from Iris Murdoch 1934–1995*, edited by Avril Horner and Anne Rowe', *Iris Murdoch Review*, 7, 2016, p. 52.
4 I. Murdoch, 'On "God" and "Good"', in I. Murdoch (ed.), *Existentialists and Mystics – Writings on Philosophy and Literature* (London: Chatto and Windus, 1992), pp. 360–1.
5 A. MacIntyre, *After Virtue* (London: Duckworth, 1981).
6 See I. Murdoch, 'Morals and Politics', in I. Murdoch (ed.), *Metaphysics as a Guide to Morals* (London: Chatto and Windus, 1992), p. 369.
7 In order to assure political stability, Rawls argues that justice should be restricted to the provision of a political and non-comprehensive form of justice, and that the conduct of politics should be limited by operating within the bounds of a delimited public form of reason. See J. Rawls, *Political Liberalism* (New York: Columbia University Press, 1993).

8   I. Murdoch, 'The Sovereignty of Good over Other Concepts', in Murdoch, *Existentialists and Mystics – Writings on Philosophy and Literature*, p. 376.

9   I. Murdoch, 'The Idea of Perfection', in Murdoch, *Existentialists and Mystics – Writings on Philosophy and Literature*, pp. 312–18.

10 I. Murdoch, *Bruno's Dream* (London: Vintage, 2001), pp. 283–5.

11 Plato, *The Republic of Plato*, trans. with an introduction and notes by F. M. Cornford (Oxford: Clarendon Press, 1961), p. 194.

12 Murdoch, 'Morals and Politics', p. 389.

13 Ibid., p. 388. See also L. Strauss, *City and Man* (Chicago: Chicago University Press, 1976).

14 See B. Williams, '*The Fire and the Sun – Why Plato Banished the Artists* by Iris Murdoch', in B. Williams (ed.), *Essays and Reviews 1959–2002* (Princeton and Oxford: Princeton University Press, 2014), p. 145.

15 See P. Conradi, *Iris Murdoch – A Life* (London: HarperCollins, 2002), p. 547.

16 Murdoch, *Metaphysics as a Guide to Politics*, p. 511.

17 D. Tracy, 'Iris Murdoch and the Many Faces of Platonism', in M. Antonaccio and W. Schweiker (eds), *Iris Murdoch and the Search for Human Goodness* (Chicago: University of Chicago Press, 1996), p. 58.

18 H.-G., Gadamer, *Truth and Method*, trans. and rev. J. Weinschemer and D. G. Marshall (London: Sheed and Ward, 1960); for a discussion of Plato's early dialogues, see H.-G. Gadamer, *Hegel's Dialectic* (New Haven and London: Yale University Press, 1976).

19 I. Murdoch, 'Manuscript on Heidegger', Iris Murdoch Archive, Kingston University, p. 206.

20 G. W. F. Hegel, *Early Theological Writings*, trans. T. M. Knox (Chicago: Chicago University Press, 1948).

21 See R. Plant, *Hegel* (London: George, Allen and Unwin, 1971).

22 See G. W. F. Hegel, *The Philosophy of History*, trans. J. Sibree (London and New York: Dover, 1956).

23 G. W. F. Hegel, *Hegel's Philosophy of Right*, trans. T. M. Knox (Oxford: Oxford University Press, 1967), p. 13.

24 Ibid., p. 185.

25 G. W. F. Hegel, *Lectures on the History of Philosophy*, vol. 1, trans. E. S. Haldane and F. H. Simpson (London: Paul, Trench and Traubner, 1892), p. 1.

26 Ibid., p. 49.

27 Murdoch, 'Manuscript on Heidegger', p. 129.

28 Plato, *The Republic of Plato*, p. 315.

29 Murdoch, 'Manuscript on Heidegger', p. 129.
30 Murdoch, *Metaphysics as a Guide to Politics*, p. 370.
31 It is worth pointing out that Hegel did see Romanticism as threatening to lead to the death of art and he did recognize the social and political world to be facing serious problems.
32 See G. Browning, 'The Night in which All Cows Are Black: Ethical Absolutism in Plato and Hegel', *History of Political Thought*, 12.3, 1991.
33 I. Murdoch, *The Unicorn* (London: Vintage, 2000), p. 100.
34 E. Dipple, *Iris Murdoch – Work for the Spirit* (London: Methuen, 1982), p. 2.
35 Ibid.
36 Murdoch, 'Morals and Politics', pp. 356–60.
37 Murdoch, 'Manuscript on Heidegger', p. 206.
38 Dipple, *Iris Murdoch – Work for the Spirit*, p. 3.
39 S. Lovibond, *Iris Murdoch, Gender and Philosophy* (Abingdon: Routledge, 2011), pp. 3–11.
40 I. Murdoch, 'Manuscript on Heidegger', p. 206.
41 C. Taylor, 'Moral Philosophy', in Antonaccio and Schweiker, *Iris Murdoch and the Search for Human Goodness*, p. 5.
42 Murdoch, *Bruno's Dream*, pp. 283–5.
43 I. Murdoch, 'Letter to Conradi', April, 1983, in Horner and Rowe, *Living on Paper – Letters from Iris Murdoch 1934–1995*, p. 500.

BIBLIOGRAPHY

Iris Murdoch

Murdoch, I., 'Against Dryness', in I. Murdoch (ed.), *Existentialists and Mystics – Writings on Philosophy and Literature* (London: Chatto and Windus, 1997).

Murdoch, I., 'Dame Iris Murdoch's Address to Kingston University Humanities Graduates, the Barbican, London, 4 November 1993', 49–53.

Murdoch, I., *Existentialists and Mystics – Writings on Philosophy and Literature* (London: Chatto and Windus, 1997).

Murdoch, I., 'The Existentialist Hero', in I. Murdoch (ed.), *Existentialists and Mystics – Writings on Philosophy and Literature* (London: Chatto and Windus, 1997).

Murdoch, I., *The Fire and the Sun – Why Plato Banished the Artists* (Oxford: Oxford University Press, [1977] 1978).

Murdoch, I., 'Interview with Stephanie de Pue', *The Iris Murdoch Review* 1, 2008.

Murdoch, I., 'Iris Murdoch Talks to Stephen Glover', in G. Dooley (ed.), *From a Tiny Corner in the House of Fiction – Conversations with Iris Murdoch* (Columbia: University of South Carolina Press, 2003).

Murdoch, I., *Iris Murdoch at War – Letters and Diaries 1939–45*, ed. P. Conradi (Exeter: Short Books, 2010).

Murdoch, I., 'Literature and Philosophy: A Conversation with Bryan Magee', in I. Murdoch (ed.), *Existentialists and Mystics – Writings on Philosophy and Literature* (London: Chatto and Windus, 1997).

Murdoch, I., *Living on Paper – Iris Murdoch Letters 1934–1995*, ed. A. Horner and A. Rowe (London: Chatto and Windus, 2015).

Murdoch, I., *Metaphysics as a Guide to Morals* (London: Chatto and Windus, 1992).

Murdoch, I., 'The Moral Decision about Homosexuality', *Man and Society* 7, 1964; reprinted in Yozo Moroya and Paul Hullah (eds), *Occasional Essays by Iris Murdoch* (Okayama: University Education Press, 1998).

Murdoch, I., 'The Novelist as Metaphysician', in I. Murdoch (ed.), *Existentialists and Mystics – Writings on Philosophy and Literature* (London: Chatto and Windus, 1997).

Murdoch, I., *Occasional Essays by Iris Murdoch*, ed. Yozo Moroya and Paul Hullah (Okayama: University Education Press, 1998).

Murdoch, I., 'On "God" and "Good"' (1969), in I. Murdoch (ed.), *Existentialists and Mystics – Writings on Philosophy and Literature* (London: Chatto and Windus, 1997), pp. 348–9.

Murdoch, I., *Poems by Iris Murdoch*, ed. Y. Muroya and P. Hullah (Okayama: University Education Press, 1997).

Murdoch, I. *Sartre – Romantic Rationalist* (London: Fontana/Collins, 1976).

Murdoch, I., *The Sovereignty of Good* (London: Routledge, 1970).

Murdoch, I., 'The Sublime and the Beautiful Revisited', in I. Murdoch (ed.), *Existentialists and Mystics – Writings on Philosophy and Literature* (London: Chatto and Windus, 1997).

Murdoch, I., 'The Sublime and the Good', in I. Murdoch (ed.), *Existentialists and Mystics – Writings on Philosophy and Literature* (London: Chatto and Windus, 1997).

Murdoch, I., '"Waiting on God": A Radio Talk on Simone Weil (1951) with a Prefatory Note by Justin Broackes', *Iris Murdoch Review* 8, 2017.

Murdoch, I. 'The Idea of Perfection' (1964) in I. Murdoch, *Existentialists and Mystics – Writings on Philosophy and Literature* (London: Chatto and Windus, 1997).

'The Sovereignty of Good Over Other Concepts' (1967) in I. Murdoch, *Existentialists and Mystics – Writings on Philosophy and Literature* (London: Chatto and Windus, 1997).

Plays

Murdoch, I., *The Servants and the Snow*, in I. Murdoch (ed.), *The Three Arrows and the Servants and the Snow* (New York: Viking Press, 1974).

Murdoch, I., *The Three Arrows*, in I. Murdoch (ed.), *The Three Arrows and the Servants and the Snow* (New York: Viking Press, 1974).

Dialogues

Murdoch, I., 'Above the Gods: A Dialogue about Religion', in I. Murdoch (ed.), *Existentialists and Mystics – Writings on Philosophy and Literature* (London: Chatto and Windus, 1997).

Murdoch, I., 'Art and Eros: A Dialogue about Art', in I. Murdoch (ed.), *Existentialists and Mystics – Writings on Philosophy and Literature* (London: Chatto and Windus, 1997).

Unpublished writings

Murdoch, I., 'Application for the Post of Tutor in Philosophy', St. Anne's College, St. Anne's College Library.

Murdoch, I., 'Letters to Micahel Oakeshott', Iris Murdoch Archive, University of Kingston.

Murdoch, I., 'Letters to Philippa Foot', Iris Murdoch Archive, University of Kingston.

Murdoch, I., 'Letters to Raymond Queneau', Iris Murdoch Archive, University of Kingston.

Murdoch, I., Letters to Brigid Brophy, Iris Murdoch Archive, University of Kingston.

Murdoch, I., Journals, Iris Murdoch Archive, University of Kingston (Diaries 1939–1996).

Murdoch, I., 'Manuscript on Heidegger', Murdoch Archive, University of Kingston.

Novels

Murdoch, I., *An Accidental Man* (London: Vintage, [1971] 2003).

Murdoch, I., *The Bell* (London: Vintage, [1958] 2004).

Murdich, I., *The Black Prince* (London: Vintage, [1973] 1993).

Murdoch, I., *The Book and the Brotherhood* (London: Vintage, [1987] 2003).

Murdoch, I., *Bruno's Dream* (London: Vintage, [1969] 2001).

Murdoch, I., *A Fairly Honourable Defeat* (London: Vintage, [1970] 2001).

Murdoch, I., *The Flight from the Enchanter* (London: Vintage, [1956] 2000).

Murdoch, I., *The Good Apprentice* (London: Vintage, [1985] 2000).

Murdoch, I., *The Green Knight* (London: Penguin Books, [1993] 1994).

Murdoch, I., *Henry and Cato* (London: Vintage, [1976] 2002).

Murdoch, I., *The Italian Girl* (London: Vintage, [1964] 2000).

Murdoch, I., *Jackson's Dilemma* (London: Penguin Books, [1995] 1996).

Murdoch, I., *The Message to the Planet* (London: Penguin Books, [1989] 1990).

Murdoch, I., *The Nice and the Good* (London: Vintage, [1968] 2000).

Murdoch, I., *Nuns and Soldiers* (London: Vintage, [1980] 2001).

Murdoch, I., *The Philosopher's Pupil* (London: Vintage, [1983] 2000).

Murdoch, I., *The Red and the Green* (London: Vintage, [1965] 2002).

Murdoch, I., *The Sacred and Profane Love Machine* (London: Vintage, [1974] 2003).

Murdoch, I., *The Sandcastle* (London: Vintage, 1957).

Murdoch, I., *The Sea, The Sea* (London: Vintage, [1978] 1999).
Murdoch, I., *A Severed Head* (London: Vintage, [1961] 2001).
Murdoch, I., *The Time of the Angels* (London: Chatto and Windus, [1966] 2002).
Murdoch, I., *Under the Net* (London: Vintage, [1954] 2002).
Murdoch, I., *The Unicorn* (London: Vintage, [1963] 2000).
Murdoch, I., *An Unofficial Rose* (London: Vintage, [1962] 2000).
Murdoch, I., *A Word Child* (London: Vintage, [1975] 2002).

Short story

Murdoch, I., *Something Special* (London: Vintage, [1999] 2001).

Other authors

Altorf, M., *Iris Murdoch and the Art of Imagining* (London: Continuum, 2008).
Antonaccio, M., 'Form and Contingency in Ethics', in M. Antonaccio and W.Schweiker (eds), *Iris Murdoch and the Search for Human Goodness* (Chicago: University of Chicago Press, 1996).
Antonaccio, M., *A Philosophy to Live By: Engaging Iris Murdoch* (Oxford: Oxford University Press, 2012).
Antonaccio, M., *Picturing the Human: The Moral Thought of Iris Murdoch* (Oxford: Oxford University Press, 2000).
Antonaccio, M. and W. Schweiker (eds), *Iris Murdoch and the Search for Human Goodness* (Chicago: University of Chicago Press, 1996).
Bagnoli, C., 'The Exploration of Moral Life', in J. Broackes (ed.), *Iris Murdoch, Philosopher – A Collection of Essays* (Oxford: Oxford University Press, 2012).
Baldanza, F., *Iris Murdoch* (New York: Twayne, 1974).
Bayley, J., *Iris – A Memoir of Iris Murdoch* (London: Duckworth, 1998).
de Beauvoir, S., 'Literature and Metaphysics', in M. A. Simons with M. Timmerman and M. Mader (eds), *Philosophical Writings*, trans. V. Zayteff and F. Morrison (Urbana: University of Illinois Press, 2004).
de Beauvoir, S., *The Mandarins* (New York: W. W. Norton, 1954).
Berlin, I., 'Two Concepts of Liberty', in I. Berlin (ed.), *Four Essays on Liberty* (Oxford: Oxford University Press, 1969).
Bloom, H., (ed.), *Iris Murdoch* (New York: Chelsea House, 1986).
Broackes, J., 'Introduction', in J. Broackes (ed.), *Iris Murdoch, Philosopher* (Oxford: Oxford University Press, 2012).
Broackes, J. (ed.), *Iris Murdoch, Philosopher* (Oxford: Oxford University Press, 2012).

Browning, G., 'Contemporary Liberalism', in G. Browning, A. Halci and F. Webster (eds), *Understanding Contemporary Society: Theories of the Present* (London: Sage, 2000).

Browning, G., *Hegel and the History of Political Philosophy* (Basingstoke and New York: Macmillan, 1999).

Browning, G., 'Hegel's Plato: The Owl of Minerva and a Fading Political Tradition', *Political Studies* 36, 1988.

Browning, G., *A History of Modern Political Thought – The Question of Interpretation* (Oxford: Oxford University Press, 2016).

Browning, G., 'Iris Murdoch and the Political: From Bohemia to the Nice and the Good', *Iris Murdoch Review* 4, 2013.

Browning, G., *Lyotard and the End of Grand Narratives* (Cardiff: University of Wales Press, 2000).

Browning, G., 'The Night in Which All Cows Are Black: Ethical Absolutism in Plato and Hegel', *History of Political Thought* 12.3, 1991.

Browning, G., 'Plato and Hegel: Reason, Redemption and Political Theory', *History of Political Thought* 8.3, 1987.

Browning, G., *Plato and Hegel: Two Modes of Philosophising about Politics* (New York: Garland Press, 1991).

Byatt, A. S., *Degrees of Freedom – The Early Novels of Iris Murdoch* (London: Vintage, 1994).

Byatt, A. S., *Portraits in Fiction* (London: Vintage, 2002).

Clarke, B., 'The Prospects for Critical Moral Perception', in J. Broackes (ed.), *Iris Murdoch, Philosopher – A Collection of Essays* (Oxford: Oxford University Press, 2012).

Collingwood, R. G., *An Essay on Philosophical Method* (Oxford: Clarendon Press, 1933).

Collingwood, R. G., *The Idea of History* (Oxford: Clarendon Press, 1946).

Conradi, P., '"The Guises of Love": The Friendship of Professor Philippa Foot and Dame Iris Murdoch', *Iris Murdoch Review* 5, 2014.

Conradi, P., *Iris Murdoch: The Saint and the Artist* (Basingstoke: Macmillan, 1986).

Conradi, P., *Murdoch – A Life* (London: HarperCollins, 2002).

Conradi, P., 'Oedipus, Peter Pan and Neghative Capability: On Writing Iris Murdoch's Life', in A. Rowe (ed.), *Iris Murdoch: A Reassessment* (Basingstoke: Palgrave Macmillan, 2007).

Derrida, J., *Of Grammatology*, trans. G. C. Spivak (Baltimore: Johns Hopkins University Press, 1974).

Dipple, E., *Iris Murdoch – Work for the Spirit* (London: Methuen, 1982).

Dooley, G. (ed.), *From a Tiny Corner in the House of Fiction – Conversations with Iris Murdoch* (Columbia: University of South Carolina Press, 2003).

Forsberg, N., *Language Lost and Found – On Iris Murdoch and the Limits of Philosophical Discourse* (London: Bloomsbury, 2013).

Friegel, L., '"Flirtatious": Review of *Living on Paper: Letters from Iris Murdoch 1934–1995*, edited by Avril Horner and Anne Rowe (London: Chatto and Windus, 2015)', *Iris Murdoch Review* 7, 2016, 56, repr. from *The Daily Telegraph* 14, 2015.

Gadamer, H.-G., *Hegel's Dialectic* (New Haven and London: Yale University Press, 1976).

Gadamer, H.-G., 'Hermeneutics and Historicism', in H.-G. Gadamer (ed.), *Truth and Method*, trans. and rev. J. Weinscheiner and D. G. Marshall (London: Sheed and Ward, 1960).

Gadamer, H.-G., *Truth and Method*, trans. and rev. J. Weinscheiner and D. G. Marshall (London: Sheed and Ward, 1960).

Gerstenberger, D., *Iris Murdoch* (New Jersey and London: Associated University Presses, 1975).

Glover, J., *Causing Death and Saving Lives* (London and New York: Penguin Books, 1990).

Griffin, G., *The Influence of the Writings of Simone Weil on the Fiction of Iris Murdoch* (San Francisco: Mellen Research University Press, 1993).

Hegel, G. W. F., *Early Theological Writings*, trans. T. M. Knox (Chicago: Chicago University Press, 1948).

Hegel, G. W. F., *Hegel's Philosophy of Right*, trans. T. M. Knox (Oxford: Oxford University Press, 1967).

Hegel, G. W. F., *Lectures on the History of Philosophy*, vols 1–3, trans. E. S. Haldane and F. H. Simpson (London: Paul, Trench and Traubner, 1892).

Hegel, G. W. F., *Phenomenology of Mind*, trans. J. B. Bailee (London: George Allen & Unwin, 1971).

Hegel, G. W. F., *The Philosophy of History*, trans. J. Sibree (London and New York: Dover, 1956).

Heidegger, M., *Being and Time*, trans. J. Macquarrie and E. Robinson (Oxford and Malden: Blackwell, 1962).

Heusel, B., *Patterned Aimlessness – Iris Murdoch's Novels of the 1970s and 1980s* (Athens: University of Georgia Press, 1995).

Hobbes, T., *Leviathan*, ed. R. Tuck (Cambridge: Cambridge University Press, 1990).

Horner, A., '"Refinements of Evil": Iris Murdoch and the Gothic Novel', in A. Rowe and A. Horner (eds), *Iris Murdoch and Morality* (Basingstoke: Palgrave Macmillan, 2010).

Horner, A. and A. Rowe, 'Introduction', in A. Horner and A. Rowe (eds), *Living on Paper – Iris Murdoch Letters 1934–1995* (London: Chatto and Windus, 2015).

Houlgate, S., *Hegel, Nietzsche and the Criticism of Metaphysics* (Cambridge: Cambridge University Press, 2004).

Hume, D., *Essays, Moral, Political and Literary* (Oxford: Oxford University Press, 1962).

Johnson, D., *Iris Murdoch* (Brighton: Harvester Press, 1987).

Jordan, J., 'Mess, Contingency and Iris Murdoch', in J. Jordan (ed.), *Chance and the British Novel* (London and New York: Continuum, 2011).

Kant, I., *Critique of Judgment*, trans. J. C. Meredith (Oxford: Oxford University Press, 1969).

Kiberd, D., 'Introduction', in D. Kiberd (ed.), *The Red and the Green* (London: Viking Press, 2001).

Leeson, M., *Iris Murdoch: Philosophical Novelist* (London: Continuum, 2010).

Lewis, R., *Living on Paper: Letters from Iris Murdoch 1934–1995*, ed. Avril Horner and Anne Rowe (Princeton: Princeton University Press, 2016).

Lovibond, S., *Iris Murdoch, Gender and Philosophy* (Abingdon: Routledge, 2011).

Lyotard, J.-F., *The Postmodern Condition*, trans. G. Bennington and B. Massumi (Manchester: Manchester University Press, 1989).

MacIntyre, A., *After Virtue* (London: Duckworth, 1981).

MacIntyre, A., *A Short History of Ethics* (New York: Macmillan, 1966).

Martin, P., 'Houses of Fiction: Iris Murdoch and Henry James', in A. Rowe (ed.), *Iris Murdoch: A Reassessment* (Basingstoke: Palgrave Macmillan, 2007).

Martz, L. L., 'The London Novels', in H. Bloom (ed.), *Iris Murdoch* (New York and New Haven: Chelsea House, 1986).

McCarney, J., *Hegel on History* (London: Routledge, 2010).

Miles, S., 'Introduction', in S. Weil (ed.), *Simone Weil: An Anthology* (London: Penguin Books, 2005).

Mill, J. S., 'On Liberty', in J. S. Mill (ed.), *Three Essays on Liberty, Representative Government, the Subjection of Women* (Oxford: Oxford University Press, 1976).

Monk, R., 'Introduction', in I. Murdoch (ed.), *A Word Child* (London: Vintage Books, 2002).

Moran, R., 'Iris Murdoch and Existentialism', in J. Broackes (ed.), *Iris Murdoch Philosopher – A Collection of Essays* (Oxford: Oxford University Press, 2012).

Morgan, D., *With Love and Rage: A Friendship with Iris Murdoch* (Kingston: Kingston University Press, 2010).

Mulhall, S., 'All the World Must Be "Religious": Iris Murdoch's Ontological Arguments', in A. Rowe (ed.), *Iris Murdoch: A Reassessment* (Basingstoke: Palgrave Macmillan, 2007).

Moroya, Y., 'Introduction', in Y. Moroya and P. Hullah (eds), *Poems by Iris Murdoch* (Okayama: University Education Press, 1997).

Moroya, Y. and P. Hullah (eds), *Poems by Iris Murdoch* (Okayama: University Education Press, 1997).

Nicol, B., 'The Curse of the Bell: The Ethics and Aesthetics of Narrative', in A. Rowe (ed.), *Iris Murdoch: A Reassessment* (Basingstoke: Palgrave Macmillan, 2007).

Nicol, B., *Iris Murdoch – The Retrospective Fiction* (Basingstoke: Palgrave Macmillan, 2004).

Nicol, B., 'Murdoch's Mannered Realism: Metafiction, Morality and the Post-War Novel', in A. Rowe and A. Horner (eds), *Iris Murdoch and Morality* (Basingstoke: Palgrave Macmillan, 2010).

Nussbaum, M., '"Faint with Secret Knowledge": Love and Vision in Murdoch's *The Black Prince*', in J. Broackes (ed.), *Iris Murdoch, Philosopher – A Collection of Essays* (Oxford: Oxford University Press, 2012).

Nussbaum, M., 'Love and Vision: Iris Murdoch on Eros and the Individual', in M. Antonaccio and W. Schweiker (eds), *Iris Murdoch and the Search for Human Goodness* (Chicago: University of Chicago Press, 1996).

Oakeshott, M., 'Political Education', in M. Oakeshott (ed.), *Rationalism in Politics and Other Essays* (London and New York: Methuen, 1962).

Oakeshott, M., *Rationalism in Politics and Other Essays* (London and New York: Methuen, 1962).

Osborn, P., '"How Can One Describe Real People?" Iris Murdoch's Literary Afterlife', *Iris Murdoch Review* 5, 2014.

Osborn, P., 'Turning the Kaleidoscope: Critics' Responses to *Living on Paper: Letters from Iris Murdoch 1934–1995*, edited by Avril Horner and Anne Rowe', *Iris Murdoch Review* 7, 2016.

Plant, R., *Hegel* (London: George, Allen and Unwin, 1971).

Plato, *The Laws*, trans. A. E. Taylor, in E. Thomson and H. Cairns (eds), *The Collected Dialogues of Plato Including the Letters* (Princeton: Princeton University Press, 1961).

Plato, *Parmenides*, trans. F. M. Cornford, in E. Hamilton and H. Cairns (eds), *The Collected Dialogues of Plato Including the Letters* (Princeton: Princeton University Press, 1961).

Plato, *The Republic of Plato*, trans. with an introduction and notes by F. M. Cornford (Oxford: Clarendon Press, 1961).

Rawls, J., *Political Liberalism* (New York: Columbia University Press, 1993).

Rosen, S., 'Letter on the "Manuscript on Heidegger"', Iris Murdoch Archive, University of Kingston, 2001.

Rowe, A. (ed.), *Iris Murdoch: A Reassessment* (Basingstoke: Palgrave Macmillan, 2007).

Rowe, A., 'Introduction', in D. Morgan (ed.), *With Love and Rage: A Friendship with Iris Murdoch* (Kingston: Kingston University Press, 2010).

Rowe, A. and A. Horner (eds), *Iris Murdoch and Morality* (Basingstoke: Palgrave Macmillan, 2010).

Ryan, K., 'Introduction', in I. Murdoch (ed.), *Under the Net* (London: Vintage, 2002).

Sage, L., 'The Pursuit of Imperfection: *Henry and Cato*', in H. Bloom (ed.), *Iris Murdoch* (New York: Chelsea House, 1986).

Sartre, J.-P., *Being and Nothingness*, trans. H. E. Barnes (New York: Washington Square Press, 1966).

Simone Roberts, M. F. and A. Scott-Baumann, *Iris Murdoch and the Moral Imagination* (Jefferson: McFarland, 2010).

Spear, H. D., *Iris Murdoch* (Basingstoke: Macmillan, 1995).

Taylor, C., 'Moral Philosophy', in M. Antonaccio and W. Schweiker (eds), *Iris Murdoch and the Search for Human Goodness* (Chicago and London: University of Chicago Press, 1996).

Taylor, D. J., '*Living on Paper: Letters from Iris Murdoch 1934–1995*, Edited by Avril Horner and Anne Rowe – Review', *The Guardian*, 22 October 2015.

Todd, R., *Iris Murdoch – The Shakespearean Interest* (London: Vision Press, 1979).

Tracy, D., 'Iris Murdoch and the Many Faces of Platonism', in M. Antonaccio and W. Schweiker (eds), *Iris Murdoch and the Search for Human Goodness* (Chicago: University of Chicago Press, 1996).

Weil, S., *Gravity and Grace* (London: Routledge and Kegan Paul, 1952).

Weil, S., *Simone Weil: An Anthology* (London: Penguin Books, 2005).

White, F., *Becoming Iris Murdoch* (Kingston: Kingston University Press, 2014).

White, F., 'Two Women in Dark Times', in M. F. Simone Roberts and A. Scott-Baumann (eds), *Iris Murdoch and the Moral Imagination* (Jefferson: McFarland, 2010).

White, F., '"The World Is Just a Transit Camp": Diaspora in the Fiction of Iris Murdoch', *Iris Murdoch Review* 2, 2009.

Williams, B., 'The Fire and the Sun – Why Plato Banished the Artists by Iris Murdoch', in B. Williams (ed.), *Essays and Reviews 1959–2002* (Princeton and Oxford: Princeton University Press, 2014).

Wilson, A. N., *Iris Murdoch: As I Knew Her* (London: Arrow, 2003).

Unpublished writing

Hinton, J. (Jennifer Dawson 1949–52), 'Iris Murdoch's Political Theory Class' (originally in *The Ship* magazine, St. Anne's College Library, University of Oxford).

INDEX

absolute 34
accident 35, 66, 110, 111
Adorno, Theodor 132
aesthetics 60
agency 31, 34, 184, 186
Alzheimer disease 3, 24
Ancient Greece 180–1
Andromeda 70
angel 49
Anglo-American philosophy 15,
    17, 43, 45, 48, 87, 91, 159,
    175
Anglo-Saxon 3
Antagoras 4, 5
Anti-metaphysical 114
Antonaccio, Maria 5, 9, 35
    A Philosophy to live By:
    Engaging Iris Murdoch 35
Aquinas, Thomas 30
Arendt, Hannah 131
art(ist) 5, 10–11, 13, 20, 28, 30–2,
    34, 35, 36, 51, 53, 57, 60–1,
    75–6, 78, 79, 80, 81, 82,
    86–7, 109, 111, 116, 145,
    176, 179
Athens 4
attention 12
Aufklärung 115
    authentic 47

Baez, Joan 145
Bagnoli, Carla 116
    Experience of Moral Life 116

Baldanza, Frank 110
    Iris Murdoch 110
Balogh, Thomas 164–5
Battersea 105
Bayley, John 24
beauty 11
Beauvoir, de Simone 13, 15, 116
    The Mandarins 117
    The Second Sex 157
behaviourism 5, 91
belief 5–7
bi-sexuality 162, 174
blacks 48
Bohemianism 19, 123, 153–4
bourgeois 187–8
Broackes, Justin 51, 85, 88
Brophy, Brigid 147–8, 153, 162–4,
    169
Buddha 41
Buddhism 41
Byatt, A. S. 16

Cambridge 15, 26, 151
Camus, Albert 116
    The Outsider 62
    The Plague 116
Canetti, Elias 148–9
catholicism 71
Cezanne, Paul 36–7
character 8, 10, 12, 39, 59, 65, 66,
    116
Christ 7, 41, 80, 86, 141
Christianity 40–1, 80–1, 176

church 72
citizen(ship) 7, 131, 136, 143
civil disobedience 135
civil society 181, 187
Clarke 100
class 186, 188
Cold War 6
Collingwood, R. G. 29
   *An Essay on Philosophical
      Method* 42
colonialism 188
comedy 29
common sense 60
communism 23
Communist China 125, 131,
   165–7
Communist Party 121, 162, 166
concept 8, 11, 17
Conrad, Joseph 39
Conradi, Peter 9, 32, 44, 146–7,
   193
   Murdoch-A Life 32
conscience 184
consciousness 13, 115, 155
conservatism 158
contemporary moral theory 113
Continental philosophy 3, 91, 146,
   156, 159, 175
contingency 11, 20, 22, 29, 33–4,
   63, 81, 132, 168
convention(s) 115
Conventionalism 5
Cornford, Christopher 86
courage 148
culture 4, 5, 13, 14, 19

Dachau 127, 158
Dasein 45–7, 52
daughter-in-law 99, 113, 115
death 7, 47, 49, 91, 93, 101, 105,
   188, 191
deconstruction 6, 31
democracy 93

demythologisation 5, 6, 13, 22,
   28–32, 35, 40–1, 53, 72, 86,
   108, 174, 192
Derrida, Jacques 29, 31
desire 40, 112, 113
Descartes, Renè 45
despair 66
devil 108
dialectic 2, 3, 20, 27, 33–6, 43, 58,
   65, 85, 87, 90, 133, 137,
   179, 191
dialogue 13, 33, 79, 179
Dickens, Charles 64–5
difference 20, 61
Dipple, Elizabeth 187
discipline 111

East European 53, 166
Easter Rising 128
egalitarian 53, 55, 188
ego(ism) 15, 19, 34–6, 40–1, 43,
   66, 93, 101, 109, 110, 112,
   124
eighteenth century 64
Eliot, George 42, 64
emotion 15, 81, 158, 165
Emperor 170
empiricism 29, 53, 61
Enlightenment 2, 40, 63–4, 107,
   135
environment 4
equality 186
eros 33, 43
ethics 115
Europe 165–6
evil 10, 12, 105–6
existentialism 15–17, 26, 43, 47,
   49, 58–9, 63, 87, 157
experience 2, 12, 20, 27, 32, 34–6,
   40, 42, 53, 107–8, 165, 176

faith 51, 53, 122
family 58, 112, 188

fantasy 35, 43, 57, 65, 75, 112, 139–40
fascism 14, 37
father 112
feminism 115, 150
Fenner, Rachel 148
fiction 5, 6, 8, 10, 25, 67, 151
Foot, M. R. D. 164
Foot, Philippa 127, 147, 153, 164–5
Forsberg, Niklas 7, 10, 86
   Language Lost and Found-On Iris Murdoch and the Limits of Philosophical Discourse 7, 10
freedom 2, 4, 5, 8, 13, 15, 16, 17, 22, 33–4, 54, 60, 65, 90, 108, 118–19, 128, 131, 166–7, 173–4, 180–2, 184
Freud, Sigmund 79, 94, 103, 162, 135
friend(ship) 112, 150–2, 168, 179, 187

Gadamer, Hans-Georg 29, 180
Gainsborough, Thomas 74
   Chasing Butterflies 74
Geist 33
Germany 166, 180
Gerstenberger , Donna 67, 100
Glover, Stephen 9
God 4, 5, 6–7, 13–14, 17, 29, 30, 32, 39, 41–3, 46–7, 49, 88, 103, 107–8, 112, 119, 165, 176
Good, the 17, 32, 34, 42, 51, 76–8, 86, 88, 96, 103–4, 107–8, 110–14, 173, 177–8
goodness 5, 6, 10, 11, 14, 21, 22, 32, 34, 36, 42–3, 53, 69, 74, 86, 8, 106, 111–12
grand narrative 121
Griffin, Gabrielle 116

The Influence of the Writings of Simone Weil on the Fiction of Iris Murdoch 116
guilt 39, 111, 112, 148
Gulag 6

Hampshire, Stuart 87
Hegel, G. W. F. 16, 18, 26, 30, 33–4, 42, 45–6, 52, 56, 61, 103, 133, 141–2, 145, 151, 180–4, 186–8
   Early Theological Writings 180
   Lectures on the History of Philosophy 182
   Phenomenology of Spirit 61, 51
   Philosophy of Right 181
Hegelian idealists 3
Heidegger, Martin 16, 21, 25, 28, 29, 44–7, 49–54, 91, 117, 180, 187
   Being and Time 41, 44–7, 50, 52
Hermeneutics 50
Hetero(sexuality) 120, 127
Heusel, Barbara 9, 69
Hicks, David 148, 152, 154–5, 169
Hinton, Jennifer 143
historian 2
historicity 7, 8, 20
history 2, 3, 6, 20, 21, 26, 27, 28, 33–4, 37, 56–7, 86–7, 96, 107, 133–4, 141, 167, 180, 182, 193
Hitler, Adolf 3, 63
Hobbes, Thomas 49, 61, 131
holism 6, 21
Holocaust 3, 6, 23
Horner, Avril 24, 68–9, 147–8
Hume, David 49, 61, 131
Husserl 16, 26

iconoclasm 7, 49
ideology 4, 6, 23, 116, 118–19, 122, 150

imagination 13, 60, 87, 117
individuals 1, 2, 4, 7, 10, 12, 15,
    17, 18, 24, 30, 34, 36–9, 43,
    49–50, 54, 58, 61, 64, 77,
    84, 87–8, 110, 111, 113,
    115
individualism 19, 57, 80, 86, 124,
    142
injustice 54
international(ism) 143–4, 188

Johnson, Deborah 135
Judaism 41
just(ice) 78, 112, 147

Kant, Immanuel 4, 30, 42, 45,
    52–3, 56, 60–2, 103
    Critique of Pure Reason 60
Kantian 11, 18
Kiberd, Don 128
Kierkegaard, Soren 39
Kingston university 3
Koestler, Arthur 65, 116, 143, 156
    Darkness at Noon 65, 116
    The Yogi and the Commissar
    156

Labour Party 127, 140, 166–7
law 37
Leeson, Miles 9
Lewis, Roy 149
liberal democracy 100
liberalism 23, 53, 63, 86, 128, 142,
    158, 186
liberty 134–5
life 26
literature 1, 2, 5, 9, 10, 11, 15, 16,
    22, 65, 115, 116, 167
literary imagination 4
lived experience 1, 7, 24, 29, 34,
    115
logical positivism 3
London 125, 163, 165

love 37–8, 43, 58, 77, 101, 111,
    159, 191
Lovibond, Sonia 115, 128, 135
Lyotard, Jean-François 121, 141–2
    The Postmodern Condition-A
    Report on Knowledge 121,
    141–2

MacIntyre, Alasdair 125
Magee, Bryan 9
magic 112
Marcel, Gabriel 26
marriage 55, 70, 71, 119, 160, 170,
    188
Marx, Karl 30, 130, 141–3, 145
    The Communist Manifesto
    143
Marxists 33, 133, 140
materialism 54
mercy 47, 93
metaphor 32, 108, 178
metaphysics 2, 4, 6, 7, 13, 15, 17,
    19–36, 42–6, 48, 51–4, 56,
    58, 66, 77, 81–2, 86–7,
    96, 158, 174–5, 178, 183,
    187–8, 191–2
migrants 188, 193
misery 66
modern(ity) 1–2, 4, 6–8, 14, 17,
    20–1, 28, 32, 44, 56, 61, 63,
    64, 66, 69, 71, 82, 86, 93,
    173, 178–9, 181, 183, 187,
    190
modern philosophy 6
Monk, Ray 55
Moore, G. E. 87
morality 1, 3–5, 13–14, 18, 20,
    22–5, 27, 29, 32, 34, 36–7,
    39–40, 43, 46–7, 49, 51, 53,
    54, 82, 86, 111, 113, 114,
    115, 117, 167–8, 174, 178,
    186, 190–1
moral perfectionism 10, 14, 76

moral philosophy 2, 5, 21, 32, 113, 143, 151, 170–1
moral subjectivism 114
moral theory 22, 86, 113
moral vision 5
Moran, Richard 17
mother 99, 113, 115
Murdoch Iris
  Fiction
    An Accidental Man 23, 66, 99, 109, 110, 120, 127–8, 139
    The Bell 22, 24, 70–2, 127
    The Black Prince 68–9, 79, 88, 128
    The Book and the Brotherhood 23, 94, 139–40, 142–3, 169, 176
    Bruno's Dream 66, 100, 105, 109, 191–2
    A Fairly Honourable defeat 12, 14, 61, 95, 105, 107, 126, 136, 149, 169–70, 188
    The Flight from the Enchanter 23, 66, 120, 124–6, 193
    The Good Apprentice 22, 39, 66, 87, 110, 111, 173
    The Green Knight 72
    Henry and Cato 41, 66, 69, 70, 72, 95
    The Italian Girl 94
    Jackson's Dilemma 41, 50
    The Nice and the Good 12, 23, 73, 75, 95, 120, 126, 128, 130, 137, 158, 168, 173
    Nuns and Soldiers 41 105
    The Philosopher's Pupil 7, 9
    The Red and the Green 120, 126, 128–9
    The Sacred and Profane Love Machine 37, 39, 74, 79, 93, 109, 137, 173

    The Sandcastle 58, 75, 120, 126
    The Sea, The Sea 41, 69, 70, 95, 109, 125, 169
    A Severed Head 94–5, 101, 105, 127
    Something Special 170
    The Time of the Angels 7, 12, 14, 49–50, 61, 66
    Under the Net 8, 15, 16, 18, 19, 20, 23, 58, 68, 95, 119, 123–4, 129
    The Unicorn 186
    An Unofficial Rose 120, 126
    A Word Child 39, 56, 95, 135
  Nonfiction
    'Above the gods- a dialogue about religion' 4
    'Against Dryness 10, 57, 63, 64, 69'
    'A House of Theory' 117, 118, 121–2, 130
    Art and Eros 81, 117
    Existentialists and Mystics 43
    'The Existentialist Hero' 57–8
    'The Fire and the Sun – Why Plato Banished the Artists' 11, 12, 21, 32, 57, 75, 79, 81
    'The Idea of Perfection ' 43, 91, 96, 102
    Journals 5, 25–6, 29, 53, 87, 95, 108, 117, 165
    Letters 1, 25, 29, 57, 149–51, 153, 158, 170–1
    Living on Paper – letters from Iris Murdoch 1934–1995 24, 26, 147–8, 153
    'Manuscript on Heidegger' 21, 25, 28, 29, 44, 148–9, 151–3, 178, 180
    Metaphysics as a Guide to Morals 6, 21, 26, 28, 29, 30, 31, 32, 36–7, 39, 42, 45,

48–9, 52–3, 75, 81, 88, 96,
104–5, 112, 117, 130, 140,
142–4, 150, 169, 178
'The Novelist as
Metaphysician' 57–8
'On "God" and "Good"' 17,
43, 96, 102, 104, 175
'The Moral Decision About
Homosexuality' 25, 127,
184
Sarte-Romantic Revolutionary
8, 15, 16
The Sovereignty of Good 21,
22, 36–7, 43, 85, 90, 96,
113, 184
'The Sovereignty of Good
Over Other Concepts' 43,
96, 107, 177
'The Sublime and the Good'
57, 60
'The sublime and the beautiful
revisited 11, 57, 61, 70
Plays
The Servants and the Snow
118, 129–30
The Three arrows 118, 129–30
myth 8, 15, 20, 117
mythology 4, 33
mystic(al) 36, 41

nation state 7
National Gallery 74
Nazi 25
Neo-Platonism 28
neurosis 35
New Review, the 9
New York 102, 111
Nicol, Bram 70, 116
Nietzsche, Friedrich 45, 58
nineteenth century 6, 57, 64
nineteenth-century realism 2
novel 2, 7, 8, 14, 15, 21, 22, 24,
25, 41, 51, 55–94, 112, 116,
158, 174, 184

Crystalline novel 10, 65, 116
journalistic novel 10, 116, 117
novelist 1–3, 8, 9, 13, 37, 59, 116,
150
Nussbaum, Martha 9

Oakeshott, Michael 134, 143, 148,
153, 158–60, 168–9
objectivism 113
ontological proof 42
ordinary 113
original sin 103
Orwell, George 116
1984 116
Osborn, Pamela 146, 148
Oxford 15, 24, 115, 139, 146, 151,
156–7

pacificism 22
painter 59
Parliament 125
particular(ity) 29
past 3, 6, 27, 29, 113
Pasternak, Boris 61
perfectionism 10, 110, 111, 113,
115
Perseus 70
personal 2, 12, 16, 20, 27, 42, 115,
116, 118, 120, 132–4, 150,
165, 176
personal moraility 11, 36–7, 132,
134, 151
phenomenology 13, 15, 16, 35,
46, 93
philosophy 1–55, 76, 82, 102–3,
111, 113, 115, 117, 124,
145, 150–1, 153, 157, 159,
167–8, 171, 179, 183
pilgrimage 111
Plato 5, 10, 11, 13, 15, 18, 28,
32–5, 39, 45–6, 48–9, 53,
56–7, 75–7, 79–81, 88, 90,
101, 113, 131–2, 142, 147,
178–90

Aspects of Plato's philosophy
  Cave 33–4, 77, 80
  Forms 33, 49
  Line 76
  Sun 77, 81
Plato's Dialogues
  Ion 77
  Parmenides 77, 182
  Phaedo 77
  Phaedrus 35
  Republic 77–8, 131–2, 179,
    181–2, 186
  Sophist 77
  Timaeus 80, 182
Platonic 4, 5, 32, 49, 74, 81, 88,
    95, 106, 114, 117, 178, 191
Platonism 32, 88, 90, 104, 192
plurality 27, 35, 43
Poland 166
political 1–3, 15, 17, 20, 23–5, 29,
    34, 37, 51, 53, 55, 64, 87,
    102, 115–45, 156, 159, 168,
    174, 176, 187, 190, 192
post-Enlightenment 45
post-Kantian 20, 190
post-metaphysical 25, 50
poststructuralism 76
post-war 50
practice 6
pre-Kantian 31
present 3, 6, 8, 16, 19, 27, 29
priest 7
prodigal son 112
progress 12, 29, 34, 39
psyche 1, 53
psychiatry 111
psychoanalysis 101–2
public 2, 27
public morality 11, 37, 132
Puerto Ricans 111

Queneau, Raymond 1, 15–16,
    26, 148, 151, 153, 156–7,
    169–70

radical(ism) 121, 129
rationalism 13, 15, 158–9
rationality 4, 34
Rawls, John 176
realism 6–7, 68–9, 192
reason 2, 3, 4, 30, 40, 107
refugee 25, 120, 151
religion 2, 4, 5, 7, 11, 13, 20, 27, 30,
    32, 34–5, 40–2, 49, 51–2,
    55, 86, 96, 105, 108, 174,
    176
remorse 112
Rembrandt, Harmenszoon van
    Rijn 75
resistance 116
responsibility 110, 115
revolution 3
rights 54, 93, 132, 134, 136, 143–4
Rilke, Rainer Maria 36–7
Roman Republic 124
romantic(ism) 19, 61–2, 107,
    111–12
Rosen, Stanley 29, 44
Ross, David 156
Rowe, Anne 24, 67, 69, 74, 147–8
Russia(n) 51
Ryan, Kiernan 14

Sage, Lorna 72
saintliness 111
Sartre, Jean-Paul 12, 15–17, 26,
    46–7, 56, 58–9, 117, 157
  Being and Nothingness 16
  Les Chemins de la Liberté 58
scepticism 4, 32
Schopenhauer, Arthur 36, 53
science 28, 30, 35, 40, 86, 113,
    122
Second World War 16, 18, 118–19,
    130–1, 192
secular 40, 112
self 92, 191
self-interest 113
selfishness 12

sex(ual) 24–5, 48, 55, 72, 90, 112, 115, 120, 144, 150, 162–3, 166, 169, 188
Shakespeare, William 145
Sidgwick, Edie 145
slavery 131, 183
socialism 13, 15, 23, 117, 121–2, 138, 151, 165–6
Soho 154–5
son 112
Soviet Empire 49, 65, 81, 117, 153
Spear, Hilda 18
   Iris Murdoch 18
spirituality 41, 70–1
Strauss, Leo 129, 177
structuralism 31
St. Anne's College 3, 25
St. Bede's School 59
subjectivism 2, 6, 53, 64
sublime 11, 61–2, 192
suffering 39, 40
suicide 128
supernatural 4, 7, 27–30, 105, 108, 126

Taylor, Charles 86, 191
technology 30
Thames, the 105
theology 42
theory 6
Thompson, Frank 147, 153–5, 159
Times, the 149
Titian 38, 70, 74
  Sacred and Profane Love 38, 74
Tolstoy, Leo 56, 61, 64, 165
Tracy, David 28, 32, 180

traditional 7, 13, 16
tragedy 61
transcendence 6, 13, 14, 44, 46, 49, 50, 63–4, 101, 112
trauma 112
Treasury, the 172
truth 7, 21, 32, 34, 49, 53, 75, 78, 80, 90
twentieth century 3, 6–7, 15, 23, 37, 57
tyranny 37, 49, 65

unity 20–1, 27–8, 32, 35, 53
UNRRA 126, 153, 155–7
unselfing 90, 108
USA 129
utilitarian 92
utopia 7, 30, 129, 131, 138

value 31, 44
Vietnam War 120, 139
virtue 12, 113
visual arts 21–2, 80
void, the 39, 112, 122

Weil, Simone 39, 40, 108, 116, 147
  Gravity and Grace 39
West, the 7, 12, 15, 148, 154, 188
White, Frances 126, 131
Williams, Bernard 32, 76, 79–80
Wilson, A. N. 9, 147
  Iris Murdoch-As I Knew Her 147
Wittgenstein, Ludwig 9, 10, 53
Wolfenden Committee 127
women 48, 56, 131, 135, 180, 186

Lightning Source UK Ltd.
Milton Keynes UK
UKHW020038291021
393029UK00009B/323